LEONARD ROSSITER
Character Driven

GUY ADAMS

LEONARD ROSSITER

Character Driven

The Untold Story of
a Comic Genius

Aurum

First published in Great Britain 2010 by Aurum Press Ltd
7 Greenland Street
London NW1 0ND
www.aurumpress.co.uk

A catalogue record for this book is available from the British Library

ISBN 978 1 84513 596 6
E-book ISBN 978 1 84513 657 4

Picture section designed by David Fletcher Welch

Typeset by SX Composing DTP, Rayleigh, Essex
Printed and bound in Great Britain by
Clays Ltd, St Ives plc

To Zoe

Contents

Acknowledgements

I would like to thank all the people who took the time to discuss their memories of Leonard Rossiter. Particularly: David Nobbs for his kindness and wit, Ray Galton and Alan Simpson for their coffee and voluminous sofa, Don Warrington for his stunning voice and profundity with regards to the business and Joe McGrath for his jolly frankness. This would be a much thinner book without all their contributions.

Special thanks are due to Camilla Rossiter. She had a difficult task in balancing her father's wish for privacy and yet also wanting to see a book in print that celebrated his life. I can only hope that I have trodden a respectful line and that she is pleased with the result. I respectfully dedicate this book to her daughter Zoe.

I would also like to express my appreciation to those who went before me, in particular Robert Tanitch and Richard Webber, whose interviews with those who knew and worked with Leonard Rossiter were invaluable in building a full picture of his life. A list of the books and other sources I have used is given on pages 291–3.

Thanks to Stuart and the rest of the team at Aurum for their hard work and support and to the marvellous Jane Donovan for dotting my 'I's, crossing my 't's and generally making it look like I can string a sentence together.

Finally, thanks to Leonard Rossiter for being good enough to merit the intrusion. He was one of our very best and if this book whets the reader's appetite for a repeat viewing of his many performances then I consider it a success.

Introduction

When approaching the life of an actor one is faced with multiplicity from the off: most of us are able to separate ourselves into the working 'us' and the one at rest. For an actor that distinction is never so simple. After all, actors are masked at the best of times – it's what they've trained for. They have the interchangeable faces of the characters they create, the face they use to talk to their audience or press, the one they share with their family and friends . . .

In some cases they even forget which face serves which purpose, becoming lost beneath a stack of peeled personalities. Peter Sellers was once asked to record a religious reading for an album of such things. After agreeing to this, he soon came unstuck. He tried it first in the crusty voice of an archdeacon but that wouldn't do . . . Then a soft Welsh lilt – perhaps thoughts of Neddie Seagoon, the *Goon Show* character, came to mind – then a thick Yiddish accent . . . No, no, the recording engineer didn't like that. Couldn't he just record the piece in his own voice? Sellers crumbled at the thought, utterly lost. 'There's no such thing,' he replied.

Then again some actors, and Leonard Rossiter was one of them, have no such mental frailty: they see acting as a job, as solid and practical as bookkeeping or car mechanics. They can analyse the business of performance unlike the frequently confused folk to whom it comes only too naturally. These performers are often unsung, the sheer technical proficiency of how they approach their work overshadowed by bigger, more eccentric personalities.

When speaking to actor, James Grout in one of the many interviews conducted for this book, he started the conversation by stating: 'There are some actors who gather amusing anecdotes at every step of their career, one can think of many I've worked with over the years . . . then there are those who simply don't. Len was one of the latter.' (And no, this wasn't the most disheartening thing I heard during an interview: that would have been the actor whose name I shan't mention for the sake of sparing blushes who, on being asked when they had first met Leonard, replied: 'Oh . . . nineteen . . . erm . . . nineteen . . . Oh dear, nineteen *something*! I couldn't be more specific, really.')

So no amusing anecdotes here then? Well no, quite a few actually. But it's true Leonard was a simple, workmanlike man – which I mean in a complimentary sense – and his home life really no different to anyone else's. When recalling her father, Camilla Rossiter brings to mind the hardworking man, buried in scripts and learning lines, or the caring father, who took her to the park or local swimming pool. It is not a childhood of glitzy celebrity parties and shocking revelations.

Actress Margaret Courtenay who worked alongside Rossiter as part of the Bristol Old Vic company in the 1960s once observed: 'Len did not seem like an actor at all. Off-stage, he might have been an accountant or bank clerk.'

So, what makes Leonard Rossiter – a man, when not working, so utterly 'normal' that he might have been mistaken for a bank clerk – worthy of a book? Quite simply: his work. Not many actors create such an utterly iconic character that they will forever be remembered, performances repeated and discussed ad nauseam on the '100 Best' shows that certain channels like to fill their schedules with. Leonard did it *twice*, concurrently, in Rupert Rigsby and Reginald Perrin. Even that frankly astounding achievement underplays the true weight of his career – indeed, it was merely five years' worth of performances while his career stretched for thirty.

'A lot of people think of him purely as a comic actor,' says Camilla, 'they will always say, "Oh, I remember your dad, he was so *funny* . . . I suppose it's because of those two series that people particularly remember but of course he did lots of work that wasn't comic, lots of different roles. I think, like with anyone in that profession, he would have wanted to be remembered as an actor across the board, someone who could play the whole range. But that's the way it goes, I suppose.

Let's be honest, an actor is glad to be remembered for *anything*!'

As director, and close friend of Leonard's, Joe McGrath says: 'At the end of the day, it's the work that's important, nothing else matters at all.' Certainly, Rossiter always thought so – he had no interest in sharing the details of his home life, nor by all accounts were they, for the most part, unusual enough to be worth sharing; he had the roles that he played, from fascist dictators to seedy landlords, neurotic businessmen to escaped convicts . . . That is where the story of Leonard Rossiter lies: in his journey to achieve the best work of which he, or for that matter anyone else, was capable.

This book looks at his life through the context of those roles, how he developed the characters and how they, in turn, may have developed him.

Prologue

'Things that make me laugh are black jokes, which some people find distasteful. I like the story about Arthur Lucan who was, of course, "Old Mother Riley". He'd been doing pantomime for about ten weeks, with the audience full of kids screaming his name. He goes off to his dressing room. Then there's a call for him, and he doesn't answer. The theatre manager has to go onstage and break the news. And he says, "Please could I have your attention? Kiddies, shush, please! I have some very sad news: Old Mother Riley is dead.' And someone from the back shouts, "Oh no, she isn't!"'

Leonard Rossiter, 'Live from Two', 1980

It's the spring of 1984 and Leonard Rossiter has just finished filming both a new ITV sitcom, *Tripper's Day*, and the lead role in *The Life and Death of King John*, part of the BBC's ambitious plan to adapt the entire works of Shakespeare for the small screen. The former will receive distinctly mixed reviews, the latter fares better.

But that lies in the future. For now, Leonard is back where he is most comfortable: the theatre. While there can be no doubt that it is television that has made him a household name, theatre is where his heart lies. Theatre offers actors the opportunity to refine a performance over an extended period and to feed off the audience as they ply their trade. It is an immediate medium, uncluttered by the complications of camera angles, lighting rigs and a performance broken up into bite-size pieces for shooting. The drama is cleanly and consecutively told – no altering the script to make an easy 'shooting

5

order' here, a process rather like asking a pianist to start in the middle and then bash out all the loud notes first, filling in the rest later. In theatre, actors tell their story: it's as simple, and potentially transcendental, as that.

The venue is the Ambassadors Theatre, the intimate London venue that carried Agatha Christie's *The Mousetrap* for the first 21 years of its record-breaking run. The play is *Loot*, Joe Orton's controversial farce. For a couple of hours, the audience will relish the grim adventures of Hal and Dennis, who, after robbing the bank next door to the funeral parlour where Dennis works, keep the cash hidden in the coffin of Hal's recently deceased mother, her ejected body going on to appear in all manner of awkward places around the house. For this dark comedy of death and corruption the theatre has been decked out in black drapes and funereal wreaths. It looks like a gaudy undertaker's parlour. In time, this will seem grotesquely appropriate as Rossiter's leading performance as the corrupt Inspector Truscott will sadly be his last.

For what consolation it may later provide – and to Leonard, who disliked the inveterate back-patting that often goes hand in hand with acting, it would be an endorsement that, while gratifying, was not to be dwelt on – the performance was to be met with glowing reviews. Jack Tinker, writing for the *Daily Mail*, will consider 'that sinister seediness in which Leonard Rossiter so excels has seldom been seen to better effect'. Michael Billington, that ever-glowing light of theatrical criticism, makes note of Rossiter's 'superb comic achievement' reviewing the play for *The Times*. It will even win the actor an award nomination, far from the first of his career, for the Best Comedy Performance of the Year in the 1984 Laurence Olivier Awards.

Inspector Truscott, Orton's unpleasant detective, was inspired by Harold Challenor, the police detective so publicly arraigned on charges of police corruption in 1963, who would avoid sentencing, being deemed unfit to plead due to his deteriorating mental health. It was a role Leonard had wanted to play since the first London run of 1966. Orton had written the part for his friend, comic actor Kenneth Williams, who played the role during the premiere production. When casting began for the 1970 film version – adapted by legendary screenwriters Ray Galton and Alan Simpson – Leonard was determined to win the part. Instead it went to Richard Attenborough who, in the opinion of Ray Galton at least, 'fucked it right up'. This would only sharpen Rossiter's determination to one day prove his mettle as the character: he was not a man to give up on such things and it is no surprise that he would eventually secure the part and make it his own.

He is joined in the cast by Gemma Craven (the young actress who shot to fame in 1976, when she was cast alongside Richard Chamberlain in Bryan Forbes' Cinderella movie, *The Slipper and the Rose*), Paul McGann (two years before his 'breakout' role in the BBC drama, *The Monocled Mutineer* and Bruce Robinson's wonderful tale of two 'resting' actors, *Withnail and I*), Neil Pearson (soon to become a household name himself due to leading TV roles in both *Drop the Dead Donkey* and *Between the Lines*), Irish actor and painter Patrick O'Connell (familiar to many audiences for his long-standing role in the BBC drama *The Brothers*) and John Channell Mills who, as well as playing the part of Meadows was to be Leonard's understudy.

The show is a hit, despite the odd first night hiccup (most memorably, McGann dropping the corpse off the stage to which Leonard casually ad-libbed: 'Well, go on then boy, ask for it back!'). And later in the year the production transfers to the larger Lyric Theatre, with David John (who had recently appeared alongside Rossiter in the aforementioned *Tripper's Day* replacing Paul McGann, who has other commitments). The seats are once again filled and the critics kind.

Patrick O'Connell recalls how tightly knit the cast became: 'Doing a farce like that you get to know people very well as exposure is the name of the game: farce exposes you to your fellow actors and the audience much more than a straight drama. We really were a team and loved working with each other. Leonard was marvellous and kept a close eye on everything. We'd heard he was a bit difficult and a perfectionist – which he was – but we all got on; we worked very hard. He was brilliant in the part: he'd been brilliant when he first turned up for the initial read-through of the play and proceeded to get better and better.'

Not that Rossiter was immune to the odd live hiccup: 'His best moment was when he dried with Gemma,' O'Connell continues, referring to that nerve-wracking moment when an actor's mind goes completely blank, leaving them stranded in the midst of a play they don't know how to get out of. 'He dried completely, just stood there looking down at Gemma. He strolled across to the prompt corner, put his hands in his pockets and pulled out his magnifying glass, walking off stage. He returned a moment later to exactly where he had been standing with Gemma and then made the sound of a tape being rewound and started the scene from the top again. It was funnier than the script.

'At one point, I was looking over at him, and thought he was so funny that I forgot I was in the play and just started laughing. He noticed, of course, and I thought, he's going to bollock me for this, but he just stood there and looked at me, waited until I'd finished laughing and then carried on the play without saying another word. He never mentioned it afterward either.'

O'Connell's concern at the 'bollocking' he might have had owing is understandable: Leonard's reputation as a man who doesn't respond well to the slightest slip in professional behaviour is well documented. Perhaps it is simply that he is happy and therefore inclined to be forgiving. He is playing a role he loves, in a medium he adores. Even the slight chest pains that send him to Brompton Hospital for a series of tests – which, in Rossiter's words, prove him to be 'fit as a fiddle' – are of little concern. He has never struggled with his health: after all, he's a voracious sportsman (his main sport being squash), who is rarely ill.

On Friday, 5 October 1984, his doctor's prognosis is proven to be incorrect.

Leonard arrives at the theatre early, as is his wont. Walking around backstage to 'get the feel of the house', he is settling into it, soaking up the atmosphere and acoustics. He chats with O'Connell, his co-star, at a party given by the Russian Embassy, who attended the production the night before and a group of them have returned. Leonard is particularly pleased by this proof – not that it is really needed – that people are enjoying the production.

The curtain lifts and the audience settles in. Truscott first appears in the second scene and Leonard offers his usual, deeply considered performance before exiting to wait in the dressing room for his character's next appearance. His dressing room has an adjoining door that leads through to Patrick O'Connell's. If the cast had contained a couple in a relationship, they would have been given these twin rooms as a courtesy. In this case, the adjoining door remains locked but O'Connell and Rossiter can still hear one another as they rehearse their lines or move around. O'Connell is changing his costume, tugging on ragged clothes that will make him look as if he's been in a car accident. He hears Leonard cough. It's a short bark of a noise and he thinks nothing of it. In the years to come he won't be able to stop himself from wondering if this was a noise that meant more than he realised.

A few minutes later he hears an announcement go out over the backstage tannoy calling Leonard to the stage, but there is no sound of movement from next door. This he does find strange: Rossiter is not an actor who needs reminding of a forthcoming cue. Often he appears in the wings early, or at the very least is heading out the door and along the corridor the very minute the call is given. A few moments pass. The silence continues until O'Connell hears footsteps in the corridor. He steps outside to meet the assistant stage manager chasing up the call. The ASM is nervous, aware as O'Connell that this is not normal behaviour for his colleague. O'Connell takes pity on the ASM, who is reluctant to knock on Leonard's door, and does it for him. There is no answer and so they open the door.

Onstage the concern is doubly felt. Gemma Craven utters Leonard's cue to no effect. A small degree of improvisation occurs, the cast desperately playing for time, ad-libbing Orton and hoping Leonard will appear at any moment. But he is nowhere to be seen. Finally, giving up on their attempts, Neil Pearson apologises to the audience and the curtain lowers.

O'Connell sees Leonard, slumped in an armchair. He is immediately struck by how pale he looks – in fact, as he will later admit: 'He looked dead.' But it's not long before he's joined by the rest of the cast. Gemma Craven, appearing as Nurse Fay in the production, lives up to her character's profession by feeling for Leonard's pulse: there is none. David John attempts to massage his heart, falsely hopeful of the air passing in and out of Leonard's mouth as he desperately pumps away on his chest. An appeal for medical help has already been sent over loudspeaker into the auditorium and three doctors run backstage, closely followed by Frances de la Tour, Rossiter's co-star in *Rising*

Damp, the show that made him a star. 'I was going to go backstage at the end of the show to congratulate him,' she would recall later, 'instead, I went backstage after only 20 minutes into the show to see him die.'

An ambulance arrives to take Leonard to The Middlesex Hospital, though all around can see he is beyond such help. His wife Gillian Raine follows in her car while reporters and photographers gather at the theatre.

The remaining cast must now do something that they feel is utterly beyond them. The management insists they conclude the performance with Leonard's understudy taking over as Truscott. They must go back onstage to complete their tale of cash and corpses. 'We were running about and playing this farce with tears in our eyes,' recalls O'Connell, 'We didn't know why we were doing it, it was a strange thing to ask us to carry on. I thought it was appalling. I thought it was really dreadful, completely and utterly cynical – they just didn't want to give the audience their money back.'

For them at least, the old adage comes into play: the show must go on. When the curtain finally falls they are told what, in truth, they already knew: their co-star is no more. Leonard Rossiter, aged only 57, has died. It is something that hits them hard, however expected. 'When you're in public,' says O'Connell 'somehow the shock is greater, you're spun right out of a public world into this strange murky place that awaits us all: death. It's incredibly disorientating. An actor's job is to create a fantasy and they immerse themselves in it. When reality intrudes into that fantasy . . .'

For Leonard Rossiter the fantasy was finally over: a career spanning 35 years and countless, varied performances had ended.

Part I

Tomorrow
Never Knows

1

A Working-class Hero

Leonard Rossiter was born on 21 October 1926 into a British Isles that was just regaining its feet. Coalminers had downed tools on 1 May of that year, with the Trades Union Congress calling a General Strike in support, two days later. Bar certain 'key' trades such as transport, workers walked away from all industries – no one wanting the political fall-out caused by bringing the country to a complete standstill. Martial law was declared as the country divided between those condemning the striking workers and their sympathisers. Though the General Strike itself only lasted nine days, the coal miners would fight on until 12 October, when they finally agreed to call an end to the strike action: many of them had no choice but to return to work, with the need to earn money to feed their families driving them back down into the pits.

Leonard was the son of John and Elizabeth Rossiter, younger brother to John Junior. The family lived in a small flat above John Rossiter's barber's shop in Wavertree, a suburb of Liverpool. Wavertree – famous for its large play area (named 'The Mystery' as it was left to the area's children for use as a sports field and recreational ground by an unknown benefactor) – would also be where George Harrison grew up 20 years later, with John Lennon also not a stone's throw away. Of course, Liverpool's geography will be forever marked by the passage of The Beatles.

Leonard's father supplemented the living he earned as a barber by working as an illicit bookmaker (betting shops only started to be legalised in the UK in 1961), offering side bets to customers as he cut their hair. The barbershop was alive to the sound of clipping scissors and the radio's crackle as his punters held their breath, listening to the matches or races, in the hope of taking home more than the usual 'something for the weekend'. John Rossiter also provided the family's only link to the entertainment industry by playing golf with George Formby's father, something that Leonard would frequently joke about in later life.

Leonard attended the local Collegiate Grammar School and soon developed a prodigious talent in both sports and languages. He was made captain of the school football and cricket teams, and was also a member of the Lancashire Colts, a youth cricket team designed to foster rising talent in the sport with a view to a professional future.

Tom Farrell remembered his schooldays alongside Leonard to author Robert Tanitch, admitting: 'Len was a hero at school, he was certainly my hero. [One day] I saw Len walking along Queen's Drive away from the sports ground where, I learnt later, our first XI had just beaten rivals Holt High School 11-nil and Len, the centre-forward, had scored all 11 goals. The fact that he was literally sauntering despite his superhuman feat was totally in keeping with his god-like image as a soccer supremo. He was a born sportsman, moving about the pitch with all-conquering, loping ease. And he was modest with it.'

Whether this was modesty or an early sign of an attitude that he would carry throughout his life – an acceptance of his talents leavened with an utter lack of interest in being praised for them – is impossible to tell. Certainly, Leonard approached everything in life as a task to be tackled with the greatest of effort, perfection the only satisfactory goal. That done, he had little interest in basking in the approval of others: achieving said goal was reward enough.

Despite these obvious sporting leanings – rumour even had it within the school that the Everton Football Club had their eyes on him – he also joined the school drama society, though it would be some years before that particular bug truly hit home. For now, his aim was to go on to attend university to pursue degrees in both French and German. Sadly, such hopes would all too soon be dashed, with the outbreak of war in 1939.

Liverpool was a target second only to London during the war, due to the strategic importance of the port. It was the main gateway to the US and provided anchorage for many nations' vessels as well as handling over 90 per cent of all the war material brought into Britain.

The bombings hit their peak in the week between 1 and 7 May 1941. Over those seven days, 681 bombers dropped 870 tonnes of high explosives and over 112,000 incendiaries. The strike knocked out half of the Liverpool docks and over 500 roads. On the nights of 3 and 4 May alone, 400 fires were attended by the Fire Department. The government was determined to gloss over the level of damage sustained by the city: to tell the truth would have been to let the German forces know how successful their targeting had been and therefore invite further attacks. Invited or not, the attacks continued over the months that followed, though never to such extremes. Over 4,000 residents would lose their lives during the bombing campaigns: John Rossiter was one of them.

John had offered his services as a voluntary ambulance driver. It was exhausting work, crews often working shifts of 48 hours or more, looking after those hurt by the bombings as well as receiving wounded troops from battles overseas. The drivers and their nurses had to wade through the darkness of the blackouts, climbing over the dead and dying in an attempt to assist and bring comfort to those still able to benefit from it. It was a hellish occupation and John was not alone in losing his life in its service.

With his father gone, Leonard had no choice but to rethink his future: he would have to help support his mother, the luxury of further education no longer an option as he needed to become a breadwinner. Having reached the conscription age of eighteen, however, Leonard still had time to consider his options as he worked through the obligatory National Service. Despite the surrender of Germany in May 1945 (and the later surrender of Japan in August of that same year), conscription in the UK continued until 1960, with young men expected to spend 18 months as part of the Armed Forces (plus a further four years on the 'reserve' list, where they could be called up in the event of war). Leonard was shipped to Germany, where he served in the Army Education Corps, teaching illiterate soldiers to read and write. At the beginning of his tenure, Germany had just surrendered but the Japanese fought on.

The task of educating the soldiers was a thankless one, as he recounted in a later interview: 'Lots of chaps resented it. Most of them were totally hardened to the idea of never needing to read or write and didn't see why they should start.' Whether his efforts were resented or not, he saw out his time teaching and helping the soldiers write their letters home before returning to Liverpool himself, eager to get on with his own life. Despite having been offered a place at Liverpool University, he concentrated on finding employment that would help support his family, ultimately joining the Commercial Union Insurance Company in 1948. Working as a clerk in the Claims & Accidents department, he earned a wage of £210 a year.

He found the work frustrating but the benefits of a secure livelihood outweighed such matters and he continued as the main breadwinner of the Rossiter household for the next six years. 'It is amazing how many entertainers started life in insurance,' he would later joke, 'and most of them will still try to sell you some, given half a chance.' Later, Rossiter's daughter Camilla would admit that her father would never talk about his family or his youth. But perhaps this was part of her desire to keep 'private life private' as per her father's wishes.

Leonard was indeed a surprisingly private and shy man: there is an assumption that all actors have an inherent 'show-off' streak in them, which Leonard, along with many of his peers, could easily dispel. 'I remember all those dances at the Rialto, Liverpool,' he later recounted, 'where I would spend every Saturday night. Well, I hated it. The whole evening was geared to [the] last half-hour – the last waltz, or whatever. Mostly the whatever.' He was equally uncertain when invited to social functions. 'I remember getting very hot under the collar at dinner tables – I was always afraid of being laughed at.' In the years to come, the laughter of others would be something he would have to get used to, though of course there is a world of difference between being laughed at and making people laugh intentionally. In fact, many of those who lack confidence are drawn towards acting as a profession for the rigidity it offers. After all, you can never be short of something to say when someone's scripting it for you.

Also working at the Commercial Union at that time was Michael Williams, who would go on to become a much-lauded actor in his own right and husband to Dame Judi Dench before his sad death from lung cancer in 2001. As well as working alongside Leonard, he also played football with him as part of an office team, where he learned how seriously Rossiter took his sport. 'Len was the most competitive man ever,' he later recalled. 'Once, he passed me the ball by an open goal: I missed it. Len wouldn't speak to me for a week, and we sat at opposite desks!'

This competitiveness and intolerance of anything but the very best is arguably what finally pushed Leonard towards the career in which he would thrive for most of his life.

2

The Amateur Stage

When later asked what drove him towards acting, Leonard would always tell the same story: his girlfriend was a member of a local amateur dramatics society and after rehearsals, he would drop by to give her a lift home. One night he was early and so he sat at the back of the rehearsal room to watch. What he saw didn't impress him and driving home, he told her so. Understandably, she was somewhat affronted – for Leonard was far too honest not to include her in his list of criticisms – and suggested that if he was such an expert, why didn't he try to do better?

A challenge like this was never going to pass him by: he simply didn't work that way. His future colleague and friend Frederick Jaeger would later explain with regard to another of Leonard's obsessions: 'When we had all moved to London, another friend of Len's, Derek Benfield, and I took Len – in plimsolls and with a borrowed racquet – on to a cold squash court at the Grampians Squash Court in Shepherd's Bush and taught him the rudiments of the game. Within an hour he had mastered the rules, within a week he was playing and within a year, he was far too good for Derek and myself – and subsequently he made himself one of the top players in our business.'

Indeed, this was a fact also attested to by his future *Rising Damp* co-star, Don Warrington (Philip Smith): 'We both played squash and he asked me if I wanted to play. I agreed and he said: "Well, you're much, much younger than me." ' That comment immediately gave Warrington hope that he had found something in which he, the young theatre school graduate, might actually beat his fellow actor (at forty-five, Leonard was more than twice Warrington's age, though hardly ancient!). 'I thought, this will be great: I'm going to get my opportunity, I'm going to show him a thing or two! He got changed and we stepped onto the court. He was very casual and relaxed, and we knocked the ball about. I was a young, energetic man: I was nimble and sprinting about.' Lulled thus into a false sense of security, Leonard suggested they commence a game and he went on to show the young Warrington precisely what he, the 'old man' was capable of: 'It was criminal what he did – he didn't only beat me, he beat me *up* – and with such ease! He played me around the court; I ran and ran and ran, and it was a real lesson. He just smiled and quickly I was exhausted. And there you are, you think: here I am, twenty-one years old and I shall show this old man a thing or two. But the "old man" had a couple of tricks I just didn't know about at all.'

Leonard's determination to excel at everything is just as clear on the rare occasions when he met his match, as his daughter Camilla recalls: 'I remember once on holiday he tried windsurfing. As with everything, he had to do it perfectly or not at all. He soon decided it wasn't working and stomped off the beach.'

And there we have it in a nutshell: 'He had to do it perfectly or not at all.'

Leonard must have been confident of his potential as an actor: faced with his girlfriend's challenge, he joined a local drama group, The Adastra Players, in 1949. In fact, so confident was he that, shortly after joining the Adastra Players, he joined a second group, the Centre Players (based in the close-by Wavertree Community Centre in Penny Lane, a street The Beatles would immortalise years later in their song of the same name). Here we see a perfect example of Rossiter's great ambition – and, indeed, impatience – as an actor. Most people would have joined only one group, felt their way in the new discipline, built up slowly if they found it to their liking . . . not so Leonard. If he was going to act then he would damn well do it to excess, like a man who fancies learning how to climb mountains making a beeline for the Andes on his very first expedition. Was it the need to challenge himself or simply that, once started, acting immediately got its claws into him? Certainly, he would become obsessive over his new hobby as time went on.

A fellow member of the Centre Players – who, like Leonard, would go on to a professional career as an actor – was John Roden: 'I first met Len Rossiter when he joined the Wavertree Community Centre Drama Group and became an acting member of The Centre Players (annual subscription two shillings!). Our theatre was the [centre] ballroom. The small, permanent stage was augmented with six boxes which gave an acting area of some sixteen feet by ten feet, with two by six feet in the wings and backstage.' It was a far cry from the voluminous theatres where Leonard was destined to travel in his future.

'He was a quiet, unassuming person,' Roden continues, 'with a wry sense of humour and a dry wit; but although easy-going and popular, Len was a very private person not given to showing his emotions or confiding in others. We got on well together and spent most of our spare time acting, producing or stage-managing. It was apparent then that he was talented, with a feeling for comedy and an aptitude for inventing comic business. On stage his nervous energy drenched him in perspiration at every performance.'

Rossiter and Roden would go on to become good friends, though the enthusiasm they shared for the stage was never far away, even when socialising: 'We spent many holidays together, boating on the Broads, hitch-hiking to the Riviera and once visiting Butlin's. Scripts were usually part of our luggage and while at Butlin's we couldn't resist taking part in the Variety Show, performing black-out sketches [brief comic pieces defined by a sudden conclusion where the lights would go immediately to black to emphasise the punchline] and a mime act.'

Like all natural performers, they couldn't resist any opportunity to perform to an audience: 'Every year there was an Open Day, with the various groups providing stalls and exhibitions,' Roden explains. 'For one of these Open Days I wrote a three-handed melodrama [hero-villain-wife], which ran for about ten minutes and which we performed every three-quarters of an hour. The audience could buy bags of rotten tomatoes and with the boos, hisses and cheers came a barrage of tomatoes from the enthusiastic audience. At the end of the day we were pretty high. Len naturally played the villain.' And was therefore, presumably, almost invisible beneath the layer of rotten fruit that would come his way. Thankfully, in the years to come it would be swapped for awards and newsprint accolades.

Though his reviews in even those early steps were extremely

positive. His first-ever production (with the Adastra Players) was in the Terence Rattigan's *Flare Path*, later adapted by the author for the big screen as *The Way to the Stars*, starring such stalwarts of British cinema as Michael Redgrave, John Mills and Stanley Holloway. Leonard played the role of Flight Lieutenant Graham and was deemed an excellent find for the company, though one reviewer criticised his penchant for delivering dialogue at too fast a pace, something he felt Rossiter would have to change, were he to achieve success on the stage. In fact, Leonard never did change the habit: throughout his career, it remained a signature of his performance style and harmed him not one bit.

Soon, even membership of two societies was not enough for Leonard as Keith Smith, who also presaged a professional career with a stint as a member of the Centre Players, later recalled: 'One of the first things that struck me about him was his great sense of fun – and by God he needed it because subsequently we joined four other dramatic societies and seemed to be learning lines and rehearsing every evening and keeping the day jobs going at the same time!'

Perhaps due to his natural flair for languages – he spoke three fluently by this time, an act of retention it is hard not to be extremely daunted by – Leonard never seemed to struggle learning lines. It was a constant in his career that he would arrive at rehearsals with the script already word-perfect in his memory. Nonetheless, to be a member of six different societies on top of his full-time position at the Commercial Union, something had to give. Acting had become more than a hobby to Leonard: it was now a skill that he relished, a business he took extremely seriously.

'One morning,' Smith continues, 'he told me that he'd started taking elocution lessons from Mrs Ackerley (a well-known elocutionist in Liverpool) and I knew then that Leonard Rossiter was taking this acting lark all rather seriously.'

In the six years during which he balanced work as an insurance clerk with his burgeoning love of the stage, Leonard appeared in over 40 productions. The acting was earning him just under £6 a week compared to the £10 weekly salary that he was now receiving from Commercial Union. Still, whatever common sense might dictate, he wanted – perhaps even needed – to pursue his acting. In 1954, at 27 years of age he gave up the security of his clerk's desk and auditioned for the Preston Repertory Company. Brave? Not according to Rossiter, who dryly remarked, when interviewed years later: 'It would have been far more courageous to have stayed in the insurance business, knowing I'd be bored out of my mind for the rest of my life.'

3

Going Pro

'In August 1954, a nervous man of twenty-seven auditioned for the Preston Repertory Company. He was a leading amateur in Liverpool and his name was Leonard Rossiter. We had to cast a small part in *The Gay Dog* and he read it pretty badly. Alan Foss, who was to direct the play, thought he was not up to it, but I sensed a talent and persuaded him to read it again; this he did equally badly but very differently, and reluctantly Alan consented to cast him.'

Reginald Salberg (quoted in *Leonard Rossiter* by Robert Tanitch)

Regional repertory theatre as an institution has all but faded from the UK, but for many years it was the backbone of the country's acting industry; a harrowing factory-floor that kept actors in wages but without sleep. The structure was simple enough: a group of actors and a technical crew would put on seasons of plays, the play changing every week. Most towns possessed a local theatre and they were a popular entertainment venue until film and television began to rob them of their audiences through the sixties and seventies. Many regional theatres closed down and the buildings were turned into cinemas or bingo halls. Now only major cities can support a theatre and they usually play home to touring productions, often supplementing their income with other live shows, touring bands, stand-up comedy or exhibitions.

To work in repertory was exhausting but for many it was the baptism of fire that set them up for the rest of their career and a far greater learning experience than a stint at theatre school. The company would usually work on three plays at any given time: making preparations (set design, learning lines) for one, rehearsing and 'blocking' (marking out the specific movements of the actors on the stage) on another and performing a third at night (with afternoon matinees on some days). For an actor, it was an act of immense concentration just to keep the mind focused on the play he was working on at any given time (and occasionally stumble onstage and begin reciting speeches from another work entirely).

Reginald Salberg would become an extremely influential figure in the world of British theatre, receiving an OBE in 1965 for his work in the medium. The foundation of a repertory company based at the Preston Hippodrome was his second such venture and he would go on to create many other companies: Leonard was by no means the only young actor who had cause to thank Salberg for the opportunity to develop a career on the stage.

The Gay Dog revolved around a story of professional dog racing. The dog of the title is owned by Northern coal-miner Jim Gay and is the central hook to a warm, comic romance later filmed with Wilfred Pickles in the lead and a young Petula Clark as his daughter (who is predictably inclined to burst into song at the slightest provocation). The play was written by Joseph H. Colton, a school teacher from Durham who was known for his rather eccentric behaviour, always turning up to a first night of one of his plays in un-matching shoes, one brown and one black. Originally titled *A Dog for Delmont*, the play was first performed in a Durham dialect by the Sunderland Drama Company in 1948. However, it was following the adaptation into a Yorkshire dialect (allegedly to encourage it to appeal to Southerners) that it became a huge success, running for 276 performances in London's Piccadilly Theatre.

Leonard's role as Bert Gay was indeed small and perhaps due to how uninspiring director Alan Foss found his audition, he made his professional debut on only a fortnight's contract – engaged solely for the one production rather than joining the repertory players. This earned him the princely sum of £2.50, quite a drop from his earnings at Commercial Union. He would later recall his mother's comment on his first professional performance: 'Very good, Leonard. In your next part see if they'll let you wear a suit.' Thankfully, there *would* be a next part for Salberg, impressed by Leonard's dedication and attitude, offered him the chance to continue with the company in the role of assistant stage manager, an opportunity he accepted.

The ASM was effectively in charge of the backstage area, ensuring all props and costumes were to hand, chasing actors for their cues and ensuring all communication between the auditorium and backstage was maintained. It was common enough that the ASM would feature in small roles in the repertory productions and this was also the case for Leonard, notching up 14 credits between that September and the following spring.

When the Preston Repertory Company ceased in the spring of 1955, Leonard had gathered a string of professional credits, including Godfrey Pritchard in R.F. Delderfield's *The Orchard Walls*, Winkel in *The Perfect Woman* by Wallace Geoffrey and Basil Mitchell and Alderman Joseph Helliwell in J.B. Priestley's *When We Are Married*, his final role, and two months later managed to secure himself a place with the Wolverhampton Repertory Company. It was here that he would first meet John Barron, future boss of Reginald Perrin and lifelong friend to Rossiter. Barron was then working as a director for the company and quickly recognised Leonard's abilities, happily casting him in a wide variety of roles. 'He was a most serious actor,' Barron would later comment, 'he was terribly serious about his career: he never bored you with it, never said what a marvellous actor he was – which so many of us, I'm afraid, do from time to time.'

The no-nonsense practicality which Leonard brought to the business, coupled as always with a determination to excel in every role he played, proved a great asset to the company. Certainly, the experience continued to hone his talents, as he later explained to journalist Jim Grace in an interview for the *Sunday Telegraph*: 'There was no time [in rep] to discuss the finer points of interpretation. You studied your part, you did it, and then you studied the next part. I developed a frightening capacity for learning lines. The plays became like Elastoplast, which you just stuck on and then tore off. It was the perfect preparation for rehearsing situation comedy on television at the rate of one episode a week.'

Not that he didn't take advantage of the small amount of free time such a schedule offered, satisfying his love of sport by watching the first half of local team Wolverhampton Wanderers' matches at the Molineux Stadium on Saturday afternoons before dashing back to the theatre at half time to prepare for his performances.

From Wildean comedy to Agatha Christie's murder mysteries (including a performance as her iconic detective Hercule Poirot in *Alibi*, an adaptation of the novel *The Murder of Roger Ackroyd*), Leonard appeared in over 50 plays in 18 months at the Grand Theatre, Wolverhampton. It was an incredible body of work in such a short time, one that would sharpen any actor's instincts and techniques when approaching the business. The skills needed to retain a huge amount of dialogue on top of the more ephemeral business of defining a character and then portraying it as a solid, believable creation became perfectly honed. Theatrical creations were shed, like Leonard's metaphorical Elastoplast, at an alarming rate.

John Bowen, a TV director who would work with the actor 10 years down the line, recalls a conversation in which the chaotic world of Rossiter's early days was brought to life: 'During his first two years, he said, everything which could happen, did happen: doors stuck, lights wouldn't come on or go off, scenery fell down, rain dripped through holes in the roof, fellow actors dried or missed their entrances and so did he; the curtain fell when it shouldn't or refused to rise, the ASM tried to prompt from the text of a different play. By the end of two years nothing could surprise him, nothing could throw him; he already knew that he could cope with it, and had the confidence of that knowledge.'

And that knowledge cannot be undersold. All over the world, countless students train at theatre schools, trying to pin down the 'art' of acting, taking whatever natural skills they might possess and building on them – all of which prepares them not one jot when they actually start working. It is easy for someone who has never worked in the profession to dismiss the mental and physical fatigue of acting: often it is difficult to convince anyone that a creative job is a job at all, let alone a tiring one. But the exhaustion a performer can experience is extreme. Repertory was the fitness training that enabled many to continue working and its presence is sorely missed in the business.

On top of his appearances in Wolverhampton, Leonard also appeared in a short run of plays at the Salisbury Playhouse, home to another Repertory Company created by Reginald Salberg. This included a production of the rarely performed, eighteenth-century comedy, *She Would and She Would Not* by Colley Cibber. Given the work's rarity on the English stage at the time, London critics made the trip from the capital to Salisbury to review it, giving Leonard some early exposure in the national press. Indeed, it was excellent exposure, with *The Times* commenting: 'The real life of the revival is Mr Leonard Rossiter who, made up to look like a frontispiece to a whole volume of roguery, often gave the plot real animation.'

Rossiter's obsessive drive was noted by a fellow actor in the production, John Graham: 'I remember that when he was not needed for rehearsal he would sit and observe from the auditorium (unlike the other actors and actresses, who retired to the dressing-rooms to gossip and do the crossword puzzle). We were all in those days committed to the theatre and weekly rep engulfed our lives to the exclusion of all else. But with Len, somehow it was more so. I remember him as a quiet, thinking man who observed and absorbed; I was told by Reggie Salberg that he was the only actor he'd actually encouraged to continue in the profession.'

And here we catch a glimpse of that same Leonard who simply couldn't join just one amateur dramatics society. While the rest of the cast try and snatch a few moments' rest, he wants to absorb more, studying the business down to the minutest detail, what works and what doesn't. He analyses the rhythms of the dialogue, tinkering with delivery to see what effect it has on the words, finding the perfect intonation, the perfect timing. Rossiter is like a watchmaker in his approach to the profession. Despite the acting business's notorious reputation as a career that can at best be described as uncertain, if anyone stood a chance of success – a goal not always achieved through skill, there are countless talented actors who have never made a solid career – it would be him. Aside from clear ability, his obsessive attention and a willingness to put in the necessary hard work gave him everything an actor needs bar that one elusive quality: a steady dose of good luck.

In 1956 a small piece of luck was to occur when Leonard was offered a bit part (Leo Borowitz) on the BBC's *Story Conference* series. This would be his first time working in the medium that would one day secure his reputation with millions. That brief exception aside, he continued to work hard in the theatre, leaving Wolverhampton to perform a handful of productions back at the Salisbury Repertory Company including *The Food of Love*, a play written by Christopher Bond, who would go on to revitalise *Sweeney Todd* in a 1973 production (in turn inspiring Steven Sondheim's ground-breaking musical). For Leonard, it was the second time in the role: the Wolverhampton Repertory Company having staged a production only three months earlier.

During this time he also appeared as Dickens' famous miser Ebeneezer Scrooge in a production of *A Christmas Carol* staged at Birmingham's Alexandra Theatre. 'He was wonderfully funny,' recalls actor Timothy West, who also featured in the production and was another of Salberg's protégés. 'He had the right style for the piece – a mad kind of vigour. It was the first time I was aware of an actor making a totally unpleasant character charming and yet never leaving you in any doubt of his unpleasantness.' A trick that might be defined as one of Rossiter's signature abilities: certainly his future would hold a surfeit of such 'charmingly' unpleasant characters.

The *Birmingham Post* was similarly struck by his performance, stating that 'Leonard Rossiter is young enough and clever enough to do justice to both the young and old Scrooge'. He was to play the part again in 1975 on a national tour directed by Michael Fabian, as well as narrating an abridged version of Dickens' novella as an audiobook in 1981.

Working with the Salisbury Repertory Company, Leonard made a new friend in actor Derek Benfield, who, alongside Frederick Jaeger, would one day introduce him to the joys of squash. Like all who worked with Rossiter, Benfield was struck by the young actor's abilities but more than that, he was impressed by his qualities as a person, later remarking: 'The greatest thing about Len – even more than his acting ability – was his enduring loyalty to his friends. Success never changed him. Unlike squash, his friendship was never competitive.'

Another member of the company who grew close to Rossiter was the actress Josephine Tewson, later familiar to TV audiences for her role as Hyacinth Bucket's much put-upon neighbour in the BBC sitcom *Keeping Up Appearances*. Appearing with Leonard in a number of productions, their friendship grew into romance, which in turn led to a three-year marriage in 1959.

Continued work in repertory saw Leonard begin to rise up the ranks, securing bigger and better roles. Indeed, once again involved in a production of *Thark* – one of playwright Ben Travers' 'Aldwych Farces', filmed in 1932 as *Thark: The Haunted House* – he found himself promoted from an earlier role as a butler with the Wolverhampton Repertory Company to the lead, Sir Hector Benbow.

On every level, things were changing for him.

PART II

The Biggest Fish in the Pond

4

At the Old Vic

The last five years have seen Leonard's life change completely, from the sedentary world of an insurance office in Liverpool to the role of an extremely busy, touring actor. He has racked up countless perform-ances and many positive newspaper reviews; he has even found time to get married, though in truth the relationship between husband and wife is not all it might be. However much Leonard's life has developed up until this point, the next few years will prove the making of him, though. It is easy for an actor's life to plateau – in truth, it could also peter out entirely, but he continued to progress: climbing into more established companies, better parts and more security. The risk that he had taken in leaving a steady full-time job to follow his dream of acting professionally finally seemed to be paying off.

His next major step was to join the much-lauded company at Bristol's Old Vic Theatre. Established in 1948 as an offshoot of London's Old Vic, the company had seen early performances from such luminaries as Peter O'Toole, Timothy West and John Neville. It was with the West End transfer of the Bristol Old Vic's premiere of the musical *Salad Days* in 1954 that the company's reputation was firmly established for it went on to become the West End's longest-running musical at that time, with over 2,000 performances. In fact, it was seeing a production of *Salad Days* as a child that inspired Cameron Mackintosh to become a theatrical producer, a decision that would result in some of the most famous musicals of all time: *Cats*, *Les Misérables* and *The Phantom of the Opera*, to name just three. Julian Slade, the co-writer of *Salad Days*, was an alumnus of the Bristol Old

Vic Theatre School, affiliated with the theatre and opened by Sir Laurence Olivier. The school's reputation has further enhanced the Bristol Old Vic name over the years: other alumni include Jeremy Irons, Daniel Day-Lewis, Ray Stevenson and Patrick Stewart. Leonard Rossiter is in extremely fertile creative territory.

John Hale, who became the theatre's artistic director that year, recalls Leonard's audition: 'In the summer of 1959 I was auditioning for my first season at the Bristol Old Vic. Len came on stage with another actor to "feed" him [lines – a common part of auditions, allowing the auditioning actor to play a scene rather than simply recite a monologue]. He was not on the list and I did not know his name. He was quiet, self-effacing and humorous. After three minutes there was no doubt.

'He joined the company and stayed for my whole time at Bristol. He was a glorious comic and a good deal more besides. Sometimes we fought, sometimes we were helpless with the jokes and situations which are so much a feature of team theatre and which do not translate to the outsider. He was always full of marvellous energy and life.'

Leonard's first role was in George Colman and David Garrick's eighteenth-century comedy, *The Clandestine Marriage*. In the story of an ageing, rheumatic fop, Lord Ogleby – played by Newton Blick – Leonard was Canton, his rather silly French companion. It was a role that would bring him more good reviews, with Peter Rodford observing in the *Western Daily Press* that 'Leonard Rossiter never fails to raise a chuckle with his ingratiating smile and bundle of twitches. [He and Newton Blick's] partnership provides some of the best of the evening's amusement and it is a pity there is not more of it.' Rodford must have enjoyed his visits to Bristol's Theatre Royal then: certainly there were plenty more to come.

Leonard's first experience of professional Shakespeare followed, with two small roles in *Romeo and Juliet*. Then came another comic part in Ben Jonson's *The Silent Woman*, about which John Coe, writing for the *Bristol Evening Post*, would say: 'Leonard Rossiter's Sir John Daw was a minutely observed piece of comedy playing that embraced those characteristics of fussy frustration and timorous anxiety associated with Robertson Hare.' Hare was a comic actor of the time who had established a career in farce, his trademark being the frequent loss of his trousers followed by the utterance 'Oh calamity!' Presumably the trousers fell down with 'timorous anxiety'.

Fellow company member Margaret Courtenay recalls: '[I] have memories of incredibly inventive comic feet and an electric form of controlled and economic energy which resulted in two small roles in *The Silent Woman* and *The Clandestine Marriage* being explosively well played and very, very funny. And what was so extraordinary was their unexpectedness for in those days Len did not seem like an actor at all. Off-stage he might have been an accountant or bank clerk.'

Leonard's observation has paid off, allowing him to develop the precise, controlled style that so impressed Courtenay. It's easy to play something quiet in a meticulous manner but to take that almost mechanical skill and bring it to the large, loud, expressive roles is clever indeed. This is unquestionably another of Rossiter's trademark skills: the controlled explosion of comic performance, where every move, however exaggerated it may seem, is planned out to the last detail. It is a skill that will naturally lead to him being cast in more prominent roles, something of a relief, having stepped up the rungs of the theatrical profession to such an illustrious company.

Understandably Leonard's roles have shrunken: he is the new boy in the company, the unknown, and is once again having to work his way up the ranks. As the saying goes, 'There are no small roles, only small actors' and while this is true to some degree – all roles are important in telling the story and must be played with the same level of competency – no actor wants to spend the majority of his time sitting backstage, for the bigger the role, the more there is to sink your teeth into.

A big jump was to come when the Old Vic decided to stage a production of *The Long and the Short and the Tall*, a wartime drama by new writer Willis Hall. The play had premiered that year in a production at the Royal Court Theatre in London, directed by Lindsay Anderson – who would work with Leonard over 20 years later, casting him as one of the leads in his bleak, satirical movie *Britannia Hospital* in 1982.

The play concerns a small group of British soldiers holed up in an abandoned tin mine in the Malaysian jungle. Cut off from the rest of their platoon, they first have to deal with a malfunctioning radio before the arrival of a Japanese soldier creates a moral dilemma: should they keep him in captivity or kill him? The soldiers are divided in their opinion with Private Bamforth forming the conscience of the group as he shifts his opinion from being only too willing to kill the Japanese man to defending him at the risk of his own life. Bamforth was played by a young Peter O'Toole in the London production – alongside Robert Shaw, Edward Judd and Gareth Thomas – but was to be Leonard's role in the Bristol production.

The guest director for the production was David Scace, who, like Lindsay Anderson, would later play an important role in Rossiter's career, casting him as the landlord Rooksby in *The Banana Box*, the play that would become *Rising Damp*. He recalls working with Leonard at the Old Vic: 'As the all-important Bamforth, Leonard Rossiter was perfect casting – he was superb. I've directed the play a couple of times since then but it's his performance that lingers in the mind. As a young, not widely known actor, he had such self-discipline as puts a guest director on his mettle: you had to be ready for him in rehearsal. He was a stimulating actor who made directing fun and his involvement was total. He could be infuriating in rehearsal but on reflection I found his intuitive interruption to be sound. I often felt he would have been a splendid director, being as he was a total professional with a wicked sense of humour.'

Leonard's suitability as a director would one day be tested when he co-directed a revival of one of his favourite plays – *Semi-Detached* – at Greenwich, an experience he would later recall to Jonathan Lynn, director of *Loot*, his final play. Lynn remembers: 'Occasionally he would come to me while I was writing a scene he wasn't in, and he would say something to me like, "Why can't they get it right? What's their bloody problem?" And I would have to say, "Well, not everyone can get it right first time, like you can." He'd say, "Tell them to do it like this." And I'd say, "Look, do you want to direct it?" And he'd say no, and I asked him why not and he said: "Because I tried directing once and it was a disaster. I upset everybody because I couldn't understand why they couldn't do it!"'

So, while he may have seemed perfect to direct on the one hand, Leonard's insistence on immediate perfection from his colleagues and impatient response when that expectation wasn't delivered meant he wasn't so suitable after all.

It's worth noting too that while many actors might be relatively subservient at Leonard's stage in their career – progressing nicely, but still with some way to climb – he himself had no such gentility. If he didn't agree with what a director was suggesting then he was only too happy to fight over it. Theatre is as prone to a chain of command as the Military and when your director tells you how something should be done, the general rule is that you do it (and moan about it to your fellow cast members later on if you disagree with the director's ideas). Not so Leonard: having worked his way through the script, he would have formulated his opinion on how a play should be produced and if the director's vision didn't tally then they could expect to have a fight on their hands.

After the seriousness of *The Long and the Short and the Tall*, there would come a change of pace with the Christmas musical *Hooray for Daisy*, written by *Salad Days*' creators Julian Slade and Dorothy Reynolds. They were already familiar with Leonard's work. 'In 1956, Angus Mackay, a friend of mine from university days, was playing a season at the Salisbury Playhouse,' Slade later recalled. 'The pan-tomime that year was *Babes in the Wood*. *Salad Days* had by then been running for two years, and Dorothy and I were in the process of completing our next show, *Free as Air*, and we were searching for the right people to appear in it.

'Angus got in touch with us to say that in his opinion there were two outstanding talents in the Salisbury pantomime: Josephine Tewson and Leonard Rossiter. He advised us to see the show, which we did, and were immediately struck by the Robin Hood and the Good Robber [the parts played by Josephine and Leonard – the former, in true pantomime 'principal boy' tradition, playing a man!].'

Slade and Reynolds were suitably impressed. Enough so, in fact, to offer the two actors small parts in *Free as Air*, thereby securing them both their first exposure working in London's West End. Leonard later commented that 'our repertory system is the best theatrical training in the world. When my London "break" came eventually, I felt ready for it.' Given how many roles he had played over the previous two years, one cannot doubt it.

While not so successful as *Salad Days*, *Free as Air* ran for 417 performances at the Savoy Theatre and an album of songs from the show – on which Leonard featured – was released by Oriole Records.

'So delighted were Dorothy and I,' continued Slade, 'with Len's outstanding presence on the stage (whether it was as a rather individual boatman, or a rather evil reporter) that when we came to write our next musical – a Christmas piece called *Hooray for Daisy!* – we created a part especially for him. This was Harry, the postman, and (in conjunction with Dorothy as the Lady of the Corner and Angus as the curate), he was hilarious.

'Indeed, my own personal theatrical memory of him is of a scene that took place in what the characters imagined to be the Giant's bedroom (actually a suite at the Savoy Hotel), which was played entirely in mime and lasted at least six minutes. I have a[n audio] tape recording of the last night at the Bristol Old Vic and this scene, due mainly to Len's incomparable clowning and timing, is one continuous roar of laughter.'

Slade wasn't the only one to record the audio of the production: an EP of 12 songs from the play was released on the His Master's Voice label to coincide with the performances. Leonard's second 'musical' album! Understandably, the silent 'mime' section was not deemed worthy of immortalisation on vinyl.

Also appearing in the production was actress Annette Crosbie, later renowned for her portrayal of the long-suffering wife of Victor Meldrew in the BBC sitcom *One Foot in the Grave*. 'I find it hard to think of Len ever being young and daft,' she later recalled. 'He had no patience with any frivolity when I knew him. All his energy, concentration and passion went into his work and he could be a frightening actor to work with because of this – you felt a kind of pressure on you all the time. And yet I remember us both playing Hide and Seek with a kitten backstage at the Theatre Royal, Bristol, and I remember that finding Len at any vast charity gala was like finding a lifebelt.'

The sense of intimidation Leonard could engender in his colleagues, conversely coupled with his generosity and warmth outside 'the office' would be a constant theme in his life. For some, a willingness to be outspoken about their fellow performers – certainly an insistence that they work as hard as them – comes with the security found in success. For Leonard, it was there from the moment he criticised his then girlfriend's amateur dramatics group and it never left him. He was never less than a professional, who gave everything he had when working, as a fellow member of the Bristol Old Vic Company, James Cairncross, confirms: 'He seemed to expend more energy – and certainly sweat more heavily – than any actor I've worked with before or since. Playing opposite him in a comic scene was something like trying to act with the fountains at Versailles.'

A charming image, and certainly one that speaks volumes about the amount of effort that Leonard put into every performance, one that certainly paid off in his role as Tony Lumpkin in Oliver Goldsmith's eighteenth-century comedy, *She Stoops to Conquer*. Tom Stoppard, a West Country journalist just beginning to write plays himself, penned a review for the *Bristol Evening World*, saying: '[Director, Dudley] Jones is fortunate in having Leonard Rossiter whose bucolic Lumpkin is outrageously overplayed. Mr Rossiter, a natural clown, could eat this part before breakfast, and indeed he makes a meal of it. As far as this vital character is concerned, all is well.'

In any other performance the accusation of overplaying the part would certainly be seen as a criticism: here, Stoppard clearly believes Leonard's judgement to be sound.

The season continued to offer a mix of theatrical styles, from Shelagh Delaney's controversial *A Taste of Honey* (concerning a working-class mother bringing up a mixed-race baby with her homosexual flatmate, a play almost designed to irritate the censors of the time, or indeed the *Daily Mail* reader of today) to *The Hostage*, Brendan Behan's bawdy mix of comedy and political commentary that allowed Leonard a role he always wished to return to: that of a lodging-house owner (and former IRA commandant). There were also a number of Shakespeare productions: *The Tempest*, *Romeo and Juliet* (again) and *The Comedy of Errors*, the latter receiving yet more praise from the critics: the reviewer 'G.M.H.' writing for the *Bristol Evening Post* offered 'an extra bouquet for Leonard Rossiter, whose expressions and faster-than-machinegun staccato of lines delivered are superbly accomplished.'

That rapid delivery, once criticised by a journalist who felt it had to go, should Leonard ever wish to achieve professional success, was now marked as a favourable quality. No one ever said the opinion of critics was a constant . . .

A sure sign of Leonard's fast-developing reputation came when a young Peter Hall offered him the chance to join The Royal Shakespeare Company, his fledgling theatre company in Stratford-upon-Avon. Established in 1960, the RSC would eventually grow to become possibly the most famous theatre company in the world and net Hall a CBE three years later, as well as a knighthood in 1977. But having now achieved roles he could relish at Bristol, Leonard was unimpressed by the parts being offered to him in Stratford. He turned the offer down, later stating: 'One of the best pieces of advice I ever received was: Never leave a pond until you are the biggest fish in it.' And so he stayed at the Bristol Old Vic until he became its leading man, performing in many more successful productions, including: Robert Bolt's *A Man for All Seasons*, *Richard II*, *A Passage to India* and Arnold Wesker's *Roots*.

By the time he left the company (in 1961), he had achieved his goal: he was indeed the biggest fish and now all he could do was to find a larger pool to swim in.

5

Semi-Detached

'It doesn't matter about dishonour as long as the money's right.'
Fred Midway, *Semi-Detached*

Semi-Detached was a play charting the desperate – and morally repugnant – steps its main character, Fred Midway, was willing to take in order to get ahead in life. It is a story of one man's desperation to work his way up the social ladder and to hell with anyone who gets in the way. Both a farcical comedy and a sharp satire on the voracious suburbanites that were a strong feature of 1960s' Britain, it was a work that perfectly captured the era and was to give Leonard one of his favourite roles: one that would set the standard for those to come, loved by audiences and critics alike. It would also be a role that would lift him to the next stage of his career, albeit not quite so swiftly as he might have hoped.

In early 1962, he appeared at the Nottingham Playhouse in a production of George Farquar's *The Recruiting Officer*, a historical comedy based on the author's experience of military recruitment at the beginning of the eighteenth century. The production had been successful, with Gareth Lloyd Evans writing for the *Guardian*: '[Rossiter's] performance is a remarkable exercise in swift, controlled fun. In a part which any sucker could make into a pseudo-Hancock parody, he never confuses expression with grimacing, or lifts his voice into contemporary fun-machine-gabbery.' Whatever 'fun-machine-gabbery' may be, Lloyd Evans has placed Leonard's precise qualities with his other comment: 'he never confuses expression with grimacing' – that perfectly controlled grotesquery clearly at work.

43

Perhaps even more important than the attendance of the critics was that of David Turner, the author of *Semi-Detached*. He recognised in Leonard's performance the abilities he had been looking for in an actor to play his lead character, Fred Midway. 'There was our Fred Midway,' he later explained, 'in the character of Sergeant Kite, breaking out of the blander style of the rest of the cast: a dynamic, galvanised, manic figure that caught the eye. We knew we needed to look no further.'

With Leonard on board, rehearsals commenced with Tony Richardson as the director. For Rossiter, the opportunity to make the part entirely his own was even more of a boon. That unerring instinct for the comic that he had long possessed could come to the fore and so he trimmed and nudged the script in the direction he felt it should go.

Actress Gillian Raine was cast as Leonard's wife in the production (a role that she would one day play for real). Thinking back to those original rehearsals she says: 'The play was well-written and very funny, but being a new production we had the chance to shape it the way we felt best and Leonard's influence was crucial to this process.' She also added: 'He was a great "company" man and a great leader of a company. He always expected them to put in as much work as he did, and because he was a good leader, they did.'

Appearing as Leonard's daughter, Bridget Turner recalls her first impression of the script: 'It seemed to me not only unfunny but somewhat lacking in taste. The machinations of Fred Midway and his ruthless manipulating of members of his own family appalled me, but at the read-through I was laughing hysterically along with the rest of the cast. The part of Fred Midway could have been tailor-made for [Len] and he gave one of those virtuoso performances for which he would be so acclaimed later in his career.'

The play opened in June of that year at the Belgrade Theatre in Coventry and ran for a week to solid reviews and good audiences. On a less happy note, however, Leonard's marriage to Josephine was on the rocks. 'We greatly admired each other, in our work,' she commented in a later interview, 'but we mistook that for love.' In 1962 they separated and, with no children to complicate matters, swiftly divorced.

It is not uncommon for actors to draw close to one another through their shared experiences. Companies – especially repertory companies – live in each other's pockets and so, naturally, emotions run close to the surface given that it is an actor's job to let them do so. Everything becomes heightened, and friendships can develop into love affairs with a weight and profundity that may seem remarkable outside the profession. Unfortunately, those same characteristics can be just as quickly dispelled once both partners are out of the unnatural environment of the job.

It is clear that Leonard was completely dedicated to his career at this point; he is the man that John Graham – Leonard and Josephine's colleague while at Salisbury Rep – observed sitting alone in the auditorium, analysing his performance rather than taking the opportunity to relax with his fellow actors. While such a man may have recognised Josephine's skills as an actress and been drawn to her as a result, it is clearly not a foundation for marriage. If, indeed, their relationship was built on such shaky ground then it can hardly be surprising that it faltered so swiftly: a marriage must be built on admiration of the person rather than their skill within a profession.

Meanwhile, Leonard pushed himself headlong into yet more work. Despite his earlier break in television with a part in the BBC's *Story Conference* series, he had not had much luck with further parts in the medium, securing only three more small appearances over the five years since that initial broadcast. A role as Harry in a one-off drama for the independent station ATV, *The Morning After* (part of ITV's long-running series *Television Playhouse*) was to change all that, however, as it led to his first recurring role on the small screen in the BBC's police drama *Z-Cars*. Arguably the first police drama that attempted to present a more realistic view of the police force (in direct contrast to the BBC's rather cosy saga of 'bobby on the beat', *Dixon of Dock Green*), *Z-Cars* was a huge success for the station. It was created by writer Troy Kennedy Martin, who would achieve great success in the industry, penning the script for that classic sixties' crime caper *The Italian Job*, as well as creating *The Sweeney* and writing the award-winning *Edge of Darkness*. The show ran for 16 years and launched the careers of James Ellis, Stratford Johns, Frank Windsor and Brian Blessed.

Leonard played the role of Detective Inspector Bamber, a somewhat unsavoury character whom the writers developed for him as director – and later, the longest-serving head of drama at the BBC – Shaun

Sutton recalls: 'The *Z-Cars* series' writers were very quick to seize an actor's strong points and write for them. They soon noticed how good he was in "sneaky" parts and his detective inspector became a very sly fellow indeed. Leonard was often cast in such roles because he was good at them: he was very different in real-life – a straightforward, no-nonsense man who knew his craft and expected others to do the same.'

Despite being asked to stay longer, Leonard only played the role on and off over a period of three months during 1963. 'They asked me to become a regular in the series,' he explained in a later interview, 'but I turned it down because I felt then – as I still do – that to go on playing the same role, year in and year out, could become very boring. I am one of those people who derive much delight in doing different things.'

Over the next few months, he was to get his wish, appearing in a handful of TV plays. These included his first starring role in *The Buried Man*, the story of Robert Bailey, an ambitious Yorkshire miner, whose attempts to better himself are met with derision by those around him, forcing him to have a nervous breakdown. The part came about quite by accident as the actor originally chosen had fallen ill just prior to rehearsals. Leonard was approached and despite concerns over his physical stature (the character had been envisaged as a much larger man), all concerned were so bowled over by his acting that he was cast.

This was followed by 'Walk in Fear', part of the BBC's *Suspense* series, in which he played a man acquitted of a murder, a judgment the victim's family refuse to accept, hounding him until he snaps. Then came *The Story of a Farm Girl*, part of a season of plays based on the works of Guy de Maupassant, and *The Fruit at the Bottom of the Bowl* by legendary American writer Ray Bradbury. Television had embraced Leonard and was offering him a rich variety of roles.

In September 1963 the opportunity to return to the character of Fred Midway in a second run of *Semi-Detached* at the Belgrade Theatre earned Leonard a break from the small screen and a return to the stage. The play was, again, a great success. Donald Gee, also appearing in the production, recalls Leonard Rossiter's performance: 'There was a sequence where Bridget Turner (who played my wife) came dashing into the Midways' living room to tell Mum and Dad that Nigel "had done it across her" and that she suspected him of staying the night with a woman in London on a trip to the FA Cup Final. Tearful and frantic, Bridget would have to conclude her report by saying to Len, "Anyway Dad, what do you think my dues are?" Dad would reply, "You'll get your alimony, there's no doubt about that, but I think if you play your cards properly you'll get possession of . . ." and here Leonard's voice rose several octaves and he would sing "the bungalow!" like an aria from *Tosca*, slapping his knee to full stop it. I watched that several times from the wings to see the pleasure that was there – and of course Biddy Turner turning upstage to recover her composure – which she did, but it took a while.'

The production was also recorded for radio, to be broadcast to coincide with the Coventry performance.

More importantly, Leonard began a relationship with his co-star Gillian Raine, which would last the rest of his life. Perhaps learning from previous mistakes, the couple would not marry for nine years, though they soon began living with one another. Perhaps, with his career clearly gathering its own momentum now, both on stage and television, Leonard was able to dedicate more of his mind to the relationship with Gillian, for it was clearly more successful than his first marriage. As with Josephine, he could not help but be drawn to Gillian's skills as an actress, though they worked together rarely, but clearly they bonded on a deeper level too. Both understood the business and the consuming nature of it, but would also manage to fuel a marriage far away from its stresses.

Things seemed perfect; there was even talk of *Semi-Detached* transferring to London, which would earn Leonard his starring debut in the West End. When he had appeared in *Free as Air* at the Savoy, it had been as a relatively minor part of a large cast: this would be an altogether bigger break. However, while the play itself made the journey to the capital, Leonard did not. It was entirely recast for a run at the Saville Theatre and the main role given to Sir Laurence Olivier, an actor whose reputation the producers felt would give their production the gloss it needed. Leonard was understandably gutted: it was a role he had crafted and now, with major success for the play close at hand, he had been cast aside.

Up until this point his career had seemed a steady, upward pro-gression. Of course there will always be setbacks, no actor plays every role for which they audition, but Leonard's trajectory had seemed so solid that this knock must have hit all the harder.

As it was, the London run proved a failure with all involved of the opinion that Olivier, – as great an actor as he clearly was – was no replacement for Rossiter. The pace of the show dropped, and where Leonard and the Coventry cast matched the hyperactive level of comedy that David Turner had envisioned, the London production dragged, being unfunny and badly reviewed. However, it seemed all might not be lost as the play was chosen by American producer David Black to be part of 'Britain on Broadway', a season of UK productions staged in New York. Of course this represented an even bigger opportunity than London's West End and when the original cast transferred to the Music Box Theatre in New York, hopes were understandably high. A week of previews went down extremely well, as Bridget Turner recalls: 'David Black came backstage, beaming, "See, I told you they would love it!" – it seemed we were set for success.'

But when the play officially opened, the production inexplicably bombed, with silent audiences and overwhelmingly negative reviews: 'This unsavoury exhibition of English morals and mores is played by a cast of players apparently under the impression that they inhabit a cartoon. They resemble nothing human. They wheeze, whinny, giggle, snort, cavort, shriek, snarl and guffaw laboriously and irritatingly, all the while performing Mr Turner's sadly inept little bravura as though this was the greatest thing since the Magna Carta,' declared Whitney Bolton in New York's *Morning Telegraph*.

In the face of such damning copy, Leonard could take some consolation in the fact that his performance was singled out by a number of newspapers as the one good thing about the play: 'But just keep your eye on Leonard Rossiter. As the monarch of this realm he is the whole story and if you watch him you can't go wrong. For a virtuoso performance is being turned in by Mr Rossiter, who has the leering grin of a Halloween pumpkin and a rubber band of a body. His is a sensational performance,' countered Martin Gottfried of *Women's Wear Daily*, New York.

Meanwhile, Walter Kerr of the *New York Herald Tribune* wrote: 'Father, Leonard Rossiter, never enters the hideous living room without doing two turns about the track. Between laps, he jams a cigar in his mouth, rips it out, flexes the muscles of his mouth until we know each of his molars intimately, and then claps his hands wildly at what I take to be butterflies.'

And finally, John McClain of *Journal American* raved: 'Leonard Rossiter, the father, has a perfectly man-eating role and he plays it with enormous vigour, running through a gamut of facial contortions unequalled since the days of Harry Langdon. He has the ideal, elastic features for a British caricaturist and he employs them tirelessly and magnificently throughout.'

Still, the writing was on the wall and *Semi-Detached* closed early despite the cast's best attempts to turn things around, altering the script for anything that might seem so peculiarly British that it could be lost on the American audience – there was even brief consideration given to altering the name to 'Duplex' so that theatre-goers might be more aware of what the title meant. Altogether, it was a dispiriting experience.

'So eager were we to escape the scene of our disaster,' recalls Bridget Turner, 'that half an hour after the final curtain fell, we were on board a boat which sailed at midnight. In order to have some respite before arriving back home after only three weeks we had traded in our air tickets for a five- or six-day voyage. It was a break we all needed. Leonard, above all, must have been deeply disappointed but we had a lot of fun on board and I remember him joking, teasing and laughing. I shall always think of him like that.'

However disappointing the American response, Leonard still had a lot of faith in *Semi-Detached* and the production of it – perhaps he was able to laugh the incomprehension off as proof of their simply 'not getting it'. It is easy to accept that the work was a casualty of the common Atlantic divide that seems to rob a great deal of English humour of its effect in America. The English have a very particular taste for dark and even cruel comedy, an enthusiasm shared by Leonard. In fact, we often like our comedy so black, so morally awkward, that it straddles the line where we're not sure if it's intended to be funny or not. While it would be a mistake to say that American humour is simpler, it is often far brighter. Maybe the piece just wasn't for them.

All was not lost for the play, however, with the BBC adapting it for the screen in 1966 as part of their 'Theatre 625' series (a title referring to the number of lines it used to take to compose a picture on a standard UK television screen). It achieved mixed reviews. Sylvia Clayton for the *Daily Telegraph* noted that Leonard 'made Fred bounce and jerk in a St Vitus dance of activity', while Maurice Wiggin in the *Sunday Times* clearly had some doubts, observing, 'It might not have seemed so funny without Mr Leonard Rossiter, a comic actor of demonic power and persuasiveness.' Though Wiggin may have been uncertain, T.C. Worsley, writing for the *Financial Times*, most certainly was not: 'That brilliant actor had a fine time with the suburban Machiavelli of a hero. But this couldn't redeem the ultimate dullness of the play: it's all very well throwing the word Jonsonian about – but this is no excuse for boring us.'

Semi-Detached was certainly not for everyone. Its humour was deemed 'morally repugnant', its performances 'grotesque'. Leonard loved it. No doubt there was an emotional attachment: it was the first time he had been so instrumental in the construction of a brand new character and Fred Midway was as much Leonard's as he was the playwright's. It was also the play where he met and fell in love with his wife, something that would add resonance for anyone. In fact, years later, once Leonard's career had reached a level where he was successful enough to create his own work, he co-directed (with Alan Strachan) a revival of the show. This was his one attempt at directing that he would later admit to Jonathan Lynn had led to disastrous fallings-out with the cast. The production opened in February 1979 at the Greenwich Theatre in London before continuing on a short tour thereafter. The cast now included Bruce Bould and Theresa Watson, the husband and wife who had recently worked with Rossiter on *The Fall and Rise of Reginald Perrin* as C.J.'s 'super' employee David Harris-Jones and his wife Prue.

Sadly the production was not so well received as the original, with Leonard's performance criticised for being over-the-top by a number of reviewers. Perrin's originator David Nobbs found himself in reluctant agreement with the general consensus: 'In my opinion it was OTT, undisciplined and wrong. I don't think he brought it off. Afterwards we all went for dinner because it was his birthday . . . or my birthday . . . or someone's birthday! But the praise from me was missing and I think he noticed it.'

Unsurprisingly, Alan Strachan disagreed: 'His Fred Midway, scheming Machiavelli of suburbia, a latter-day Jonsonian figure plotting and manipulating his way up the social ladder, was another performance marked by a quality of high-octane energy which approached that of a dancer. It was always a particular pleasure to watch him work on a character's body language in rehearsal, cutting through stage space like a whiplash; his body, his very fingertips seemed to dance with a kind of gleeful grace as another of his sequence of audacious stratagems began to form and shape itself before the hapless victims were even aware of his tactics.'

Whatever the final verdict, nothing can take away from the fact that Rossiter's Fred Midway was one of the crowning points of his illustrious stage career and for all the production's ups and downs, it was a part that he was to cherish for the rest of his life.

6

The Kitchen Sink

Having established himself as a force to be reckoned with on the British stage and having started to make solid steps in the world of commercial television, in 1962 Leonard Rossiter appeared in his first feature film. Based on the novel by Stan Barstow, *A Kind of Loving* was one of the highlights of the recent trend in British cinema that saw movies lean more towards a grittier, *cinéma vérité* style of film-making. The British New Wave movement, as it was later dubbed, often looked to the working classes for inspiration and not in the frequently comic, soft-glossed manner of years gone by – where poor people were usually immaculately turned out in their waistcoats and cloth caps – but instead offered a grim, uncomfortable view of the late fifties/early sixties in which the movement took root.

Instead of glittering cocktail parties and lavish stately homes, dramas would just as often be played out in damp bedsits or smoke-stained terraced rows, the air redolent with boiled cabbage and misery. They were filled with characters suffering from alienation, depression and empty wallets. 'Angry young men', a phrase often used to describe the writers as well as the characters, became a dramatic staple found in the novels of Alan Sillitoe, the cinema of Tony Richardson and John Osborne's plays. The 'kitchen-sink' drama, so-called after an expressionistic painting by John Bratby, would become firmly entrenched over the years that followed, ultimately conventionalised in the world of the soap opera, with *Coronation Street* and *EastEnders* being 'kitchen-sink' to their very core.

Leonard was already familiar with this type of drama, having played

Peter, the mother's boyfriend, in Shelagh Delaney's *A Taste of Honey* at the Bristol Old Vic. It was also a style he felt comfortable with. 'I felt much more at home in those types of plays and films,' he later commented, 'I would never have made it at all as an actor if there had not been that sort of revolution in English theatre.' For all his love of exaggerated comic gesture and grotesque characters, his performances always fought to be recognisable as 'real' – even if they had the volume turned up on them a little – to accentuate the characteristics that were so recognisable in the first place. This was nothing so simple as a caricature – they were too well fleshed out for that – but an illustration of a character so detailed you couldn't miss every bit of linework and shading. The stylised drama and comedy of previous years were not to his taste at all – indeed, he would have seemed utterly misplaced within them.

A Kind of Loving was directed by John Schlesinger: it was the first of a number of films in a career that would take him to Hollywood and his CV was to include such award-winning fare as *Midnight Cowboy* and *Marathon Man*). It charted the uneven relationship between its stars, Alan Bates and June Ritchie, as they try to achieve the premise of the title. Leonard's role was small, appearing in only one scene as 'Whymper', a work colleague of Bates's lead.

The following year brought Leonard another small role (*two* scenes this time!) in *This Sporting Life*, the first fictional film from director Lindsay Anderson. It was one of the last movies to be classified as part of the New Wave and told the story of a young northern rugby player (played by Richard Harris) whose success on the pitch is not matched by his life away from it. It was Harris's first leading role and earned him a Best Actor Award at the Cannes Film Festival, as well as a nomination for Best Actor in a Leading Role (he lost out to Sidney Poitier for his performance in *Lilies of the Field*). As a pop-culture side-note, it was the performance of actor William Hartnell in the film that convinced a young BBC producer to cast him as the lead in a brand new science-fiction show she was working on, called *Doctor Who*. Despite the minor role, Leonard left his mark and was to work with Anderson again, this time in the satire *Britannia Hospital* (1982) towards the untimely end of his career.

Often the entertainment industry can seem a distinctly small world due to the chains of circumstance frequently running through it. Everyone ends up working with the same people time and again, disparate careers frequently seeming to synchronise briefly as one actor (or writer or director) bounces around another's CV. *A Kind of Loving* was adapted from Barstow's novel by Keith Waterhouse and Willis Hall (author of the play, *The Long and the Short and the Tall*, in which Leonard recently starred at Bristol). The pair went on to adapt Waterhouse's novel, *Billy Liar*, initially for the stage and then as a feature film for, again, John Schlesinger.

Billy Liar (1963) was to offer Leonard the first movie role that he could really sink his teeth into. It tells the story of a perpetual dreamer, Billy Fisher, who spices up his unfulfilling life with fantasies and daydreams. Leonard plays Emmanuel Shadrack, director of a funeral parlour and Fisher's boss. Shadrack was a slimy creature, just the sort of character that Leonard had already established a reputation for playing. Like many of the people the protagonist Fisher dislikes, he 'dies' in a hail of imaginary machine-gun fire as punishment for the way he treats his employee.

'He gave a superb, subtly comic performance,' Waterhouse later commented, 'perfectly cast, perfectly played – I always hoped to work with him again. He was always very high indeed on that "What about . . .?" list that writers compile when discussing casting with their directors. But the reply to "What about Leonard Rossiter?" was always, alas, that he was already spoken for.'

Indeed, Schlesinger adds: 'Leonard made me laugh so much behind the camera that it was I who often ruined takes.'

7

A Television Star Cometh

'For most people of my age – over forty! – you get a much greater sense of doing the job more successfully working in the theatre than in any other medium. Consequently, when you're offered jobs in theatre, most actors jump at the chance to renew acquaintance with the boards. It's very difficult to get good work in the theatre, there's very little now, particularly in the provinces.'

Leonard Rossiter, *Live from Two*

He may have loved working onstage but Leonard Rossiter was being offered so much TV and film work that he had to start turning the theatre jobs down. However much he may have loved live performance there was no doubt what paid better and common sense must be allowed to prevail occasionally, even in such a foolish and emotional business as acting.

As 1963 drew to a close, Leonard featured alongside Patrick Macnee's John Steed and Honor Blackman's Cathy Gale in the hugely popular series, *The Avengers*. The episode 'Dressed to Kill' was written by one of the most well-regarded script-writers the UK has ever produced, Brian Clemens. People are being bumped off at a New Year's Eve fancy dress party – that really, just to add to the party atmosphere, is being held in an abandoned station as the train it was originally taking place on has broken down there. Leonard plays a somewhat boorish Northerner, William J. 'Billy' Cavendish, who saunters around the platforms (and drinks optics) in his Robin Hood outfit. Cavendish was a typical Rossiter creation: harmless, but cringeworthy – you certainly wouldn't want to get caught next to him at the bar.

1964 brought Leonard his first of two appearances on the classic sitcom, *Steptoe and Son*, written by Ray Galton and Alan Simpson. It is one of the most successful – and, for that matter, funniest – sitcoms of all time. Galton and Simpson had spent seven years writing for Tony Hancock, creating all the scripts for *Hancock's Half Hour*, the radio (and later, TV) series that had established the comic's reputation. In 1961, Hancock broke off his association with the writers, abandoning three film ideas they had created without even reading them. He was notoriously difficult and Galton and Simpson were fortunate that the BBC offered them a contract to write six one-off comedies for a new series, *Comedy Playhouse*. One of those plays would be 'The Offer', a comedy about a father-and-son team of rag-and-bone men, *Steptoe and Son*. The show was so well received that it was immediately commissioned as a full series. *Comedy Playhouse* would go on, with many different contributing writers, launching many future shows such as: *Till Death Us Do Part, The Liver Birds, Are You Being Served?* and *Last of the Summer Wine*.

Steptoe and Son was one of the first sitcoms to employ actors rather than comedians (both Galton and Simpson believe the distinction to be crucially important in ensuring a true performance as opposed to just a comic chasing a punchline) and ran between 1962 and 1974. At the height of the show's success, it achieved record audience figures of 28 million and led to two feature films: *Steptoe and Son* and *Steptoe and Son Ride Again*.

Leonard's first appearance in the show was in the 1964 black-and-white episode 'The Lead Man Cometh' as a rather eerie visitor to the Steptoe scrap yard, offering a considerable quantity of cheap lead. 'Huw the Pew' (as Galton and Simpson refer to him, given that he also likes selling off church pews when he can get hold of them) has, in fact, stolen the lead from the Steptoe house, something that becomes all too clear when the old man and his son are left running around with buckets, trying to trap the torrential rain leaking into their home.

Leonard avoids any temptation to play the part up, offering instead a softly spoken and somewhat scary Welshman who sidles around the scrap yard: he is the perfect conman, seeming unconcerned whether they buy his lead or not. The role could have easily been one of Leonard's 'big' grotesques but works all the better for being quite the opposite. With the two leads playing their parts with the customary vigour, Huw the Pew wonderfully undercuts them.

As a side note to the show's popularity, a repeat of the episode later that year was rescheduled as it coincided with a General Election and it was feared so many people might stay in to watch that it would affect the attendance at polling stations!

When Leonard returned to the show, almost ten years later, it was as one of a pair of prisoners who have recently escaped from the nearby Wormwood Scrubs, breaking into the Steptoe house with designs on a hot meal and some cash. Of course they have found the only place in London less hospitable than the prison they've just left. The prisoners also happen to be a father and son and in no time, it's clear to the audience that they endure pretty much the same love/hate relationship as Albert and Harold.

'The Desperate Hours', stands as Galton and Simpson's favourite episode of the whole Steptoe series, in no small part thanks to Leonard's involvement. 'It was towards the end of the series,' explains Alan Simpson, 'after about fourteen years and Harry [H. Corbett, who played Steptoe Junior] was getting into a bit of a rut – he was phoning the performance in a bit.' Corbett was famously bitter about his failure to define a career as a serious actor and sick of being typecast as the young Steptoe. 'He'd developed a few mannerisms,' Simpson continues, 'and he was relying on them to get him through. When we got into the rehearsals, though, Leonard was playing it at such a great level that it became a battle between them – Harry couldn't help but raise his game.'

'He realised he was going to have to start acting!' adds Galton.

Leonard's father is played by the Irish actor J.G. Devlin, who manages to be even more disgusting than Wilfred Brambell as Old Man Steptoe: 'We always said that if Wilfred couldn't, or wouldn't play the old man,' says Galton, 'then J.G .was our second choice for the part. Having them there was perfect, the episode worked because of the balance. The sons both had the same feelings about their fathers, and the fathers had the same opinion of their sons.'

In the end, accepting there's no way he can make a getaway with his father in tow, Leonard's character decides to return to prison.

Besides, he's hungry and the food is certainly better than any on offer in the house he has had the misfortune of breaking into.

Back in 1964, another ATV 'Play of the Week' role was offered to Leonard (alongside his fellow Bristol cast-member, Annette Crosbie) as well as his first encounter with director Joe McGrath in *Justin Thyme*, a one-off comedy co-written by John Bluthal, a regular collaborator with Spike Milligan and familiar to today's audiences as Frank Pickle in *The Vicar of Dibley*.

Next up came a part in a romantic play written by actor/writer Douglas Livingstone, the first in an association that would extend over four different plays in the next 10 years. 'When I started writing,' Livingstone explained in a later interview, 'Len was right at the top of my "if only I could get him in a play of mine" list. I loved the colour he brought to every part he played; he seemed to me to manage something very difficult and very rare – to bring the size and excitement of a theatre performance to the television screen while always remaining totally believable. I never considered that television would take only "chuck away" acting and neither did Len. He always made you sit up and watch – and listen – because he was terrific with words, he loved to use them.

'I was very lucky. He was in three plays of mine, and he played three very different parts, although I wrote all of them with him in mind. The first was in the play *Beggars and Choosers*, which was in the 'Love Story' series. Len played a long-time bachelor sergeant, in love with a NAAFI girl. It was a beautifully tender performance that avoided any sentimentality and I still gratefully remember the quality he brought to the love scenes with Avril Elgar, who played the girl.'

Shortly after *Beggars and Choosers*, Rossiter and Livingstone were to appear together again, this time in the *House of Glass*, a play written by Mike Watts and directed by Michael Currer-Briggs. Set in a military detention centre, Leonard plays the role of a fastidious prison officer while Livingstone is an imprisoned conscientious objector (CO). Needless to say, Leonard's character made no bones about his disgust towards Livingstone's. 'When we acted the scenes he could really frighten me,' Livingstone admits, 'but Len had a great ability to switch on and off very quickly, to be absolutely in character and almost at the same time to be quietly sending up the whole business of "make-believe".

'I remember that when we got into the studio – the old Rediffusion studios at Wembley – we had great technical trouble getting a canteen scene to work. I and several other "prisoners" sat around a table while Len stood beside the table, watching over us as we ate. Lining up the shots is always a long process and one of the problems for the actors is that while they can't see the director sitting up in his box, he has got the cameras and microphones trained on them and can hear everything they say. (I got my warning on my first television part when I made some little comment about the director "aside" to another actor and a voice boomed over the studio loudspeaker, "I can hear you, Livingstone!")

'In this particular canteen scene the director was having a lot of trouble trying to decide where to position the soup plates. As usual, his instructions were relayed through the floor manager: "Move the plates a little to the right. No, a little to the left. No, put the plates on the other side of the table. Give Doug Brian's plate. No, give Brian's plate back. Why hasn't Davy got a plate? Move every plate one plate to the right." And on and on went the game of "Change the Plates" until I became aware that not only were the plates shifting about, but that the cutlery had got very unsteady too and I looked up to see Len standing, apparently rigidly in character, no tell-tale expression on his face, but his thighs vibrating against the edge of the table as his whole body shook with laughter. The rest of us visibly broke up and got the rocket, but he never gave himself away.'

Strangely, the play was never shown, the popular belief being that Rediffusion pulled the plug on it as the Army used to spend a lot of advertising money with them at that time and the work was rather damning in its portrayal of the military.

Leonard's next role with Livingstone was also a military man, albeit retired. In *Harry-Kari and Sally*, written by Livingstone for ATV, Leonard plays Harry, an ex-sergeant-major whose repressed homosexuality drives him to murder when he catches the object of his affections in bed with his female lodger.

'Leonard Rossiter's Harry was an extraordinarily vivid piece of work,' wrote Jessie Palmer in her review for the *Scotsman*. 'Which caught the devious twisted mind, the violence behind the apparent ineffectualness with horrifying realism.'

1973 saw their final collaboration together. Leonard appeared in Livingstone's *After Loch Lomond* for London Weekend Television as 'the life and soul of many a coach party,' says Livingstone, 'disappointed in his fellow passengers on the last night of a coach trip to the Highlands. A superb performance – funny, bitter and moving, a combination Len could manage uniquely well.'

The play's director John Gorrie agrees: 'The characters Leonard played were often extroverts and apparently content; but inwardly the same characters were full of doubts and fears. Lots of actors can play those life-and-soul bores with their stories and their egging people on to have a good time; what Leonard was able to do was to reveal the very sad man beneath it all. There was always in his best moments a corner of desperation – not just comic desperation but genuine desperation. He brought a tragic dimension to comedy, he was unique – there was no one like him at all.'

One could argue that Rossiter was far from unique in bringing an element of tragedy to comedy. Many actors, and indeed writers, have realised that nothing makes a character soar more than playing on that polarity when telling their stories. After all, *Steptoe and Son* – to use an example conveniently close at hand – thrived on it: this was a tale of sadness and desperation, of a pair of men trapped by circumstances and family, all of which made it funnier than had it just been about a pair of rag-and-bone men. When the sadness is real then we, the audience, invest in what we're seeing, we believe in the characters and laugh all the more when something comic happens, having grown to care. It's not an easy balance to achieve, however, and certainly something that Leonard excelled at. Gorrie is also right when he states that it became a backbone to Rossiter's career: Reggie Perrin and Rupert Rigsby would have been nothing without their private tragedies.

Despite all the TV work that 1964 offered, Leonard did manage one performance in the theatre, appearing in *Hamp*, a First World War story written by John Wilson originally presented at the Theatre Royal in Newcastle before it transferred to the Lyceum Theatre in Edinburgh for that year's Edinburgh Festival. The 'Hamp' of the title is a young lad unable to take the fighting anymore, who snaps and attempts to walk away from it. Leonard plays one of the officers defending Hamp at the inevitable court martial (though his character is acting partly out of self-interest, convinced that should Hamp be convicted, he will have to lead the firing squad assigned to carry out the sentence). Leonard was joined by his fellow actors John Hurt, Malcolm Tierney, Tom Watson and Richard Briers, who recalls complications with the set: 'The director, for reasons best known to himself, decided to build the stage up, thus increasing the rake six or seven times. The tables and chairs also had to be adapted to this angle and their upstage legs were duly cut by half. Unfortunately, this could not be done to the actors. The result was that they would enter from the wings with a highly pronounced Richard III limp, turn to face the audience, hurtle downhill to the footlights, brake sharply and then trudge up the slope in second gear. The sight of Leonard's face registering mock-exhaustion as he trudged upstage after almost tipping over into the front stalls is something I shall treasure always. Ever after the play was known affectionately as *Ramp*.'

8

That Was the Career That Never Was

The year 1965 brought about a brief change in direction for Leonard, thanks to Ned Sherrin and his new show (which was pretty much the same as his old show) entitled *BBC 3*.

In 1962, Sherrin devised, produced and directed the hugely influential *That Was The Week That Was* (or *TW3*). Hosted by David Frost, a new face at the time, who went on to enjoy a long career in political broadcasting – including a confrontation with disgraced US president Robert Nixon deemed such a TV landmark that they made a film about it! He also had a knighthood ahead of him. *TW3* was the last scheduled show on a Saturday night and was satirical, anarchic and frequently open-ended. Consistently controversial due to its willingness to lampoon any fair target (whatever the potential consequence), it became extremely successful and stood at the forefront of the satirical boom that was such a part of the 1960s: Peter Cook & Dudley Moore, *Beyond the Fringe* and *Private Eye* magazine . . . you couldn't move for satirists in that decade.

The BBC were determined to curtail the programme's tendency – aided by the fact that it was broadcast live – to simply run as long as it wished, working its way through the material devised with little consideration of the slot it was supposed to occupy. An extra programme was added to the schedule: repeats of the BBC adventure series *The Third Man* (loosely inspired by the movie adaptation of Graeme Green's novel). As *The Third Man* now ended the evening's scheduled entertainment, it was assumed Frost and Sherrin would have no choice but to ensure that they finished on time so the programme wouldn't begin late. Not wishing to give in so easily, Frost began reading the full synopsis of that evening's episode of *The Third Man* so there was no point in watching! In the end the BBC ditched the repeats and allowed the show to be once more open-ended.

TW3 ran for two series before taking a break due to the BBC's coverage of a General Election (it was thought the show could cause problems for the channel's statute of political impartiality). When it returned late in 1964 (with Harold Wilson and the Labour Party just settling into their newfound authority over the country), it was retitled *Not So Much a Programme, More a Way of Life* with Willie Rushton joining Frost as host. The following year, 1965, saw another change of name – and Robert Robinson replacing Frost as host – with the show now titled *BBC 3*.

BBC 3 proved just as capable of controversy as its forebears, most famously when theatre critic Kenneth Tynan proved himself wrong by announcing that the word 'fuck' had lost its ability to shock. It was the first time the word had ever been uttered on British television and a certain vocal minority was only too happy to show how shocked they were by phoning the channel and shouting at the hapless receptionists. Moaning at the BBC for being indecent isn't the modern sport many might think.

Many famous actors and comedians had been given a considerable boost by being part of the 'ensemble' cast on these shows and to Sherrin, Leonard Rossiter seemed an obvious choice. 'I had admired his work in *Semi-Detached*,' he explained in a later interview, 'and [director] Robin Philips had told me graphic stories of how funny he had been at the Bristol Old Vic . . . he seemed a natural choice. His bold style and compelling personality promised wonders.'

Sadly those 'wonders' would prove few and far between.

'Unfortunately he was prevented from settling into the team by a combination of complications,' continues Sherrin. 'During the first weeks he was still filming *Hotel Paradiso* in Paris because the film's schedule had overrun. He would fly in on Friday and leave on Monday, and did not get a chance to become part of the team. Moreover, in the early weeks much of the material used by Eleanor Bron, John Bird, John

Fortune and John Wells [all performers involved in the show] was improvised or written by them. Leonard's appearances were perfunctory and supporting – nothing to do with Leonard's skills or his ambition.

'Meanwhile I was trying to assess his range and to encourage the contributing outside writers to find opportunities for him. I had discovered on *TW3* that it is usually not until an actor has been seen to do something funny that scriptwriters start to write for him. Then they send in sketches along those lines. If he strikes out amusingly in a different direction, in comes a batch of sketches exploiting this new departure. Indifferent writers simply identify their favourite performer and assume he will supply enough idiosyncratic behaviour to make their material funny.'

One of the outside writers who did submit material for Leonard to use was Tim Preece, who would go on to work with him as an actor, both in 1972's *Machinegunner* and more famously, as Perrin's 'bearded prig' of a stepson in *The Fall and Rise of Reginald Perrin*. Clearly, he was something of a rarity, though: 'Leonard soon became impatient at the lack of good sketches for him and asked to be released from his contract. By an irony, for his last show – the fifth in the series – decent scripts had just started to arrive for him. On his last appearance he did a marvellously subtle impersonation of Groucho Marx, written by Dick Vosburgh, which was a five-minute hint at the sure-footed pastiche Vosburgh was to write, some 15 years later, in *A Night in the Ukraine* [a one-act play based on Anton Chekov's *The Bear*, adapted to be played like a Marx Brothers' movie. Presented alongside "A Day in Hollywood", a musical revue, it would achieve considerable success both in the West End and on Broadway]. But Leonard had committed himself to a theatre role and when the usual batch of scripts rolled in after his superb Groucho, it was too late.'

It's no great surprise that Leonard excelled in his impersonation of Groucho Marx for he was a big fan, as his daughter Camilla remembers: 'He hated Chaplin, I remember that strongly – hated the sentimentality of him, I imagine – but the total anarchy of the Marx Brothers appealed a great deal. We watched them whenever possible.'

Leonard was to work with Ned Sherrin again in 1978 and once more don a Groucho greasepaint moustache, wig, glasses and cigar to do so. Sherrin was hosting a series called *Song by Song*, which looked at famous comic lyricists. One edition concentrated on the work of E.Y. 'Yip' Harburg, the American lyricist whose work included the standard, 'Brother, Can You Spare a Dime?' as well as all the songs (and indeed some of the dialogue) in the movie of *The Wizard of the Oz*.

Leonard was asked to perform 'Lydia the Tatooed Lady' (written by Harburg alongside composer Harold Arlen). The song was one of Groucho's signature tunes, originally heard in the Marx Brothers' movie *At the Circus*. It was a performance he laboured over, listening to the original time and again in an attempt to capture every single nuance of Groucho's performance. Once again that analytical mind came into play, breaking the performance down into a series of notes and pauses, defining how best to stress the lyrics and replicate it perfectly.

'Leonard sang,' recalls Sherrin, 'splendidly, pouring concentration liberally into characterisation and spilling perspiration all over the studio floor.'

Had things worked out differently, Rossiter might have gone on to become an entirely different type of performer, though given his earlier decision not to linger in *Z-Cars*, it's doubtful he would have lasted long as a variety comedian without his feet beginning to itch.

9

Witches, Whisperers and the Wrong Box Entirely

Just as *Z-Cars* had seen Leonard's TV career blossom, so *Billy Liar* opened the door to a number of movie performances, partly due to the support of the celebrated British writer and director, Bryan Forbes. Forbes had begun his career as an actor before moving into writing. He penned scripts for the war film *The Cockleshell Heroes* (1955), but it was his work on that hugely influential caper movie in which he also appeared, *The League of Gentlemen* (1960), that really established his name. Setting up a production company with his friend and colleague Sir Richard Attenborough, Forbes moved into directing and built up a reputation as one of the UK's foremost filmmakers.

In 1964, he adapted James Clavell's novel, *King Rat*, concerning conflict between an English lieutenant and an opportunistic American corporal within a Japanese prisoner-of-war camp. Forbes cast Leonard as a fellow prisoner, Major McCoy. Sharing screen time with a young George Segal (who played the corporal) – in a role originally planned for Frank Sinatra – *King Rat* gave Rossiter his first true Hollywood appearance. Forbes was so impressed that he tried to cast him in every film he made thereafter.

'Perhaps the performance I enjoyed most,' recalled Forbes in a later interview, 'was a a scene he played with the late Eric Portman in my film of *The Whisperers*.' The movie told the story of an elderly lady – Edith Evans in a role that won her multiple awards – struggling to deal with her criminal son, played by Portman. 'It is always the test of an actor,' Forbes continues, 'when he is put up against somebody of the calibre of Eric Portman and although Leonard was then comparatively inexperienced in the art of film acting, he possessed to a very large degree the gift of ignoring the camera and "being" rather than impersonating.'

Two more cameos followed: one in Forbes' *Deadfall*, a diamond heist movie and another in the black comedy, *The Wrong Box*, both of which starred Michael Caine. 'To my lasting regret,' Forbes continues, 'I was never able to find a part that completely challenged [Leonard] – for happily, after *Deadfall* he became so much in demand, both on stage and television, that our professional commitments never timed out and, though I offered him other roles, he was not available to play them.'

As well as Forbes, the mid-sixties saw Leonard work with several other British cinema icons. A small role in the screen farce *Hotel Paradiso* provided the opportunity to act alongside Alec Guinness, who starred as a meek fellow conducting an affair with the sultry Gina Lollobrigida. Perhaps this was a surprising pairing but then as Lollobrigida's husband is played by the loveable cinematic toad Robert Morley, her taste is already questionable!

In 1966, Leonard appeared in a movie for the famed Hammer Studios. *The Witches* offered a script by Nigel Kneale, creator of *Quatermass* and future writer of the controversial *Year of the Sex Olympics* (in which Rossiter would also star) and concerned a some-what twee witches' coven operating in a quiet village. It predates *The Wicker Man* by seven years and with Kneale writing, it should have been one of the better examples of sixties' British horror – but the film actually manages to be utterly awful. Joan Fontaine stares around her as if baffled as to why she has agreed to star in the picture (and indeed it would pretty much mark the end of her screen career) and Leonard turns up now and again as her doctor, offering a soothing word and the offer of counselling as she becomes more and more convinced of the devilry at work in the village.

Kneale can't quite account for how bad the movie is – though he certainly took pains to distance himself from it in later interviews – alternately saying that the director (Cyril Frankel) either missed his intentions to write a black comedy, the villagers being inherently ludicrous in their rites, or contradictorily, fell into the trap of letting the villagers' rites seem ludicrous and thereby ruining the film's chances to be creepy! Truth is, it just doesn't work and, as is usually the case in cinema, the blame can lie squarely on many people's shoulders. Leonard manages to escape blameless – as indeed does a handful of the cast – delivering a suitably simple and realistic performance, but the character is bland and hardly provides enough enjoyment to salvage things.

Jimmy Sangster, a long-term scriptwriter for Hammer Studios, was the writer on another project released that year featuring Leonard, though *Deadlier Than the Male* was written for a different studio to his norm. It loosely resurrected the fictional character 'Bulldog' Drummond, originally an ex-First World War veteran-turned-private-detective and now an ex-Korean war veteran turned insurance investigator because nothing defines 'thrilling' more than insurance fraud! Drummond was played by Richard Johnson, who was director Terence Young's original choice to play James Bond in the first movie adaptation of Fleming's hero, *Dr No*. The movie plays an audience-pleasing hand by casting Elke Sommer and Sylvia Koscina as a pair of glamorous assassins, with Nigel Green offering a suitably dastardly villain (as he was frequently wont to do).

Leonard has a small role, playing an odious member of a board of directors. He is swiftly dispatched, though not before managing to get in a quick snog with Elke Sommer, paralysed by a poison in her ring and then rolled off the penthouse balcony, aware of all that's happening but unable to do anything to stop it. Not the nicest of deaths, certainly, but only ten minutes earlier a man had been shot to death by a rigged cigar, so it could have been worse. For those concerned that these lovely ladies might get away with such naughtiness, let me reassure you that Drummond does save the day. And an insurance company chairman sleeps peacefully once more.

As the fifties became the sixties, Leonard had been balancing a new marriage with his work as part of the Bristol Old Vic theatre company. Now, a few years later, he was divorced (but in a new relationship) and becoming thoroughly entrenched as a TV and film actor. He had appeared on Broadway – however briefly – worked with Michael Caine and Alec Guinness, and acted alongside Harry H. Corbett and Wilfrid

Brambell in one of the most highly regarded sitcoms of all time. In addition, he had appeared in a big-budget Hollywood movie and narrowly avoided a change of career as a satirical comic in Ned Sherrin's *BBC 3*. It had been a tumultuous time but the rest of the decade held greater changes still.

10

Cuckolds and Assassins

In 1965, Leonard had the opportunity of working with Keith Waterhouse and Willis Hall for the third and final time in a TV adaptation of *Celebration*, a stage-play they had written together, four years earlier. *Celebration* tells the story of a large family wedding followed by a funeral that takes place six months later. Leonard plays the part of Frank Broadbent, the uncle and – during the second half – corpse.

'I had the rare fortune to work with Leonard three times,' Hall later commented, 'We remained good friends over the years and often talked about doing something else together but never, alas, got round to it. But there remain these three superb performances that I take out of the recesses of my mind, occasionally, and separately dust them off and run them for a private chuckle.'

It is a sure sign of the success of Rossiter's career that Hall – like Bryan Forbes before him – laments the fact that he was unable to work with him again due to Leonard's availability. Even now, the television roles kept coming with a string of one-off plays, a format extremely common in the sixties and often adaptations of stage plays that offered actors a speedy accumulation of varied roles in much the same way as Rep had. *Between the Two of Us* concerned a lonely man and woman who, despite their need for companionship, can never help arguing whenever they meet. Writer Rhys Adrian was particularly impressed with Leonard's performance. 'He brought an eccentricity to the role,' he explains, 'the sort of eccentricity you find in normal people, and he did it so well that he didn't seem to be acting at all.'

Mr Fowlds by John Bowen followed, in which Leonard plays a prison visitor who ends up turning to crime. 'It was a part tailor-made for Len,' says Bowen, 'inasmuch as he could bring to such a fantasising and fantastic character an absolute conviction and truthfulness of playing. It seemed to me that when, later on, he achieved success as a comedian it was because his comedy technique was always based on consistency and conviction; the character might grow outrageously, but always from the inside.'

Both Rhys Adrian and John Bowen brushed against Leonard's skill of making the eccentric, outlandish and funny come from enough core truth that it stays rooted as part of a believable character – the skill that will see him achieve the height of his fame soon enough, when brought to bear on a seedy landlord and an office worker in the throes of midlife crisis.

In 1966, a translation of a modern French farce, *Dr Knock*, saw Leonard taking pulses (and liberties) as a medical conman who uses jargon and a convincing personality to strip his patients of cash. But it was his next project, *Death is a Good Living*, which saw him once again risk audience discomfort by insisting on a truthful performance. Leonard plays the role of Norman Lynch, an assassin for hire. The four-part series was adapted from Philip Jones' original novel by frequent collaborators Brian Degas and Tudor Gates – the following year they would pen the script for *Barbarella*, the surreal sci-fi romp that offered the world lots and lots of Jane Fonda.

Death is a Good Living was directed by Gerald Blake, who recalled his experiences when working with Leonard: 'He was a joy to work with, and during particularly difficult filming in rain and mud on the West Coast of Ireland he kept the whole unit laughing with his off-the-set jokes and pranks. The character is shot at the end, and when rehearsing this he released a hideous noise as he "died".

' "What are you doing, Len?" I asked.

' "It's a death rattle," he said.

' "No," I said, "you can't do it, it'll upset the audience."

'He gave me a long look.

' "Do you want the truth, or don't you?"

'No argument – that's what he did. And he was completely right: he taught me never to pull punches.'

Blake also points out the meticulous nature of Leonard's working methods: 'He planned out every minute detail of his performance which could sometimes make other actors in the scene a little bored. But that was Len's style of work – making his acting look ad lib and impromptu where he had put in a tremendous amount of care and effort and intellectuality.'

One cannot help but be reminded of Woody Allen, whose signature style of performance, packed full of pauses, 'ums' and 'ahs' seems utterly naturalistic but is actually planned and scripted in every detail. Sometimes it takes a performer a Herculean amount of time and practice to appear truly spontaneous.

In theatre, the role of Pastor Manders in Henrik Ibsen's play *Ghosts* (1965) would gather Leonard some of his finest critical notices yet. 'Leonard Rossiter's Pastor Manders,' wrote Alan Brien in the *Sunday Telegraph*, 'is one of the funniest and most savage portraits of a hypocrite I have ever seen.'

It is easy to forget now how scandalous Ibsen's play was when originally written in 1881 – but then, what wasn't scandalous in those days? The work focuses on corruption within marriage, with a widow revealing to her spiritual confidant and former lover (Manders) that her husband had been a philanderer throughout their married life and now his 'evil' has been passed to their son in the form of hereditary syphilis. To make matters worse, the son (Oswald) has returned to the family home, hoping to marry Regina Engstrand, his mother's maid. What he doesn't know is that she is the illegitimate product of one of his father's affairs and therefore his half-sister.

Written in a period when family honour and a belief that living according to a decent set of morals would provide its own reward, the play was seen as utterly repellent by the critics of the day. As a memorable quote in the *Daily Telegraph* put it: 'Ibsen's positively abominable play entitled *Ghosts* . . . An open drain: a loathsome sore unbandaged; a dirty act done publicly . . . Gross, almost putrid indecorum . . . Literary carrion . . . Crapulous stuff.' Somehow one suspects they didn't enjoy it very much.

This production which, thanks to a shifting in society's moral compass didn't manage to cause its audience to haemorrhage with outrage, was directed by Adrian Rendle. Tellingly, he found himself working hard to deal with an entirely different issue of societal convention: the difference in age between the mother (played by 61-year-old Catherine Lacey) and Leonard, who was only 39, so that an audience might believe they could once have been lovers. 'Len, of course, was a good deal younger than Catherine Lacey,' he explains, 'and at the dress rehearsals this became a more noticeable feature, for Katie Lacey wasn't one to use a lot of make-up. I found myself going between their respective dressing rooms, which were on either side of the stage. My function became one of suggesting more age for Len and less for Katie. By the last act all seemed well and I made no reference to their appearances. At the end of the notes Len said to me quietly: "Is he grey enough, do you think?" but before I could answer Catherine Lacey quickly flashed: "Oh yes, Len, any greyer and you'd be my father!"'

Rossiter's former life at the Commercial Union also seemed to come in handy: 'Len was meticulous about his insurance papers as props,' Rendle continues, 'and told me of his experiences in the insurance business before becoming an actor. He had to have those papers exactly right and, without a word, he manufactured the most authentic-looking documents for his scene.'

Barry Warren plays Oswald, the syphilitic and soon-to-be-heart-broken son. 'Len tended to make all his parts an aspect of himself,' he says. 'He was never invisible – Leonard Rossiter was always there. I could see bits of Manders in Rigsby. I liked the way he rubbed his hands; it helped me (as Oswald) to dislike him. The insincerity was so subtly played.'

1966 saw Leonard cast in a production of *Volpone*, which was presented at the Oxford Playhouse before transferring to London's Garrick Theatre a year later. A Jacobean comedy written by Ben Jonson, it tells the story of Volpone, a Venetian gentleman who pretends to be dying in order to dupe three greedy fellows into offering him gifts in an attempt to curry favour and be remembered in his will. Leonard played Corvino, one of the victims of Volpone's plot. So desperate is Corvino to be heir to Volpone that he offers the man sex with his wife – played by Maureen O'Brien, having recently left her role as a companion in *Doctor Who*.

The production reunited Leonard with actor Leo McKern, with whom he had recently appeared in the movie, *A Jolly Bad Fellow*.

McKern was suitably impressed with his performance, saying: 'Leonard's Corvino was, in my opinion, definitive. It was paranoic jealousy personified, a superb performance which I never tired of watching and enjoying; it was a rare experience, an amalgam of delight and immense satisfaction to share the stage.

'Offstage,' he adds, 'I thought him prickly, unpredictable, companionable and splendidly entertaining, difficult, a worrier, cynical (about certain things), passionate, insecure: a multi-faceted gem of an actor who adorned every production lucky enough to have him.' He also commented that Leonard was 'wonderfully fortunate in his lady', though whether that means McKern was enamoured of Gillian or that his fellow actor was lucky to have someone who could tolerate him when he was 'prickly', 'unpredictable' and 'difficult' is hard to say. Of course we are all contradictory in our personalities depending on circumstances and to highlight the negatives from McKern's comment is somewhat unfair.

The director Frank Hauser was also struck by Leonard's performance: 'He had this extraordinary ability of turning the sadistic into the comic. Playing a jealous husband who nevertheless is persuaded that his way to great inheritance lies in getting his young wife to go to bed with the rich donor, he menaced her constantly with a knotted handkerchief. This would have been nothing but unpleasant, except that in his outburst of rage at her refusal, he kept hitting himself with the knot. In one image he conveyed the brutality and comic impotence of the man.'

That same year, Leonard played Leone, another willing cuckold – though it must be noted Volpone doesn't succeed, however determined in his lust – alongside Judi Dench in a production of Luigi Pirandello's comedy of manners, *The Rules of the Game*. It's a vicious triangle between a woman, her husband and lover. The woman has left the marital home and now lives with her lover but in order to maintain the appearance of honour, the husband visits them every night. Disgusted by her husband's willingness to let her go – unaware of how much he hates her for her infidelity – she forces him into a duel with a stranger by contriving a violation of her honour in public. She expects, in fact *wants*, her husband to die in the duel – it is her revenge on him for his civility. He agrees calmly, on the understanding that her lover will be his second; he then dictates terms for the duel that will leave him at a distinct disadvantage, eventually – as per 'the rules of the game' – withdrawing from the duel so that the lover is forced to take his place. Of course, the lover is killed and the wife's plan of revenge backfires.

'Mr Rossiter,' wrote Don Chapman for the *Oxford Mail*, 'breathing the calm, mannered confidence of the compulsive melancholic, handles [his wife] with the self-amused fatalism of a bomb-disposal expert.'

Meanwhile, Judi Dench was 'overwhelmed by his technique and brilliance in the part'.

Sixteen years later, Leonard would return to the role in a production directed by actor Anthony Quayle, who described him floridly as 'Brilliant, absolutely brilliant! There was a kind of inner concentration and focus. He was definite. Everything – whether he was acting, talking, playing squash – everything came to a point. He was not malleable, he knew his own mind; he was as sharp-minded as his features, in every way a cutting edge. He was a sharp dagger of concentration. He was not a magnanimous man, he was not an open oven-door giving out general warmth, but a very concentrated burning glass. It was a very rare talent. I had the most enormous adoration.'

The reviews were, again, glowing. Francis King, writing for the *Sunday Telegraph*, was particularly struck by the climax when Leonard (as Leone) stands alone on the stage, having just seen the execution of his plan – and therefore his wife's lover. 'Few actors other than Mr Rossiter could hold for so long the pause at the final curtain, while a whole succession of emotions pass across Leone's face: mockery, vengefulness, pain, resignation, triumph. This is great acting of a kind rarely to be seen.'

Sometimes the greatest sign of an actor's art can be seen in his silences; in the moments when the face needs to be so clear, so controlled, as to do all the actor's job for him. It's no great surprise that Leonard could manage such a performance – he was, after all, as Quayle described him: 'a sharp dagger of concentration'.

The two characters, Corvino and Leone, were marvellous counterpoints to one another. Both were jealous men, one forced to ignore the fact in order to gain material wealth, the other feeding off the jealousy to save his own life and enact revenge while he does so. They were perfect Rossiter creations, one repugnant (and yet still amusing), the other morally ambiguous but attractive for all of that.

It's not difficult to see what drew Leonard to the theatre. For an actor, the chance to explore characters as rich and multifaceted as these night after night was attractive indeed. In turn, not many actors would be capable of pulling off such challenges, so one can see why theatre directors were equally drawn to Rossiter!

Though forced to balance his theatrical work with TV and film, he was making the parts he did play count. In the year to come, 1967, he would be hard at work on a glut of performances before the cameras and only manage one theatrical play. It was to be the most lauded play of his career and a character that he would play over the next three years.

11

The Irresistible Rise

'Do not rejoice in his defeat, you men. For though the world has stood
up and stopped the bastard, the bitch that bore him is in heat again.'
The Resistible Rise of Arturo Ui, Bertolt Brecht

After nearly 100 stage performances, 1967 would see Leonard Rossiter
play the part that, for many, still ranks as the pinnacle of his stage
career. It was a character, and indeed production, that seemed doomed
to failure. Certainly London theatre producers were reluctant to stage
the work (it would take two years of cajoling for them to do so).
But then Leonard thrived in roles like that. Not only did he excel in
making dislikeable characters compulsive viewing, he also transformed
material that might at first seem unpalatable into compelling entertainment. One only has to look at *Semi-Detached* to find a perfect
example of this – a play that even some of the cast thought repugnant
eventually turned into a palpable success.

'Do you want the truth or don't you?' Leonard had asked director
Gerald Blake while filming *Death is a Good Living* the year before,
proving how little he cared for the sensibilities of an audience when
there was a story to be told. Combining that bravery with the unerring
sense of comedy that had guided him through everything from *Steptoe
and Son* to Ned Sherrin's satirical *BBC 3*, he was eminently prepared
for the most important role he had undertaken thus far.

In 1933, as Adolf Hitler came to power, the German dramatist and
committed Marxist Bertolt Brecht fled his home country for fear of
persecution. He travelled to Denmark and then, in 1939, as war seemed

inevitable, to Sweden. When Hitler invaded Norway and Denmark, Brecht fled yet further, marking time in Helsinki while he awaited a visa that would allow him to move to the United States. It was during this period that he wrote his clear and damning parable of Hitler's ascendance to power: *The Resistible Rise of Arturo Ui*. Completed in just three weeks, it likened the dictator to a fictitious Chicago gangster – the 'Arturo Ui' of the title – who, determined to control the 'cauliflower racket', rose up among the organised crime families through a combination of merciless violence and political huckstering.

Brecht had always intended his script to be performed in English, intentionally using the backdrop of Chicago gangsters as a draw for getting the play performed on the American stage. However, it was not to be. The play eventually premiered in 1958, two years after his death: it was presented by the renowned Berliner Ensemble, a company Brecht himself had established alongside his wife, Helene Weigel, in 1949.

In 1967, the actor-turned-director Michael Blakemore had been working at the Citizen's Theatre in Glasgow – he would in fact become its artistic director a year later – and was determined to bring the play to the theatre. Mainly, as he would later admit, due to the fun he would have in producing the overtly theatrical and bombastic piece on a British stage. Brecht's work was famous for its unconventional and non-realistic style; his plays were brash and wore their theatricality on their sleeves, often directly addressing the audience. While the celebrated members of the Berliner Ensemble had had a full six months to rehearse and stage the play, Blakemore did so in just under three weeks. He was never in any doubt, however, as to the actor he wished to cast in the central role: the grotesque Arturo Ui was perfectly suited to a performer of Leonard Rossiter's power and drive.

Leonard was less sure, being far from convinced that he could pull off the Chicago mobster accent that the part required. He visited Blakemore at his flat in London, insisting that he should read for the part to allow the director to judge his suitability. Blakemore insisted he read perfectly and thus assuaged Leonard was on board. Later, the director described Rossiter's approach to the role: 'He saw the part as an opportunity to deploy the full range of his gifts and, swooping between the comic and the grotesquely sinister, he went for the throat. As an actor he had much in common with the great performers of an earlier generation, a self-sufficient talent forged out of necessity in the provinces. He was enormously inventive and from the outset had a clear idea of what he wanted to do with the part.'

While impressed with Rossiter's ideas, Blakemore was concerned with a necessity to adhere to the theatrical principles Brecht had taught – and of course, imbued in his plays. 'During the rehearsals Len would arrive each morning, his scenes already structured with moves, bits of business and theatrical climaxes. I was full of admiration but continued to fret about Brechtian correctness. I felt it necessary to pose some questions. Len took this as criticism, which of course it wasn't. Indeed, as an ex-actor I was secretly on his side. I could picture him at the end of the day's work returning to his digs and after a preoccupied dinner, going to his room and with a fierce concentration pacing out his part in front of the gas fire until the early hours of the morning. In weekly and fortnightly rep it was the way all of us had to work if, as actors, we wanted to achieve anything at all.'

Eventually he allowed Leonard to play the part the way he wished: 'What Leonard was offering was so alive and charged with comic intelligence that it simply couldn't be denied.'

Again we see that ferocious determination to craft a role the way he believes it should be done, the conviction that he knows best. As with Fred Midway in *Semi-Detached*, Leonard had an almost blank canvas for Arturo Ui for the play was virtually unknown to a British stage. Unlike the weight of previous performances that often make Shakespeare such a task to keep fresh, he had the chance to offer a definitive version of the role.

As the production drew closer, the play came together and after a ludicrously long dress rehearsal that saw them working until one o'clock in the morning, it was clear that they had a successful production on their hands. One terrifying uncertainty was left unrehearsed: the climax would see Leonard carried forth over the stalls on a large tower, giving his final speech of the play. The construction of the tower in question was completed a mere half an hour before the opening curtain and while Leonard had had chance to scale it (mainly to ensure he could!), there was no time to rehearse the scene and it would be performed for the first time with the complete staging in front of the opening-night audience.

The production was a success with full houses and exuberant critics, but attempts to stage the play in London met with failure. Brecht was deemed far too unpopular for the West End and no one was willing to back a production of one of his works. It was revived the following August as part of the Edinburgh Festival, performing for a run at the Lyceum Theatre. Again, the production was deemed an artistic and commercial success but a backer for a London run still couldn't be found.

In the interim, Blakemore staged a play at the Glasgow Citizen's Theatre that also looked to Nazism for its theme. *The Strange Case of Martin Richter* by Stanley Eveling concerned a Jewish butler who leads the servants of an old German house to rebel against their ex-Nazi masters. The lead in Scotland was played by the Austrian actor Martin Miller, but when the production transferred to London for a performance at the Hampstead Theatre Club, Rossiter took over the part.

Eveling was critical of Leonard in the role: 'I just found that Rossiter didn't sound or look Jewish or defeated. In a way I felt he lacked a real comic talent. I equate the comic – not the satirical or merely laughable – with a certain sort of obdurate, courageous helplessness. Looking back, I think Ui was his best part: a combination of the absurd and the threatening, the anarchic and controlled, the deliberate and the wilful. I felt he did not understand or even respect maybe the character of [my] play. His performance was thrust into it and was not a part of it. It says a lot for him that the critics liked his performance but when Miller did it, they also liked the play.'

The critics certainly did like the performance: 'Leonard Rossiter, manipulating every nuance of megalomania with masterly shifts from the comic to the sinister, gives the role of Richter an enigmatic, ambiguous but always compulsive fascination,' wrote Milton Shulman in the *London Evening Standard*. While Robert Cushman, of *Plays and Players*, said: 'Leonard Rossiter, whose attributes apparently include the enviable ability to walk effortlessly with his body arched back at an angle of forty-five degrees, solves the problems of playing an outsize character by going out and creating a world of his own, and daring the rest of the play to match up to it.'

Arturo Ui's thus far wholly *resistible* rise towards London success eventually turned in Leonard's favour in 1969. There was a brief stint of the production in April 1969 at The Playhouse in Nottingham before finally, backed up with enough stellar reviews and packed houses, it opened at the Saville Theatre in London's West End during June of 1969 – the same theatre that had seen *Semi-Detached* bomb (without Leonard) five years earlier.

It was to prove a hugely successful run, with critics and audiences alike aghast at the production and the performance of its star. John Wells, the satirist, actor and writer who had begun his career through Ned Sherrin's *TW3* and *Not So Much a Show, More a Way of Life* was in one of the London audiences: 'You could see the underpinning of his comedy because it was absolutely real and he did have extraordinary power too – in the way that Spike Milligan has on stage – in that he actually could bring the whole audience to him. He didn't go out to the audience, he could actually bring *them* in, by the intensity of his concentration.'

David Graham, appearing alongside Rossiter in the play, observed: 'He blazed with energy and liked you to blaze with him. I always found him very generous as an actor. His Arturo Ui was an unforgettable experience: a great performance, one of great power, dazzling comic invention and marvellous physical dexterity.'

The critics too were equally exuberant in their praise:

'. . . Leonard Rossiter's virtuoso performance. This is the most vivid, compelling and hilarious acting currently on view on the London stage. It can best be described as volcanic: it alternates between menacing, brooding inertia and eruptions of hysterical violence. The loathsome obsequiousness, the foxy charm, the startled backing into the furniture, the ever-present awareness of himself as an actor calculating effects, make up not only a great performance but a great *Brechtian* performance.'

Frank Marcus, *Sunday Telegraph*

'The part of Arturo Ui gives a wonderful opportunity for a virtuoso performance and this production is fortunate in having discovered just the virtuoso actor for it. Leonard Rossiter is, in my opinion, better than even the Berliner Ensemble's star Ekkehard Schall in the part; Schall, basically, is a heroic actor and had to work harder to bring out the seedy, middle-aged, born-to-failure aspect of Ui, which Leonard Rossiter, a character man from the start, does to perfection. Rossiter's performance is Chaplinesque in the best sense of the word – it is grotesquely comic and yet displays the control of movement one associates with ballet. And each movement has its own transparency, behind the actual gestures one senses the process of thought or emotion which has led to it.'

Martin Esslin, Plays and Players

'A tremendous performance, the funniest and technically the most brilliant in the West End at the moment. Eyes popping like eggs, he lopes across the stage, fawning on the eminent, baring his deadly smile, squawking in terror when a chair gooses him.'

Jeremy Kingston, Punch

'Mr Rossiter is perfect – a trampled paranoid, comically mean-minded with the timing of a comedian and, stealthily developing, the arrogance of a madman. Even at his funniest, Mr Rossiter never lets us forget the gas chambers, the bombs, the slaughter.'

Clive Barnes, The New York Times

The role would earn him awards from the Variety Club of Great Britain, the Scottish Television Theatre Award and, voted by London theatre critics, the *Plays and Players* Award. Leonard dealt with the accolades with his usual apparent indifference – he knew he had done a good job and that was all that mattered to him. Talking to Byron Rogers in an interview with *TV Times* magazine, he admitted: 'I am at my best at strong characters with a manic streak. I like roles such as Hitler: where you can go from outraged hysteria to assumed calm in seconds. I think I am better equipped to do that than most.'

That furious physicality that is so much a part of any Rossiter performance – and hell for the costume department as the perspiration began to flow – was certainly beyond many performers, especially on a nightly basis. The sheer size of character, a not altogether realistic grotesque, was also a trap for most actors: underplay it and you miss the point; overplay and you create a mess. The precision needed to sustain such a larger-than-life character but always hit the necessary mark had always been one of Leonard's skills and in Ui, he had found the perfect vehicle.

For years to come, Arturo Ui would be the touchstone of Leonard Rossiter's career, a part talked about with reverence and one that would divide people into those who adored it and those who somehow failed to see it. Because of its transience, theatre is particularly prone to exaggerated reminiscence: performances are offered then gone, never to be successfully captured. Even if you film a theatre production an essential atmosphere is lost by not being in the same room as the actors and audience. If you miss it, it's gone forever. That ethereal quality often sets a production so high on a pedestal that it's impossible to touch it. Nothing can ever be revisited, or re-analysed. If a production was deemed perfect, then perfect it shall forever be. Sometimes that can even become a curse for an actor, as the shadow of the one 'perfect' performance hangs over them for the rest of their career. Sometimes an actor can achieve such success that the only way forward is down.

Not so for Leonard Rossiter: he was on a direct course for the roles that would eclipse even Arturo Ui in the public's affection (helped, of course, by the fact that they would be in a medium that, unlike theatre, was regularly watched by millions). His career had a good distance to climb yet.

12

More Movies

Arturo Ui's rise may have been resistible, but it was certainly time-consuming too. Between the production's Glasgow premiere and the eventual run at the Saville Theatre was a period of two years. Not that Leonard Rossiter had simply been kicking his heels during that time. He was not a man who naturally spent a good deal of his time at rest: when he wasn't working, he would be playing sport (particularly squash, of course), anything to raise sweat and a smile. Rossiter was man with unbelievable energy: indeed, he bristled with it and if it couldn't be released on stage, then a squash court would do just as well.

Not that work would ever be scarce for him: not any more, his successes had assured he would always be in demand. 1968 brought three more of his movie performances to cinemas. First up was Sir Carol Reed's adaptation of the Lionel Bart musical, *Oliver!* – itself an adaptation of Charles Dickens' novel, *Oliver Twist*.

In 1960, Lionel Bart had unveiled his simplified (and far more jolly) tale of Dickens' orphan at London's New Theatre (now the Noël Coward Theatre). Jewish actor Ron Moody was in place as Fagin (countering some of the accusations of anti-Semitism his character had faced since Alec Guinness' performance onscreen 12 years earlier) and the production ran for over 2,000 performances. Over the years it has been revived many times and has launched the careers of several actors and musicians, including somewhat strangely, Phil Collins, who played the role of Fagin's favourite pickpocket, the Artful Dodger.

The screen version was fairly true to the stage musical, though some of the numbers were removed. Leonard played Mr Sowerberry, a part originally performed on stage by Barry Humphries, the Australian satirist and painter most famous for his alter ego Dame Edna Everage. The Sowerberrys are Oliver's first adoptive guardians after his stint in the workhouse and they employ him to work in their undertaking business, though Oliver doesn't last long in the job.

Rossiter was not a great fan of the style of the film: 'I don't like Dickens being "prettied up",' he said in a later interview, 'David Lean's *Oliver Twist* is more to my liking [Lean's version, released in 1948, is still considered a classic of British cinema and by far the best adaptation of Dickens' novel despite many other attempts since] but it was a pleasant experience.'

A modern-day role followed quickly in Oliver's footsteps, with Leonard taking the part of Inspector Dudley in Christopher Morahan's comedy crime movie, *Diamonds for Breakfast*. The English-language debut of Italian superstar Marcello Mastroianni, *Diamonds for Breakfast* was a lightweight affair about a Russian fashion designer who recruits models to form a team of jewel thieves. Good things lay ahead for Leonard, Mastroianni and indeed, Morahan.

The swinging-sixties staple of silly spy movies reared its head again, with Rossiter once more reunited with Tom Courtenay. Courtenay played the title character in *Otley*, a film adapted by *Likely Lads* and *Porridge* creators Dick Clement and Ian La Frenais from a novel by Martin Waddell. Clement also directed. 'It was my debut as a film director,' he later admitted, 'and I knew that my best bet was to surround myself with the finest possible cast. I asked [Leonard] to play a rather offbeat assassin called Johnston, my theory being that although it was not a comic role, Len would bring an extra dimension to it through his talent for comedy. Johnston was an ex-commando who ran a fleet of coaches ("Sixteen days in the Dolomites for thirty-six quid – very reasonable"), but who was happy on occasion to terminate life for extra pocket money. Len was funny but also quite sinister and always believable. I was quite sorry when he got his comeuppance at Notting Hill Gate tube station.'

The film followed the mishaps of Courtenay's Gerald Arthur Otley, an antique dealer and thief (often a tautology) who is mistaken for a spy and therefore spends the next 90 minutes stumbling from one misadventure to another. Clement doesn't exaggerate when he says that he surrounded himself with the best possible cast. As well as Courtenay and Rossiter the film features such familiar British faces as James Villiers, Freddie Jones, James Bolam, Geoffrey Bayldon, Phillida Law and Ronald Lacey. While Waddell's character starred in a series of novels over the next few years, the film was a one-off.

It's worth noting that Clement already thought of Rossiter as a comic actor. Leonard was always happy to introduce humour into his roles (he was even able to give a scene of domestic violence grim laughs in *Volpone*, as noted earlier by director Frank Hauser), but if one looks at his work as a whole it is far more varied than just comedy. It is always an actor's lot to be typecast as a certain kind of performer. Certainly, once Leonard had appeared as Rigsby and Perrin, the straight roles that he would normally be offered diminished considerably, having become a sitcom actor in the short-sighted eyes of many a casting director. His time as a general character actor was fast diminishing.

13

The Year of the Sex Olympics

It is easy, when discussing the creative media of the sixties, to overuse the expression 'groundbreaking'. By the very nature of cultural history, the further back one goes when discussing it, the more frequently ground will be seen to be 'broken'. Television, in particular, was still a clunky and primitive medium throughout the decade – certainly by today's standards. Those working in the medium were weighed down with ludicrously heavy and immobile cameras, shooting on video tape that was extremely hard to edit, which necessitated long scenes with little action so as to create longer, more practical sections to work with.

Whereas film had been presenting spectacular vistas for decades, and theatre had developed its own creative trickery to lend atmosphere and scope to productions, television was still a small box that attempted the miraculous via a repetitive sequence of 'two' and 'three' shots (the number of actors' faces in frame). It is worth offering a comparison to highlight the limitations: the story of the British fighting the Zulu Army at Rorke's Drift was famously put on film in 1964, in the hugely successful epic, *Zulu*. The movie, directed by Cy Endfield, offers audiences the daunting spectacle of hordes of charging Zulus in a breathtaking manner – prompting most to call Michael Caine to mind, uttering the completely apocryphal line: 'My God, there's thousands of them out there!' A few years earlier, the BBC had presented a live play on the same subject and when faced with the practical complications of an actual Zulu army, they were reduced to having a refined lieutenant poke his head out of the tent flaps only to turn back, ashen-faced, with the news that there were indeed 'thousands' of Zulus advancing on their position.

Television was constantly at war with its own limitations and while it is possible – indeed, necessary – to view footage from the time with a focus on its creative qualities rather than technical hiccups, the sheer weight of one can sometimes cut into the other. However, between 1967 and 1968, Leonard starred in two films produced by the BBC that earn the right to their 'groundbreaking' label in spades, despite being littered with the sort of limitations, clunkiness and rough art that epitomised the medium at the time.

1967's *Drums along the Avon*, part of the 'Wednesday Play' strand, was an early example of the 'mockumentary' style of comedy that gained considerable popularity, with such later successes as Robe Reiner's 1981 movie *This is Spinal Tap* and Ricky Gervais 2001 sitcom, *The Office*. While Leonard Rossiter's appearance at its centre as a white man 'blacked-up' so as to impersonate a Sikh might bring to mind such racially awkward images as Peter Sellers in *Goodness Gracious Me* or *The Party* (or indeed Sellers' fellow Goon Spike Milligan in various comic turns beneath a turban), *Drums along the Avon* is saved by the fact that it actually has a point beyond comic-book impersonations. Charles Wood's sharp satire takes an edgy look at racial relations in the UK during the sixties, with Leonard's role being that of an ex-colonial officer-turned-liberal, who is convinced that by 'becoming' a Sikh he will help bring the white and Asian communities together. The play was well reviewed, funny and prescient.

A string of one-off TV dramas followed. Leonard appeared in an adaptation of Roald Dahl's short story *Taste*, taken from the author's 1954 collection, *Someone Likes You*. Rossiter played a wine snob who bets the always-chilling Donald Pleasance his daughter's hand in marriage if he can guess a particular vintage.

Michael Keir's *The Unquiet Man* saw Leonard play a ventriloquist whose dummy convinces him to murder his wife, perhaps inspired by the segment of Ealing's 1945 portmanteau horror movie *Dead of Night*, which offered a similar tale. Certainly the latter, with Michael Redgrave as the nutty ventriloquist, inspired William Goldman's 1976 novel and 1978 movie *Magic* (with Anthony Hopkins offering a career-defining performance as the chilling lead).

The Fanatics couldn't be more different: giving Leonard the chance to portray famed French writer and philosopher Voltaire. It was a dramatisation of a true story concerning Voltaire's attempts to clear the name of tradesman Jean Calas, who was falsely labelled a murderer and tortured to death due to his Protestant beliefs. Writing in the *Observer*, George Melly commented: 'Leonard Rossiter as Voltaire demonstrated how it is possible to express the spirit of the man through minute observation of physical mannerism.'

But it was with the broadcast of *The Year of the Sex Olympics* in July 1968 that Leonard took part in the second, truly groundbreaking drama of the time. Written by Nigel Kneale, the play was a considerable force in British television's early decades of experimentation. Kneale was the creator of the *Quatermass* serials, which had famously emptied the streets in the 1950s as people gathered around their sets – or those of their neighbours if they didn't own one personally – in order to follow the chilling sci-fi adventures of Professor Bernard Quatermass and the various alien invasions he encountered. Returning to the limitations of TV for a moment, it's worth pointing out that the terrifying giant monster that clambers atop Westminster Abbey at the climax of *Quatermass'* first series was nothing more than Kneale's hand in a gardening glove, covered in twigs and stuck through a photo of the building!

Set in a dystopian future of those who make television and others who simply watch, *The Year of the Sex Olympics* details the attempts of the broadcasters to find material that would stimulate – though not too much – their audience. The population explosion has been curbed by broadcasting live sex all day, gluttony and violence are desires itched by a channel of fat men flinging food at one another while the populace has learned to 'watch not do'. But how can the programme makers make their audience laugh? What is the elusive 'fruitskin' that will provoke humour in the doughy-faced rows of spectators that they monitor on their audience feedback screens?

When a man accidentally dies during a live broadcast – the camera zooming in on his blood-spattered face – the peals of hysterical laughter from the viewers point the way forward. Creating *The Live Life Show*, where hidden cameras will broadcast a never-ending feed of two rebellious citizens from the studio as they try to survive on a primitive island, re-learning all the old skills society has lost – even making fire or preparing their own food is beyond them. Little do they know the producer has ensured they're not so alone as they believe, smuggling in a deranged killer so as to ensure the audience gets some of the riotous 'comedy' they have recently learned to love.

The drama is astonishingly prescient not only in its presentation of 'reality' TV but also the failings of a society that has grown numb to real experience, satisfied with a dull diet of programming in its place. Interviewed shortly before his death in 2006, Nigel Kneale explained his inspiration to the author Andy Murray: 'It was written at a time of people saying, "Let it all hang out" or "Let's have lots of porn". I thought, OK, but where do you go with porn? You've got to show everything, all the days and all night, and the reason for that would be to calm the population. If they got too lively and had lots of children, this would cause a huge population explosion. But if they've got it all on television, why try? They're sat watching happily and if they're fed, they'll just carry on being couch potatoes. But suppose you did have that: how long would it last? Some of them would get sick to death of television. A lot of them were dying of boredom. That was the story.'

Leonard was cast in the role of co-ordinator Ugo Priest, a modern spin on the BBC's Director-General. Originally, the part was offered to Leo McKern but he was unavailable and so the director, Michael Elliott, wrote to Rossiter, insisting it was 'the most important [television] play Nigel Kneale has written since *Quatermass*'. Lasar Opie, the somewhat twisted – by our standards, at least – producer who ends up helming *The Live Life Show* and relishing every heart-rending moment would be played by Tom Courtenay, with whom Leonard had worked on numerous occasions. But Courtenay pulled out at the last minute, having been offered the chance to star in a production of *Hamlet*. Elliott decided to offer the part to someone he had known from his work in the theatre, a young actor called Brian Cox, who would go on to be cinema's first – and in this author's opinion, finest – Dr Hannibal Lecter in Michael Mann's 1986 film *Manhunter*. A long and varied career in Hollywood has followed. The central role of Nat Mender, the producer of the Sex Olympics, who opts out of society and volunteers to take part in *The Live Life Show* was played by another newcomer, Tony Vogel, who mostly manages to deal with the complexities the script offers, requiring him to deal with concepts and responses that must have had his brain in a twist.

For all the occasional awkwardness of presentation the final third of the play is desperately chilling; the climax utterly unmerciful. The script would certainly cause ripples if it were broadcast today, over 40 years later. It is unsurprising therefore that it nearly wasn't made then.

A copy of the script was leaked to self-styled TV 'watchdog' Mary Whitehouse, president of the National Viewers and Listeners Association. 'I don't think she'd read anything but the title,' Kneale admits in the interview with Murray, 'and [she] said, "This must not be put on! I will have the producer sacked!" She went after the producer, Ronald Travers, who was a nice, rather self-effacing man, and she did her damnedest to get him booted out of his job. However, she was overruled.'

Nor did the problems end there. An electricians' strike during production looked set to bring the whole project crashing down. The striking electricians actually stood on set, blocking the shooting so that – even with someone else trying to operate the lights – the filming had to be stopped. The BBC's Director-General at the time, Hugh Carleton Greene, had as much sympathy for the electricians' feelings as he had for Mary Whitehouse. He ordered Travers to select one of the troublemakers and have him physically thrown out of the building. A BBC commissionaire was brought in to do just that, carrying him to the front gate and throwing him out of it! Sure enough, the rest stayed well clear for fear of suffering the same fate.

During location filming Vogel fell and broke his wrist – particularly bizarre given that his daughter in the play does exactly that at the very same location. Even then the troubles weren't over: the delays having knocked the whole production impossibly behind schedule, the final ten minutes of the play were left unfilmed when the allotted studio time was over.

'I remember they all came back to our house,' said Kneale, 'Leonard Rossiter, Brian Cox and the others. They all just sat about here in acute gloom wondering if they'd ever finish the thing, because there was no logical reason that they should be able to. The studio time was now lost, gone to some other show. There was the question of cost. It was a kind of stand-off for some weeks. They then decided to go ahead with it, get Leonard and Brian and the others back, and finish the thing. And it looked very, very good.'

Certainly, it was colourful: one of the first handful of colour productions from the BBC, it made considerable use of the fact. The 'High Drive' TV makers were draped in garish fabrics and gold paint, inhabiting a world of visual excess. TV reviewer Nancy Banks-Smith remarked during her highly favourable review that those viewers who had only seen it in black and white – as colour TV owners were still few and far between in those days – 'hadn't seen it all.'

Sadly, today, that means we can't see it either as all that exists is a 16mm black-and-white print. Indeed, for many years the play was thought lost altogether due to the BBC policy of either recording over video once it had been broadcast or simply junking the tapes altogether. In the days long before home video and digital repeat opportunities television was also somewhat disposable.

Thankfully, a black-and-white print is certainly better than none at all and the British Film Institute released the film on DVD a few years ago with a commentary from Brian Cox, in which he recalls the experience of working with Rossiter: 'Len was an incredible, dynamic and gifted actor,' he says, 'he was kind of an inspiration. He had this phenomenal energy. He became obsessed with Charles Macready [a nineteenth-century actor, renowned during his lifetime for performances weighed down with considerable research and precision, a man one can easily imagine him seeking to emulate]. He would go on these long walks and I'd see him as my gym used to be around the corner from where he lived. He'd be out of breath when I met him, having just walked from Hampstead. "Macready used to do it," he'd say, "so I think I can do it as well" – ever the athlete.'

Despite the string of difficulties Leonard's performance is up to his usual, pitch-perfect level. His Priest is a man who remembers the old days but is determined never to return to them, though at the climax the viewer is not quite sure whether he maintains that belief. He plays the gentle advisor, telling the younger men what it was like before the civilised 'watch not do' society they enjoy today, nodding towards their baffled faces as he talks of such terrifying concepts as 'feelings' and 'war'. While the last few minutes of the play are astonishing from all quarters, Rossiter takes the last line, creating a definite shiver and an ambiguous conclusion.

According to research conducted at the time, much of the audience found the whole thing impenetrable, despite Banks-Smith's glowing review the following morning: 'Quite apart from the excellent script,' she wrote, 'and the "big big" treatment, the play radiates ripples. Is television a substitute for living? Does the spectacle of pain at a distance atrophy sympathy? Can this coffin with knobs on furnish all we need to ask?'

It certainly did 'radiate ripples' as the same writer found when reviewing a new programme from Channel 4 in 2000: *Big Brother*. She was quick to make the association between the new show and the programme she had reviewed 32 years earlier. As was scriptwriter and actor Mark Gatiss, a great fan of Nigel Kneale, commenting in a piece written for the *Guardian* newspaper shortly after the *Quatermass* creator's death: 'When *Big Brother* began on Channel 4 in 2000, I took a principled stand against it. "Don't they know what they're doing?" I screamed at the TV. "It's *The Year of the Sex Olympics*! Nigel Kneale was right!"'

The year 1968 also saw Leonard consolidate his place in the annals of sci-fi movie history by appearing in Stanley Kubrick's *2001: A Space Odyssey*, possibly the most highly regarded work in this genre ever made. With an accent as thick as borsch, Rossiter appeared as a Russian scientist trying to get to the bottom of the strange occurrences on earth's moon. His was a brief appearance but then *2001* was not about the characters: it's a movie of ideas, images, landscapes and soaring classical tunes.

He would work with Kubrick again, however, seven years later in the director's adaptation of W.M. Thackeray's *Barry Lyndon*. As the cowardly Captain Quin, Lyndon's rival for his first love, Nora Brady, Leonard's role was a little more substantial than in *2001* and both his performance and indeed the film itself are exceedingly well regarded. Writing for the *Telegraph*, columnist Tim Robey re-evaluated the movie prior to an extended screening at the BFI on London's Southbank in 2009. 'Watching it now,' he says, 'is a spellbinding experience on many levels, but it makes you realise that the most undervalued aspect of Kubrick's genius could well be his way with actors. The supporting cast is a glittering procession of cameos, not from star names but from vital character players. Leonard Rossiter makes the first unforgettable impression as Captain Quin, the pompous and prickly suitor of Barry's cousin Nora (Gay Hamilton) – he raises snobbish indignation to an art form.'

As the sixties drew to a close, it took with it a decade of varied and lauded work from Leonard Rossiter. The 34-year-old man who had entered that decade must still have sensed the uncertainty of his chosen career. Relieved that his hard work in repertory had seen him accepted into Bristol Old Vic, yes, and as a lover of theatre he would have felt no sense of limitation in the medium. Thinking in terms of a career, however, times were already changing for actors and the notion of surviving financially just by working in theatre was becoming a less viable goal with each year that passed. Film had always been a more affluent industry, with many an actor weathering a dry spell of employment, thanks to a reasonable fee for movie work, but it's little brother – television – was also beginning to blossom. Leonard entered the decade with a small handful of inconsequential TV appearances and no film roles whatsoever, he left it as an actor who frequently had to turn down theatre appearances as he was so much in demand elsewhere.

His timing was impeccable, bringing a style of acting that matched the size of a theatre performance with the precision and attention to detail needed when working to camera: he was there as TV finally took off. For just as the sixties had seen a massive change in Leonard, they had witnessed a similar change in the medium that would all too soon make him a huge star. While TV started the sixties with small audiences and limited skills, it finished the decade with video recording, colour transmission and a captive audience. The majority now owned a television set and it was that 'coffin with knobs on' that the population now looked to for entertainment. The audience was there and waiting, and soon they would take Leonard Rossiter for their own.

14

The Winter of Discontent

While the blossoming of television might be cause for celebration it certainly had its drawbacks. All over Britain, repertory theatres were closing down, the lack of attendance making them financially unviable. There can be no doubt that the draw of television – entertainment you didn't even have to leave your house for – was the major culprit. Theatre had somehow weathered the drop in numbers caused by cinema, but it couldn't do the same again.

Leonard was still able to secure some theatre work, however, though the reviews of 1970's production of *The Heretic*, a new play by Morris West about a sixteenth-century man put on trial by the Roman Catholic Church, might have given someone with less self-conviction cause to regret his involvement. 'Leonard Rossiter literally sweats to endow it with individuality,' noted Irving Wardle in *The Times*, 'But his labour is impotent. I doubt whether Mr Rossiter is heroic martyr material in the first place, his great talent lends itself more to grotesque satire. Here he produces a violent sequence of facial and vocal convulsions, twisting his features into foxy snarls and driving his voice through a chaotic jumble of vowel sounds, sometimes posh, sometimes cawing, sometimes suggesting the slurred cadences of an American drunk. The effect, on the whole, is undisciplined and vulgar.' Ouch!

He fared no better from the pen of Felix Barker, writing for the *Evening News*: 'The star of *Arturo Ui* proceeded to give the sort of performance I thought went out with The Lyceum. Has there been such a grotesque since the hunchbacked Laughton swung from the gargoyles of Notre Dame?'

Unfortunately, Leonard was suffering a backlash following his performance in *Arturo Ui*. Raised to such heights of expectation, either the critics cannot help but be disappointed, or perhaps he still had a foot in the exaggerated Brechtian performance demanded by *Arturo Ui*, a style now doing him no favours with the critics here.

His next stage appearance, in 1971, would be better received – including by Irving Wardle. Writing again for *The Times*, he said of Leonard's performance in *Disabled*: 'Barker is a character squarely within Rossiter's grotesque range and comes over with rasping comedy, physical pain and humiliation, and no trace of irrelevant sympathy.' *Disabled* was a new play by the author Peter Ransley, premiered at the Hampstead Theatre Club. Leonard was playing a ventriloquist, who was sexually impotent due to being paralysed from the waist down. That doesn't stop his urges, however. Milton Schulman, writing in the *London Evening Standard*, was similarly impressed: 'Leonard Rossiter's display of gloating, sneering, leering humanity, needed to protect himself from being smothered by pity, is brilliantly irascible and funny.'

In *Disabled*, he was joined by Pauline Yates, who would work with him again in a few years' time as his long-suffering wife Nicola in *The Fall and Rise of Reginald Perrin*. 'I was rather frightened of him then,' she later admitted to the author Robert Tanitch, 'mainly because my scene was at the end of the play and rather difficult. I remember thinking that I mustn't ever let him down after all his hard work. I played a social worker and I tied up the ends of the play – it felt quite a responsibility. Leonard never made you feel easier about your responsibilities. He never said, "Oh, don't worry, it doesn't matter." It mattered very much to him and it *had* to matter to you too – otherwise you would have to go, or be ignored, which was worse.

'I haven't made him sound amusing,' she continued, 'but of course he was. He could suddenly do something very funny, but later he would be in a corner quietly going over his words. We came from the same background. I grew up in Liverpool, only about a mile from where he lived. His humour was often very "Scouse" – that rather laconic insult which could be a backhanded compliment. So sometimes when Southerners would say that they didn't like Leonard because of his brusqueness, I would say, "You just don't understand him, it's Liverpool humour."'

That same year, an iconic role followed in the form of *Richard III*, a production directed by Peter McEnery for the Nottingham Playhouse. As was common, McEnery was eager to find a fresh take on the frequently performed play, turning it into a hellish pantomime, with Richard the macabre court jester. Leonard was pitch-perfect, the psychopathic clown perversely funny and yet terrifying at the same time as he hangs the corpses of his victims from a bloodthirsty merry-go-round that dominated the stage.

Leonard was cast purely on the strength of his *Arturo Ui* performance, as McEnery explains: 'Out of the handful of really great performances I have been privileged to witness, including two by [Laurence] Olivier, Leonard's Arturo Ui was one of the greatest. His natural talent apart, it was the perfect example of the actor meeting the character head on and fusing into one, combining concentration and energy into an awesome performance. I think great actors can show flashes of greatness – or rather uniqueness – in many parts, but it is usually with one particular role [that] we associate an actor. For me the role was Arturo Ui and the actor Leonard Rossiter.

'It was this display of energy that prompted me to ask him to play Richard III. With all the great challenging roles, regardless of individual or directorial interpretation, Olympian energy above all is required: Leonard had it.'

And the press agreed. Writing in the *Financial Times*, B.A. Young said: 'Leonard Rossiter, in a vividly macabre performance, gives full rein to his graveyard humour. He's not much deformed, a slight hump at the shoulder, a stiff-kneed walk; but the quizzical turnings of the head, the swivelling of the eyes, the knowing nods (all so characteristic of Mr Rossiter that he must beware of letting them become mannerisms) suggest a deformity of spirit more alarming than any physical defect.'

Whereas Frank Marcus, for the *Sunday Telegraph*, was struck by the amount of humour that Rossiter brought to a role not usually associated with such things. 'Gradually, but inevitably, the unctuous dissembler turns into a raving psychopath but on the way he garners more laughs than any Richard I have seen. Mr Rossiter assumes the stance of a maimed hero; he stalks about, lurches and jerks his head bird-like from side to side. He is often quite still, and occasionally erupts into dangerous rages.'

While the clownish interpretation was effective by all accounts it's a part that Rossiter always wished to return to, this time with a more traditional performance. Sadly he would never have the chance.

15

Turning to Crime

In 1971, writing team Bob Baker and Dave Martin had just finished work on a couple of scripts for a children's historical adventure series, *The Pretenders*, when HTV producer Patrick Dromgoole made them an offer they couldn't refuse: 'He said, "Do whatever you like, write me a thriller set in Bristol,"' Baker recalls, 'and so Dave and I looked at one another and thought, we have a canvas, let's paint it.' In doing so they would paint a backdrop for one of Leonard Rossiter's stand-out performances: that of Eddie Dobbs, safecracker.

'We did an incredible amount of research,' Baker continues, 'and we happened to know a few villains, which helped. We asked our closest "villain", "How do you blow a safe?" and he said he would put us in touch with someone. So we met this guy in a pub in Bedminster, which is the darkest part of Bristol, and he asked, "So where is this safe you want done?" We said: "No, no, no! – we don't want a safe done, we just want to know *how* to do it!" He was delighted to tell us.'

On hearing of the writers' endeavours, Leonard – always a lover of research – was eager to meet the man himself.

'He said, "I've got to meet this guy,"' continues Baker, 'so we arranged another meeting.'

Late at night, in a deserted shopping arcade, the two writers and Leonard met a pair of bank robbers. They all got on rather well despite some nervousness when told that one of them – 'Dave' – had once been shotgun to the notorious Kray twins.

'Len and Dave got on well,' recalls Baker, 'though there was a moment of silence when Len asked right out, "How many jobs you done then, Dave?" Dave thought for a while and then announced, "I've done 147 egg-packing stations and once we did 30 cinemas in one night, coming down the A4."

'Len just sat and listened to this guy, picking up the threads of the way he thought, felt, the way he stood, how he used his hands, but mainly he picked up this manic laugh. Finally, Len said: 'I've got him – he's there.'

That technique of absorbing a character and finding the 'hook', the single detail that makes a character lift from the page and become 'real', is one of the most ethereal parts of an actor's – or indeed a writer's – job. One can well imagine Rossiter, a man who approached the business of acting as just that: a business, relating to Dave's workmanlike attitude towards his own criminal career. Without necessarily approving – this was a man who freely admitted to having shot people, after all – they both shared a brass tacks attitude towards their livelihoods: there was no mystique, no airy-fairy gloss. It was a job, simple as that. Leonard was to make a superb, and extremely believable onscreen villain – helped no end by an excellent script.

'We put our hearts and souls into it,' admits Baker, 'we were new writers, really – we hadn't done much, a couple of *Doctor Who's* – but that doesn't really count in this game. [Bob Baker and Dave Martin would go on to write a number of *Doctor Who* scripts over the years, most famously creating the character of the Doctor's robot dog, K-9, a character still on our screens today.] But we got the research right and I think that we knew the sort of people these were.'

And Rossiter wasn't above a touch of improvisation, despite his usual precision and preference for nailing every single move and detail before getting in front of the camera.

'Len's character is racist,' explains Baker, 'which doesn't reveal itself until they have done the robbery because until then they are not black or white but just villains together. He got that element beautifully: the minute they blow the safe and start looking at all the money coming out, he kisses the black guy on his head. A wonderful moment as none of us knew he was going to do it.'

Again we witness his almost-defining quality as a performer, the thing he did that stood him apart from many of his contemporaries: he took the unsympathetic, the dislikeable and rooted it in an inarguable truth, fleshing out that character as a human being defined by all of his characteristics, good and bad, turning him into someone his audience could relate to. He made the dislikeable watchable, he gave a humanity to the seedy characters he was so often offered and caused us to empathise with them, if not necessarily like them. It's a skill that really cannot be undersold.

Thick as Thieves was a great success, with Leonard Buckley noting in *The Times*: 'Rossiter played Eddie as a hands-in-pocket, marrow-cold little ne'er-do-well, whose every word was a cross between a sneer and a snarl. This was his best performance.' The play also won what Bob Baker defines rather self-deprecatingly as a 'Pie Oscar' for Best Regional Drama in that year's Royal Television Society awards.

'It was like being voted the "Best Dog in the Street" really,' he says, 'though of course we were delighted to have won it.'

A few years later, in 1976, the success of the play brought both the writers and Leonard the chance to work together once more. 'We had done our bit for HTV again,' explains Baker, 'writing episodes for the children's dramas *Arthur of the Britons*, *Sky* and *King of the Castle*, and we were offered another drama as a sort of thank you.'

This time the play was called *Machinegunner* (West Country slang for a debt collector, named after the interminable rapping on doors that was a mainstay of the profession). 'I was constantly being chased by creditors,' admits Baker, 'and that's how the story came about.'

Here Leonard is given another rather unpleasant character to add to his increasing repertoire, that of Cyril Dugdale, employed by Felicity Ingram (played by actress, Nina Baden-Semper at that time most famous for her role as the long-suffering wife in the contentious sitcom *Love Thy Neighbour*) to take photographs of a local property developer in bed with his mistress – Kate O'Mara before her roles in *Triangle* and then *Dynasty* would immortalise her in the public eye as a glamorous, yet cold-as-ice ball-breaker with shoulder pads you could land a seaplane on. This rather immoral sidestep from his usual business of collecting rents embroils Dugdale in a criminal plot to capitalise on land sales. The whole film plays out with Bristol an unpleasant backdrop as bleak as Newcastle in the 1971 classic *Get Carter*. Despite the grim quality that overshadows the whole, Rossiter still finds the odd moment to add touches of physical comedy.

'That was Len ad-libbing,' Baker admits, only too happy with the additions, 'though there was a lot of black humour in the dialogue, he couldn't resist a couple of slapstick opportunities when it came to filming.' It all feels perfectly natural given the ineffectual nature of the character Leonard is playing: a man way out of his depth for the whole story.

'[Cyril] was trying to come to terms with everything,' explains Baker, 'and be the big, cool detective, but he was, in fact, just a debt collector. What Len did well – as in *Rising Damp*, really – is that belief that he was far more revered than he actually was: a little man getting involved in things above his head. It was full of these little innuendoes, which Len did beautifully, especially with Nina. He had this wonderful love/hate relationship with her. He sees her as being inferior [because she's black] but she was earning at least twice as much as he was, something he simply can't get his head around. "She's a black woman, why is she earning more than me?" That was always underneath what he is saying.'

Felicity Ingram was intended to be the wife of the black thief in Baker and Martin's earlier *Thick as Thieves* and it must be remembered that you had to search high and low for a black actor in a strong lead role onscreen in those days. Though certainly, as with the previous film, *Machinegunner* features dialogue that would cause a modern censor to have a conniption. At the time however, the censors were suitably immune to racial slurs, as evidenced by their response to Rossiter's line when, having just escaped a murderous beating, he confronts Ingram, infuriated and terrified by the situation she's got him into. 'What are you!' he shouts at her, desperately trying to cover himself with a towel, having just stepped out of the shower, 'nothing but a la-di-da, black-enamelled, bloody jungle bunny!' The censors thought long and hard about the line and, deciding it simply couldn't stand, removed the word 'bloody' from it.

Baker firmly believes that while racism shouldn't be tolerated, honesty in writing a character's dialogue should be adhered to. Whether or not the writer shares those beliefs has nothing to do with it, he must stand by the truth of what his characters would say.

'I remember,' he said, 'I did some teaching and I showed a part of *Thick as Thieves* to the students, three or four of whom were black.

We reached one bit where Len says, "I've got this guy on the job," and in comes black actor Horace James. When the character leaves, one of the gang quips, "You didn't tell me there was a monkey on the job!" The students were outraged, but that's what the character would have said. You're not allowed to do that now.'

Contentious aspects aside, both dramas hold up extremely well when watched today.

Director Patrick Dromgoole shares his recollections of Leonard: 'He was a tetchy perfectionist, impatient of laziness and circumstances in which he could not do his work. Some perfectionists enjoy this tetchiness that goes with it, but I do not think this was true of Leonard. He was also generous, very generous, and sharply aware of the strains on those around him. When I as director and another man as production manager tried without success to get someone to move a car which was in the way of one of our shots, it was Leonard who went and spoke to the car owner and persuaded him to move it out of our way.'

'We were very, very proud of the films,' admits Baker, 'but mainly because of Len's tremendous dynamism: he really took the part by the throat. He was amazing, doing so much for the play that you didn't even realise was there. He would keep the dialogue as it was, but my goodness he would give it energy you didn't expect, lifting out the tiniest of details and elevating the whole thing.'

There would be a third opportunity for the writers to work with Rossiter – on 1982's *Escape to the West* – though this time Bob Baker was on the production side, leaving the script to Dave Martin.

'Dave and I had worked together for 10 years,' explains Baker, 'until, eventually, he said, "I don't want to write TV anymore, I want to write books," which was fine, as I wanted to get more involved in the production side of things. I went off to become script editor on *Shoestring* [a private detective show produced by the BBC, starring Trevor Eve]. Then I went to HTV for six years and during that time I was able to commission Dave to do *Escape to the West*, once again with Len. It's an interesting piece. I don't know if it really works, but it's good.'

Escape to the West was a play within a play, detailing a production team's attempts to tell the tale of an escaped Russian author, the resultant 'documentary' being a farcical twisting of the facts.

'It's the same character as in *Machinegunner*,' says Bob Baker of Leonard's role, 'Cyril is now an extra for the TV company making the film. The budget for *Escape to the West* was really small, though and Len wasn't happy with the part. He suddenly realised halfway through that Joss Ackland had the much better role!'

Ackland, as the Russian author who is the subject matter of the fictional documentary, was justifiably lauded for his performance. However, the linked story concerning Leonard – who, mirroring the Russian's escape wants to break out of his failed life in downtown Bristol to the affluent, western suburb of Clifton – was deemed trivial in comparison and the play as a whole never quite achieved the quality it was aiming for.

Despite this, Baker and Martin remained in touch with Rossiter, always hoping for the opportunity to work together again. In fact, Leonard put them forward as writers for the mooted feature film based on the characters that he and Joan Collins played in the highly popular Cinzano adverts, though ultimately the project never bore fruit.

Still, the association was something that Baker frequently enjoyed: 'We used to go out to eat at Keith Floyd's restaurant [Leonard would eventually write the foreword to the chef's first cookbook, *Floyd's Food*, published before Floyd went on to establish a successful TV career. At the end of his life in 2009, Floyd was also the partner of Dave Martin's widow, the writer having sadly died in 2007]. Len just would not stop joking. I think my second wife actually wet herself as he just got more and more funny as the evening went by. You couldn't stop him: he was like a rollercoaster. He had us completely transfixed as an audience – everyone would just stop and listen to him. I admire him so much for his acting. He was a craftsman, he could make you feel sorry for him and laugh at the same time.'

16

The Caretaker

Playwright and actor Harold Pinter earned a reputation for offering the blackly comic buried deep within the surreal, unsavoury or just plain disturbing. If ever there was a playwright whose work was crying out for the attentions of an actor like Rossiter, it was Pinter. Leonard had already proven time and again that he could offer performances balanced on a knife-edge between the comic and tragic, realistic or absurd. His style was perfectly suited to Pinter and his 1972 performance as Davies, the tramp and emotional lynchpin in the playwright's three-handed play, *The Caretaker*, is one fondly remembered by theatre audiences and critics alike.

Pinter's play is the tale of Aston, a man damaged by mental illness and electric shock therapy, who invites a tramp – Davies – back to his house. But Aston's younger brother Mick doesn't take to Davies and the play unfolds as the three characters interact with one another. It was a role that Rossiter first played back in 1961, fresh from his stint at the Bristol Old Vic. The production, directed by Gareth Davies, was staged at the Leatherhead Theatre Club, a surprisingly successful venture run out of the somewhat dilapidated Ace Cinema on Leatherhead's High Street.

Established in 1951 by Hazel Vincent Wallace as a base for her previously London-based Under Thirty Theatre Club, the club had always managed to secure rising names in theatre, mostly due to Wallace's unstoppable tenacity in booking them. Vanessa Redgrave and Nyree Dawn Porter had appeared together in panto, Richard Briers and Carmen Silvera also starred in productions there. *The*

Caretaker premiered in London the year before (with Donald Pleasance playing Davies, Alan Bates and Peter Woodthorpe as the brothers), the production going on to run for 444 performances. Wallace, as always determined to have her club present the newest and most exciting theatre, secured the rights for a recast production to play alongside the London show.

Leonard's Davies was singled out for review, with 'E.W.A.' writing in the *Surrey Advertiser*: 'the centrepiece is always the tramp and Leonard Rossiter plays him with humour and compassion. This is the true picture of the familiar drifter: stupid, idle, yet not without his streak of human dignity – and pomposity. One recoils from the sight of him; one can almost smell him; yet one can feel sorry too.'

Not that this familiarity allowed Leonard to approach reprising the role 11 years later with anything less than his usual obsessive attention to detail. Director Christopher Morahan, who had cast him in *Diamonds for Breakfast* (Morahan's debut as a movie director), recalls: 'He combined a restless energy with a comic invention which, with a single-minded search for truth, revealed the part and the play in a way which audiences had not previously conceived they could be played. He worked at the play, worrying the part like a dog with a bone, searching, trying, rejecting, perfecting business and character, never putting himself before the play or the other actors till in the end he had built a memorable, funny, dangerous, revealing and moving portrait.'

In the production Leonard was joined by John Hurt and Jeremy Kemp and over the following years the latter frequently crossed paths with him on the Fulham Road as they both lived in the area: 'The memory is of Leonard swapping foul abuse and "V" signs with passing lorry drivers, who would lean out of their cabs and offer some choice insult – kindly meant – on the subject of *Rising Damp* or more likely Joan Collins! As they accelerated away from the lights he would pursue them, still gesticulating, grimacing and shouting abuse. It was the irreverence of the man which appealed to me.'

And the reviews were as good as ever. Writing for the *Daily Mail*, Peter Lewis declared: 'It was a peach of a performance easily holding comparison with the original production and well worth anybody's money.' While Derek Mahon of *The Listener* said: 'Rossiter, especially, on whom everything depends is continuously fascinating to watch. Every look, every gesture, reveals the comical agony of unease in a bullying nature stranded without leverage.'

Back on television, *The Baby's Name Being Kitchener* was a rather grotesque period comedy written by Peter Everett for BBC 2's 'Thirty-Minute Theatre'. Rossiter took the central role, a lascivious army sergeant who courts a rich society lady while really having designs on her 15-year-old daughter. His performance, particularly as he continually tries to murder the mother, was suitably over the top.

The mother (Sophie) was played by Margaret Courtenay who had worked with Leonard when they were both part of the Bristol Old Vic. 'He took his comedy very seriously,' she recalls, 'and would beaver away, worrying at a feed-line until it was absolutely right and in focus. He was a taskmaster. Rehearsals were never easy, and sometimes it hurt, but I loved working with him and learned a lot from him.'

'Never easy, and sometimes it hurt' – not a description one can easily imagine applying to the rehearsal of a period television piece. But then to Leonard Rossiter, a half hour's script was no less solid and in need of mining than a coalface.

17

Camilla

Throughout this period of expansion and success as an actor, Leonard's private life had also burgeoned. He and Gillian had soon started sharing a London flat together, though nearly jeopardised their tenancy in 1966 on the night of the World Cup Final when, so enthused by England's win over Germany, they brought down the ceiling light in the flat below theirs by jumping around so much!

In 1972, everything changed beyond measure when Rossiter witnessed his finest co-creation: a daughter, Camilla. Finally marrying, he and Gillian bought a house in West London backing onto Brompton Cemetery. 'They're good neighbours,' joked Leonard, 'very little noise and no late-night parties.'

Stamford Bridge, the stadium of Chelsea Football Club, was nearby and on Saturdays the air would fill with the sound of cheering (and the occasional ribald song). Not that Leonard would mind that, he still loved his sport – though he was an Everton man, through and through. He played squash twice (sometimes even three times) a day and had advanced to the level of being one of Britain's foremost amateur players. He also played cricket, as screenwriter Dick Clement recalls: 'We saw each other fairly frequently on the cricket field since I used to run an occasional side called the "Bushwackers". Len used to bowl outswingers, if I remember correctly [a fast-spin delivery that veers the ball to the left], looking faintly crafty as he approached the wicket. But he was a natural athlete and took his games quite seriously. I have fond memories of sitting in deck-chairs discussing art, life and Liverpool.'

Leonard joined the Chelsea Casuals, a football team made up of writers and actors who would play weekend fixtures at Hyde Park. One of their regular opposing teams was made up by the staff of Leonard's favourite Italian restaurant and if he had a table booked for the night of the game, he had to play with extra determination. Nothing sours the digestion like conceding victory!

Leonard loved food and wine, teaching himself to be an expert in the latter after being encouraged in the hobby by his close friend John Barron (with whom he was soon to work again on *The Fall and Rise of Reginald Perrin*). 'I had given 15 years of close attention to wine,' explained Barron, when interviewed for *The Unforgettable Leonard Rossiter* (screened on ITV, then later released on DVD), 'and Leonard soon became addicted. He tasted many of my fine clarets and burgundies, and was soon building a superb collection himself. I had installed a temperature-controlled cellar in part of my basement floor. Leonard was not to be left behind. He was adding an attic floor to his house and the refrigeration engineer, arriving to make a survey, was puzzled to be directed upstairs. Only a man who could so closely catch [the absurdity of] Reggie would put his cellar in the attic!'

Rossiter became a regular bidder at auction houses and his attic 'cellar' was soon host to a very fine collection indeed, despite the practical complications offered during dinner parties when guests might already be several bottles worse for wear.

'It was very narrow, with racks on either side to hold the bottles,' Camilla recalled, when writing for *Intelligent Life* magazine in 2009. 'This meant that the only person small (and sober) enough to get down the far end, to the really good stuff, was me. Dad loved Dickens, so I was nicknamed "the Artful Dodger". For me, part of the fun of dinner parties was waiting for Dad to launch into his best Fagin performance and announce to the guests that he needed to "send for the Dodger!" I would then proudly retrieve whatever was required from the far reaches of the cellar and emerge to loud applause.'

HTV producer Patrick Dromgoole, who worked with Rossiter on the crime dramas *Machinegunner* and *Thick as Thieves*, also shared his love of wine: 'On my farm, where I have an extensive and distinguished cellar (in my own opinion), we once played the game of recognising wines by tasting them blind. Leonard was better than most, but when losing points was anxious to establish – quite correctly – the invalidity of such a game. The act of recognition, and therefore the naming of wines by their flavour and bouquet is a false one; appreciating wine, as he knew very well, lies more in the capacity to appreciate than the delineation of their pedigree. But if he had won more clearly on the points scale, would he have expressed the same reservations?'

Probably not: we already know that Leonard did not like to lose, as illustrated again by Camilla: 'Dad bought himself an electronic chess game, about the size of a modern laptop. He pitted himself against the computer, which soon became the bane of his life. Whenever it won, it would trill: "I win, I win, I win" while flashing green lights at him. To his great delight, he finally beat it and ran up and down the stairs, shouting in triumph. The machine, rather sulkily, emitted just one "You win" and switched itself off.'

'I like to win,' Leonard admitted in a newspaper interview, 'I think fooling around in sport is very tedious. It needs a fairly good player to outclass me now. I enjoy fundraising activities provided we can field a good side in both games – it's only fair to the spectators. To pay good money just to see a few celebrities knocking a ball about is not very worthwhile, is it?'

Sometimes he and Gillian would play tennis but that was often awkward as she was always in the position of irritating her husband. Either she would win, in which case Leonard would be cross with himself for having lost, or he would win and would then berate her for not trying harder! When it came to sport, he was simply competitive down to the core.

Looking back now, Camilla recalls those early years, with her father often learning lines or rehearsing dialogue. But the predominant memory is that of a quiet (Saturdays excepted, naturally), happy and above all, normal life. 'When a person is known for their comic roles,' she says, 'known as someone outgoing and sensational, the expectation is that the person in question will be like that themselves. And of course they're not necessarily like that at all. The business was a part of our lives as so many of the people Mum and Dad knew were involved in it in some way or another but it was always separate from "normal" life.

'I remember him focusing on his work, sitting on the sofa and learning his lines. I was aware he was an actor, though he didn't like watching himself on the television, so we never sat down and watched the programmes. But he was a fun dad certainly, always playing games, going out to parks – all the sort of things you would expect and want a dad to do.

'He had a great sense of humour – he was always laughing or making someone else laugh. There would always be a lot of laughter and fun in the house. He would be serious about his work, yes, but he wasn't in the least bit a dour person.'

But he certainly was private, always avoiding questions about his personal life. To Leonard, his home and family were completely removed from his public persona. That house, with its gently decaying neighbours and roaring sports fans, was a world outside work. It was a privacy he fiercely defended and one that his family respects to this day.

In 1973, he would take on the role that – while setting him up as a star name – also threatened to strip that privacy away. It was time for Rigsby to be born.

Part III

Rising Damp

18

The Banana Box

Since his success as Arturo Ui, Leonard had had little choice but to bias his work towards television. The few plays he had worked on, however, had all been fairly weighty, with parts he could really sink his teeth into. From Pinter's tramp – Davies – to Morris West's Giordano Bruno, they had all been dream roles and characters crying out for his particular style (though in the case of the latter he may have taken that style too far). 1973's *The Banana Box* couldn't have seemed more different: a new play by young writer, Eric Chappell, it had a message or two about racial intolerance but was, at heart, a fairly raucous comedy. Not that Leonard would have been in the least snobbish about comedy, he was far too good for that, appreciating the challenge and importance of the medium, but it was certainly a far cry from the meat-market carousel of Peter McEnery's recent production of *Richard III*.

Perhaps that was the play's biggest draw. Leonard could never abide standing still in his career; he was always striving for variety and freshness. Little could he have guessed, though, that this particular production would turn his career on its head more than any other role he had ever played. He wasn't the first, or even the second actor to play the role, but *The Banana Box*, not altogether successful in itself, would lead to *Rising Damp* and this was the first chapter in the story of one of the most successful television comedies of all time.

Considering his later profession, the play's writer, Eric Chappell, didn't have the most auspicious start. Born in the Lincolnshire town of Grantham in 1933, his parents treated writing with a level of suspicion that would have ensured a lesser man never touched a pen creatively for the rest of his life. 'My mother didn't really approve,' he would joke in a later interview, 'she thought it unwise to put something on paper in case it was held against you at a later date.'

Despite his working-class background, Chappell fostered a love of storytelling from an early age, something he ascribes to a defensive strategy in the playground: 'If you weren't popular for something people tended to pick on you. I was quick with my tongue so kept out of trouble by being entertaining.'

His obvious enthusiasm for fiction was encouraged by his English teacher but it wasn't until he was in his mid-twenties and after studying and ultimately failing to qualify as an accountant that he turned to writing with a professional mind. He got a job as an auditor with the East Midlands Electricity Board but would get up early so that he had extra time in the day to sit behind a typewriter, beginning work on a novel. Ultimately, and commonly enough, a period of rejections followed. He wrote a handful of novels but none of them were published, something he simply puts down to the fact that they were 'bad – looking back, I'm ashamed of them; they weren't good enough for publication'.

After deciding that novels were too lengthy and obviously not where his strengths lay, he turned his mind toward plays. He knew he had a good ear for dialogue, an ability to put words in a character's mouth that had that vital ring of truth. It was a far better medium for him and within a few months, he had produced his first script. *A Long Felt Want* was a comedy centring on a pair of boys and their developing interest in the opposite sex. Though never produced, it was strong enough to get him on the books of the Curtis Brown literary agency in London. For a while he concentrated on producing half-hour plays, one of which – *My Brother Peter* – was finally produced by the BBC for their anthology series, 'Love Story'.

In the summer of 1969, while taking a break from his work as an auditor to have lunch, Chappell read an article in the local Leamington Spa newspaper about a black man who had conned a hotel into letting him stay there for free by masquerading as an African prince. Amused and inspired by the idea, he began work on his second play. *The Banana Box* got its title from an old saw about immigration countering the suggestion that all it took to be British was to be born there. 'If a cat has kittens in a banana box,' the argument ran, 'what do you get: kittens or bananas?'

The commitment of his day job was such that it wasn't until the following year that Chappell actually took the idea and began to write. By this time his idea had shifted somewhat: the story was now set in a grotty letting house rather than an upper-class hotel. The landlord 'didn't become a fussy, blazered hotelier but a rather seedy old sweat,' says Chappell. His character was influenced in part by someone he had known and also the prevalent post-war attitudes to immigrants. He called the character Rooksby, a name that would change, a few years later.

It took him three months to complete *The Banana Box*, working weekends and early mornings. While he had always intended his characters to be equally balanced with no single lead, Rooksby soon came to the fore. Chappell then sent the play to his agent and waited while they sought the financial backing of a theatrical company. They approached a number of producers and arranged a 'rehearsed reading' at the Hampstead Theatre Club in the Swiss Cottage Centre, London. Rehearsed readings were a common way of showcasing new writing. A director would assemble a cast, who would then read the scripts aloud – with no set or costume – bringing the words to life and highlighting the potential, were it to be fully dramatised.

Peter Woodthorpe was the first actor to step into the worn slippers of Chappell's seedy landlord. Woodthorpe had earned a considerable reputation as one of the country's finest character actors. During the 1950s, he had established his name in the theatre and became highly sought after for leading roles despite being only in his twenties. Later he would concentrate on film and television, appearing in such movies as *The Charge of the Light Brigade*, *Hysteria*, *The Hunchback of Notre Dame* and *Merlin*. He was a familiar face on the small screen, too. A regular in the first two series of ITV's phenomenally successful adaptations of Colin Dexter's *Inspector Morse*, he also appeared in *Only Fools and Horses*, *Coronation Street* and *Minder*.

Clifton Jones, one of the most well-known black actors at that time having appeared in such high-profile shows as *Jason King* and *The Persuaders*, took on the role of Phillip, the ersatz African prince.

Miss Jones – soon to be a name impossible to utter without the extra application of that fabled, nasal Rossiter tone – was played by Heather Canning, a face known to many theatregoers after her body of work at the National Theatre.

Finally, Noel Parker – a character later rewritten for the series as Alan Moore, the long-haired student immortalised by Richard Beckinsale – was played by Geoffrey Burridge, who sadly died from an AIDs-related illness at just 38, in 1987. Before his career was so tragically cut short he had appeared in films such as *An American Werewolf in London* and *The Internecine Project*.

The director was John Tydeman, a former producer at the BBC who had also directed Chappell's first radio play, *Like Achilles*.

The reading went extremely well. Performed to a full house, Tydeman later observed that 'it was funny and unusual for its time and the style of humour a little more upmarket than what you see in *Rising Damp*; the play was rather offbeat and worked beautifully'.

Michael Codron, a highly respected theatre producer, clearly felt the same way. He bought the rights and decided to try the play as a regional production before committing to a West End run. It was offered to the Phoenix Theatre in Leicester. Stephen MacDonald, newly promoted from his role as assistant director of two years to director of productions, was handed the play by the outgoing director and began to read. But the title didn't sit well with him and he admits to initially approaching the script with low expectations. By the end of the day he had changed his opinion entirely and was sold on the humour and enamoured of the fact that it had a local appeal, something he was determined to bring to his upcoming schedule.

MacDonald met with Chappell to discuss possible refinements. He had no doubt as to Chappell's ability to write good comedy but felt the play needed bringing together more as a whole. In a comment that with hindsight would be proved spot-on, he told Chappell that the script was 'material for a television series, but for a play there needs to be more development of the characters' relationships and how they affect one another'.

However, MacDonald's enthusiasm for the material wasn't universally shared among the theatre's management, who were far more comfortable with a steady stream of 'classics' than a more challenging contemporary piece but he soon silenced the opposition when he secured Wilfrid Brambell as his leading man. Brambell was a big star at the time, famed for his portrayal of Old Man Steptoe in the hugely successful sitcom *Steptoe and Son* (in which Leonard Rossitter had already featured in a guest role).

Ironically, Brambell hadn't been MacDonald's first choice for the role – despite his undeniable pedigree in plying seedy characters and his status as a box-office draw. In fact, the director had considered Leonard Rossiter. Having worked with Gillian Raine before, he relished the idea of casting her in the production alongside her husband but unfortunately Leonard was booked at the time and therefore unable to accept.

Cast alongside Brambell would be Keith Drinkel (fresh from success as Parker in the long-running TV series *Family at War*), Janet Michael (Miss Jones) and Neville Aurelius as Philip.

Gathering reasonable – if not stellar – audiences and a handful of mixed reviews, the play was a moderate success. Though complimentary of Chappell's script, the critics considered there was room for improvement. Eric Shorter, writing for the *Daily Telegraph*, said: 'though its theme of home counties-born blacks seeps through in an emotionally overwrought last act, it comes too late to give the comedy that theatrical shape which would affect us more deeply.'

Criticism of the ending aside, Chappell was universally declared a 'talent to watch' and no one questioned the play's ability to raise considerable laughs. At the time, however, Michael Codron passed on the opportunity to take the production to the West End: he was unconvinced by Brambell's performance and considered the whole venture too high a risk. Though disappointed, Chappell knew that the play had its flaws and could understand the producer's decision.

Two years later, *The Banana Box* would get a second chance, thanks to a new producer in the shape of South African Leon Gluckman. It was entirely recast, taking the final steps towards the version we are more familiar with: most particularly in that Leonard Rossiter was now available for the part that would go on to make him a household name. Chappell recalls the initial read-through: '[Leonard] came, looking rather suspiciously at the text. [He began to read] and people started to laugh – people who didn't normally laugh. I could see Len, his eyes began to lighten up and he really went for it. Suddenly they were falling about like anything. So we knew we'd got one good part in the play at least.'

He was joined by the black actor Don Warrington, who would later become synonymous in the role of Philip; fresh from drama school, he recalls the experience of being cast alongside Rossiter: 'I'd seen Leonard when I was at drama school – in my first year, we got tickets to see *The Resistible Rise of Arturo Ui* and I thought he was amazing. I wasn't very experienced in theatre, but what I saw in front of me was extraordinary. I carried on being a drama student and then when I left, lo and behold, the first job I get is working with him, so it was a bit daunting on many a level. As the play was a comedy, I wasn't really prepared for that coming from the drama school I went to, so when we started it was amazing to watch Len going about his business technically. It was a lesson, like being in a permanent masterclass. He challenged the other actors around him – he had a kind of energy you had to respond to.

'He was very specific with what he did and would talk a lot about the tempo of performance. He would have his tempo on stage and what you had to do was to have your own: to find what your character's beat was. If you think in terms of music: is it a waltz, a tango, what is it? Because when you found it and matched it with his, you could find the drama or comedy, or whatever you were trying to present. When the performances matched properly, you got the relationship and it was from those relationships that everything else came through. So that was my first experience of him.

'He was nice to me, he was helpful: he would talk to me about comedy, about what worked and what didn't. He was frank – if I did things *his* way they were funny, if I did them *my* way, then they were not! But the thing was, he was always right. I was young and happy to be taught by someone like that.

'Acting is collaborative and he knew that. He was a very generous actor because he knew it wasn't about him. He was very concerned that *everyone* be good because he realised that a single performance doesn't make a play. A play is about all the people on stage: it's about what each character brings, and if you don't have that dynamic you don't have anything.'

Paul Jones, still most famous as the lead singer of sixties' group Manfred Mann despite considerable critical and commercial success as an actor, took on the role of Noel Parker.

The play opened at the Adeline Genee theatre in East Grinstead on 12 March 1973 and would go on a short tour of venues in Oxford and Newcastle before finally debuting in the West End at the Apollo Theatre (25 June 1973), where, with Frances de la Tour now featured as Miss Jones, it would run for a month.

Director David Scace, who was responsible for de la Tour's and Warrington's casting, was overjoyed to be working with Leonard again, having previously directed him in a Bristol Old Vic production of wartime drama, *The Long, the Short and the Tall*. 'The amount of energy he put into a role was unbelievable,' he later commented. 'He must have worked for hours on his performance.'

Reviews were unanimous in their praise for Rossiter:

> 'Utilising his entire, very considerable repertoire of grimacings, shufflings and nervous twitches, Leonard Rossitter creates a memorable character.'
>
> 'P.H.', *Stage and Television Today*

> 'All the Rossiter mannerisms are there: the angled stance, as if everyone around has chronic halitosis, the corkscrew head movements suggesting a cobra rising from a wicker basket, the stiff-legged gait as of a man parading on stilts, the compulsive buttock-scratching as if ants were lodged in the pants.'
>
> Michael Billington, *Guardian*

> 'Mr Rossiter hilariously personifies the pinched little souls who make up the Soho mackintoshed brigade.'
>
> Milton Shulman, *London Evening Standard*

Overall, however, there lingered the view that the play lacked some cohesive element with criticism once again levelled at the depth of its script:

> 'Mr Chappell has a gift for phrasing a paragraph, but the stylistic device, by the end of the second act, seems overused. This is a strangely empty evening only rarely bashed into life by some flashing piece of outrageous behaviour by the indomitable Mr Rossiter.'
>
> Michael Coveney, *Plays and Players*

'There are plenty of funny lines and the director has whipped a pretty froth on top of the trifle. The weakness of Eric Chappell's play is that amusing to-ing and fro-ing gives only a superficial view of growing up.'

John Barber, *Daily Express*

However, the audiences clearly enjoyed the production, as did Yorkshire Television's acting head of light entertainment, John Duncan. There would be a future for Chappell's scripts and characters yet . . .

19

Situation Comedy

'I've never felt any affinity for any part I've played, really. Obviously some are more suited to what gifts – or otherwise – you have but very, very rarely, on perhaps two occasions I suppose in 28 years have I thought, Ah! This gives me all the things I can do really well. One of them was *Rising Damp*, the other was a play about Hitler, so clearly I have a dictator *manqué*.'

Leonard Rossiter, interviewed by Russell Harty

There is a degree of snobbery aimed at sitcoms: they're an inarguable example of populist entertainment and there's nothing culture likes to turn its nose up at so much as a 'bums-on-seats' ethic. The half-hour, frequently studio-bound and cheap format aims to do little more than amuse its audience – as much, one hopes, as the recorded audience laughter that often accompanies the soundtrack, in itself a style that has become much derided in recent years. However, there can be little doubt that creating a successful situation comedy is exceptionally difficult. Like all television it takes a combination of everyone's effort, excellent scripts, good performances and solid technical presentation. As *Reginald Perrin* creator David Nobbs comments: 'TV is like an airplane: I sometimes think it only takes one thing to cause a crash.'

Bearing all that in mind, there's still nothing so subjective as humour and shows that live on in our national memory as having made millions laugh week after week deserve a considerable amount of respect. Sitcoms hold their own in any list of 'classic' TV, from

Hancock's Half Hour to *Only Fools and Horses, Last of the Summer Wine* to *Open All Hours*, they have attracted sizeable audiences and devoted fans. At best, they offer strong, iconic characters that capture the hearts of a nation. Like an amusing, if somewhat embarrassing old friend, there can be few TV viewers in the UK who don't have a strong affection for the likes of Basil Fawlty, Stanley Fletcher, Albert Steptoe and, of course, Rigsby. Writing for the *Guardian* in 2009, journalist Catherine Shoard notes:

> There are two sitcoms from the 1970s that don't feel dated today. *Fawlty Towers* still zips along, its pace largely down to its then-innovative fast cutting style. *Rising Damp* is similarly snappy – but that's more because of the speed of Leonard Rossiter's delivery. So rapidly did his Rigsby rattle out dialogue that writer Eric Chappell was forced to churn out reams of extra script to fill episodes.
>
> The shows share a lot: a farce structure (doors endlessly burst open, people pop up from behind plants), a sublime four-piece cast, and a main character who's a miserly, middle-aged snob, forever tripping as he scrambles up the social ladder. Yet *Rising Damp* has arguably worn better than *Fawlty*, perhaps because it was always meant to look faded; it's hard to think of a less snazzy title sequence than a long shot of an old front door, soundtracked by a clapped-out pub piano.

That 'faded' quality is certainly synonymous with the show. The world of *Rising Damp* is one of ageing, mildewed furnishings, patchy carpets and wood that peels as if with psoriasis. Such a grim – yet perversely, nostalgically comfortable – world is perfectly placed in the seventies, an era that abounded with beige fabrics and looming wallpaper. It's a world perfectly described by Eric Chappell (via Rigsby/Rossiter) in the pilot episode:

> 'I know it looks small – that's the heavy wallpaper. I should have used paler colours. Look at it: functional, with just a hint of luxury. There's nothing between this house and the Urals. You're breathing the same air as the Tartars up there and look how long they live. I should charge you extra.'
>
> Rigsby, 'The New Tenant'

It's a perfect thumbnail of both the era and the intimate, studio-bound world of the sitcom: TV that comforted, reflected, amused and entertained.

Given that Chappell's play was often, albeit pejoratively, said to be material that would suit a sitcom better than the stage, one might assume that it would have been an easy commission. William Franklyn, Rossiter's friend and fellow actor, went to see a performance of *The Banana Box*, later commenting: 'We had a wonderful evening, and when we went round to Leonard's house later. He said: "Well, what do you think?" And I said: "You've got a very successful TV series there. You've got the first four episodes." And he said: "Don't be ridiculous! You don't know what you're talking about."'

Such an attitude seems bizarre in hindsight, especially as Rossiter would become a driving force in encouraging Chappell to rework the material for the small screen. But hindsight makes fools of us all, the future is never so easily predicted.

Despite both its later success and the early approval of many reviewers and audiences, the transition from stage to screen did indeed take some time. The acting head of light entertainment for ITV, John Duncan, came to see the show during its time in Newcastle. 'I didn't think it would make it to the West End,' he admits, 'it was no good as a play. But it contained wonderful writing and was clearly the most brilliant blueprint for a sitcom: the characters were strong, the situation right – everything was in place.'

Despite his earlier comments, Rossiter encouraged Chappell to turn the basic elements of the play into a sitcom pilot. The writer was, perhaps surprisingly, reticent. Still very fresh to the world of professional writing, he was concerned that he wouldn't be able to pen a full series of such material. Writing plays and one-off radio scripts was altogether a different prospect to committing to three-and-a-half hours of comedy script: would there enough material in the characters? And even so, would he be able to find it?

Eventually, with the constant encouragement of both Rossiter and his own literary agent, Chappell wrote a pilot script, entitled *Rooksby*, which was submitted – and subsequently rejected – by numerous production companies. Despite John Duncan's initial enthusiasm, the script sat unread on his desk for some time until it was finally commissioned as a one-off play, part of a series of comedy pilots to be broadcast by ITV in the autumn of 1974.

The notion of pilot episodes is often confusing to viewing audiences: generally, pilots are only produced for viewing by the commissioning TV company rather than broadcast onscreen. If the commission goes ahead and a full series is produced, the pilot is often broadcast as part of that series – as long as sufficient changes haven't been decided upon, the recasting of characters and altered plots, for example, that would make such a broadcast impossible. Comedy lends itself favourably to the notion of broadcast pilots, however, and already there had been numerous precedents for a TV company testing the water for potential shows by producing a series of individual plays.

In 1973, the BBC produced a series showcasing Ronnie Barker, *Seven of One*. The first episode, 'Open All Hours', featuring Barker as a tight-fisted corner-shop owner, Arkwright, would go on to become a highly-successful series in its own right and the second episode, 'Prisoner and Escort', gave birth to Stanley Norman Fletcher and the much-lauded *Porridge* (a series that would end up vying with *Rising Damp* for awards over the next few years). Previously, the long-running 'Comedy Playhouse', which ran for 15 series between 1961 and 1974, had launched *Steptoe and Son*, *Last of the Summer Wine*, *Till Death Us Do Part*, *The Liver Birds* and *Are You Being Served?*

By the time John Duncan commissioned the series of pilots, he was already committed to leaving the Light Entertainment division. His background firmly in documentaries and satirical programming, he had never felt truly comfortable there. Former BBC chairman Sir Paul Fox had recently taken over at ITV and brought numerous talents with him, including Duncan Wood. 'He made all the difference,' Sir Paul commented in a later interview, 'Duncan was the creator of *Steptoe and Son* and *Hancock's Half Hour*.' It was a credible pedigree indeed. ITV had always struggled to match the BBC's success in the sitcom medium: looking back at the classic examples, the BBC manages to steal most of the limelight. It was a balance that Fox hoped Wood might be able to redress.

For *Rooksby*, Wood cast Richard Beckinsale in the newly created role of Alan Moore without the need for a read-through. Beckinsale had only just finished filming the first series of the aforementioned *Porridge* and was already a familiar face to British audiences after his success in the Jack Rosenthal scripted sitcom, *The Lovers*. Perhaps surprisingly, Wood was less certain about keeping Leonard Rossiter in the central role: 'The producers wanted someone who had sitcom experience,' reveals Chappell, 'someone totally dependable. And although Len Rossiter was a great actor, he hadn't done that much comedy. He'd never carried a show before so they wanted strong support beside him and I think Richard quickly came to mind.'

That concern seems bizarre given that Leonard had done a great deal of comedy by that point – indeed, had already begun to risk typecasting as a comic performer – but there's no one quite so cautious as TV producers. Given how much money they're about to spend in making a show, it's a wonder any of them dare make a decision. Besides, Chappell is right in that Rossiter had no experience of being a regular in a sitcom. His appearance in *Steptoe and Son* had been a one off: indeed, he hadn't been a series regular in anything since *Z-Cars* in the early sixties (and even then hadn't appeared in every episode). It was something he simply hadn't been interested in. Still, if it was the workload they were concerned with, the regular long hours and the fast turnaround of script to screen then they need look no further than his theatre background. The workload of a TV sitcom was nothing to daunt Leonard: he'd survived far worse.

Despite the producer's concerns, Leonard made himself heard when it came to casting the other characters. Frances de la Tour and Don Warrington were both held over as Ruth Jones and Philip Smith, the roles they had played in the most recent run of *The Banana Box*. 'This shows his shrewdness again, I think,' says Warrington. 'He thought we were ideal for those parts and if he wanted the sitcom to work, he had to get the right people in the roles with him. It was also extremely generous though, he really didn't have to do it.'

The name of Chappell's seedy landlord became a concern. Interviewed by a national paper just prior to shooting, Leonard commented: 'If you didn't like Hitler, you certainly aren't going to like Rooksby,' going on to describe the lascivious landlord in terms that would antagonise a genuine landlord by the same name! The 'real' Rooksby was quick to complain and so Chappell was forced to rethink. Finally, he plumped for 'Rigsby' as an alternative after trawling the phonebook for something with a similar ring to it.

As the pilot was to have taken its title from the landlord's name – the more philosophical *The Banana Box* deemed unsuitable for the new medium – losing the name Rooksby also made Chappell rethink the title of the show as a whole. He could simply have plumped for *Rigsby*, but he wanted something completely different.

ALAN: I've got rising damp – my furniture's coming to pieces.

RIGSBY: How can you have rising damp in the attic? You're higher than the crows up there! It should be very healthy, like Switzerland.

On re-reading his script the term 'rising damp' struck Chappell as suitably dreary and depressing, a phrase that evoked the world of Rigsby's house only too well. Eager for a second opinion, he sent the suggestion to Leonard. 'He liked it,' Chappell recalls, 'he loved anything of the macabre or sombre that was funny. He never played soft comedy so he thought the name was ideal – and I stuck with it, although I must admit, I remained unsure about it for some time.'

Rossiter was adamant that *Rising Damp* was the right title despite Chappell's concern that it was something the critics could throw back at them if they didn't like the show (indeed, one of the few bad reviews that the pilot received would take the opportunity offered, observing that they had watched *Rising Damp* and it was 'a little wet'). In the end, director Ian MacNaughton told Chappell to get used to it: the Graphics department had finished the titles and they weren't going to change them now.

The newly christened *Rising Damp* was scheduled alongside five other potential series: *You'll Never Walk Alone* (written by Hancock and Steptoe writers Ray Galton and Alan Simpson), *Brotherly Love*, *Badger's Set* (Barry Took), *Slater's Day* and *Oh No, It's Selwyn Froggitt!* (starring Bill Maynard and the only other show to be commissioned as a full series). Broadcast on 2 September 1974, it achieved a respectable audience of 6.1 million viewers.

The reviews were predominantly positive, with Rossiter receiving a good deal of praise:

'Leonard Rossiter's bragging, conceited Rigsby is a precisely conceived role superbly executed.'

Stewart Lane, *Morning Star*

'Leonard Rossiter is worth a quarter-mile start to any comedy show.'

Shaun Usher, *Daily Mail*

'The sort of professional performances that just make you purr.'

Peter Fiddick, *Guardian*

'Leonard Rossiter's Mr Rigsby established himself at once as a memorable personality.'

Sylvia Clayton, *Daily Telegraph*

'It is marked as a winner straight away.'

Gerard Dempsey, *Daily Express*

'The series has been a personal triumph for the versatile and hard-working Leonard Rossiter. He plays it so frantically at times that it seems he'll spoil everything by going right over the top. But he knows just what he is doing and always stops short by a hair's breadth.'

James Thomas, *Daily Express*

Still nervous about how he would deliver enough material, should the pilot be commissioned, Chappell was particularly relieved when he watched the live recording: 'I was thinking, how are we going to get through week after week? because I wasn't always going to write stuff that was hilariously funny. And then I realised how we were going to do it – when I saw Len's reaction that first week when he realised he was stuck with an African student and the audience roared with laughter. I thought, he hasn't said anything yet, and so I thought, Eric, you're home and dry because when you're stuck for a line, he's going to finish the scene for you.'

Don Warrington also praised Leonard's unerring ability to hit the jokes head-on in the script: 'The big surprise of the pilot was me. It was all set up that this prince was going to come and live in the house. And given the character of Rigsby he expects Prince Charles. So what they had to do was hide me from the audience. It came to my moment: I walked in and the audience just erupted, they couldn't stop laughing. And [Leonard] just held the moment, he kept it going for ages and ages and ages.'

The pilot was directed by Ian MacNaughton, who had worked as a producer for Spike Milligan and Monty Python; he had never been in any doubt that the programme would be a success, pointing to the quality of the characters as a defining sign of the show's strength: 'I recognised the landlord, Rigsby, immediately. I'd been an actor myself for years and lived in digs all over the place, so it wasn't difficult putting a human touch to him.'

McNaughton was to work with Rossiter again in the Galton and Simpson comedy about a real-life 'professional farter' Joseph Pujol, *Le Pétomane* (1979), and rated the actor extremely highly: 'Leonard had perfect timing and was tremendous fun to work with, and so was Frances. But the show was full of such wonderful conflicts: Rigsby adoring Miss Jones, who in turn likes Philip, so Rigsby is jealous of Philip – all these situations were classic set-ups for situation comedy.'

So, the pilot was broadcast and – whether a comfortable choice for the producers or not – Leonard proved himself perfectly capable of being the show's star. Familiarity with the character of Rigsby makes it easy to forget what an incredibly successful portrayal it is. Rossiter delivers a masterclass in sitcom acting, the energy and focus never slipping for one moment. And yes, as both Chappell and Warrington observe, he holds the audience's laughter purely on the strength of his facial expressions once Philip is revealed – a tremendous skill indeed.

20

Series One

After the success of the pilot, Yorkshire Television commissioned a full series of *Rising Damp* and, with that, work began in earnest. Chappell was commissioned to write the scripts piecemeal: 'Duncan Wood commissioned very slowly,' he recalls, 'after one show he'd say, "Do you want to write another one?" Then two more, and we crept through the first series until we'd completed seven shows.' It would take him, on average, three weeks to write each episode: one week of notes, another for a first draft and then a further week for a second draft.

Once the script was finalised, there was then only one week to produce it: a tight schedule but not uncommon in TV during those days. Preparations would begin with a London read-through (conducted at St Paul's Church Hall in Hammersmith for the first series, moving to the Sulgrave Boys' Club, Shepherd's Bush for the latter shows).

Ronnie Baxter, an old hand in TV sitcoms, having worked on such shows as *For the Love of Ada* and the controversial *Love Thy Neighbour*, took over from Ian McNaughton as producer and director. 'The read-through would always take place on a Sunday at the rehearsal room in London,' he explains, 'that was the first time the cast read the script together. Other people from Wardrobe, Make-up and Design would be there to pick up on any requirements. They would then return to Leeds, leaving the rest of us to carry on with rehearsals for the remainder of the day.'

Studio times were then booked with another two-and-a-half days of rehearsals, the Wednesday afternoon being used for a technical run with the Film and Sound departments on hand to judge how best to achieve their aims. On the Thursday, the cast would travel up to Leeds. Then, on the Friday they would rehearse within the studio sets and finally film the show in front of a live audience that evening.

Baxter describes the working environment: 'The show was a delight to be involved with. Richard [Beckinsale] had an old head on young shoulders and knew all the tricks. He would scare you to death in rehearsals if you didn't know him and how he worked, but experience tells you not to panic in situations like that. Leonard was the total opposite and soaked his part up like a sponge. You'd give him the script and the next day he'd know his lines perfectly, which tells you a lot about Leonard Rossiter.'

Indeed it does, but it's no surprise to us, Leonard's working methods being all too familiar by now. No doubt he would have been one of the first people to be 'scared to death' by Beckinsale's laid-back attitude but there was no question that the younger man could do his job, one only had to see the results, and it wasn't long before the two of them became very close friends.

'Rehearsals were very professional,' Baxter continues, 'and Leonard appreciated his fellow cast members' – and in particular Frances de la Tour's – acting ability. She brought a lot to the character of Ruth and made her part twice as good as it might have been. Despite what's been written or said, I never saw a single argument between Frances and Len during my time on the show, and that was partly down to the fact that the cast weren't a lovey-dovey, back-slapping group – we had a job to do, the clock was against us and we had to get the comedy right. It was a very professional atmosphere to work in and it ran like a clock.'

The suggestion that Frances de la Tour and Leonard did not get on can partly be founded on the actress's refusal to discuss her part in the show after moving on to other projects. In truth, her decision was simply based on a wish to move on and not become forever associated with the part, though naturally this is easier said than done: for many she will always be 'Miss Jones'.

Also, the two were polarised in their politics, something that always leads to heated debate though rarely any genuine ill will. Camilla recalls many of her parents' dinner parties erupting in good-natured rows as Leonard's staunch Conservative views clashed with the left-wing attitude of many of his guests (acting produces a distinctly liberal majority among its practitioners). Frances de la Tour was a member of the Workers' Revolutionary Party at the time (and later the Marxist Party and Respect) and so was bound to clash strongly with her host's views.

'In 1978 all the [television] companies were going through a lot of union problems,' explains Vernon Lawrence, producer and director of the fourth series of the show, 'and Yorkshire Television was having a lot of trouble with the ETU [Electrical Trades Union]. This was disruptive to a lot of shows that we were making, including *Rising Damp*. I had a phone call from the studios one day to say that the management were actually doing the lighting and would that be acceptable to the cast? So I went out and asked the cast. Frances de la Tour, who had very positive political views, smiled weakly and said yes, for the sake of the show, she was happy. But she then said: "Don't ask Len, because we know what *he'll* say!" Because Leonard was slightly left of Attila the Hun, so they had very different views politically, but as far as work was concerned they both had enormous respect for each other. And when they were on screen, they were absolute magic.'

The whole series of *Rising Damp* was produced and filmed within the allotted seven weeks and the first episode broadcast shortly after 13 December 1974. The show was filmed in front of a live audience, common practice at the time. Ever since the beginnings of television there had been a concern among producers that comedy needed to recreate a live experience, surrounding the viewer at home with the notion of an audience. It was thought that people needed encouragement to laugh and that a laughter track would provide that encouragement. In America it was common practice throughout the 1950s and 1960s to manufacture a false laughter track, pre-recorded laughter being spliced in at the correct moment to highlight jokes in the script. This was not a cost decision, though it could sometimes be restrictive to film 'live', rather it was deemed preferable to using a genuine audience – which could not, after all, be relied to laugh on cue.

There is also the difference in medium to be taken into consideration. Sometimes live audiences laughed at the 'wrong time', throwing the actors timing much as they might in the theatre, whereas a certain breakdown in naturalism is more easily tolerated and no one minds if the characters pause to allow the laughter to continue. But if an actor stops during a television programme any sense of believability is lost. Having said that – and contrary to popular belief – in the UK, live audiences have always been preferred, even with shows that, due to the amount of location filming or special effects, were not filmed in front of an audience, later being shown to one so their response could be recorded and added to the sound mix. These days it has become fairly common practice for comedy to be broadcast with no laughter track at all: indeed, many producers, performers and audiences prefer it.

For *Rising Damp* the presence of an audience was deemed vitally important, though Eric Chappell admits to worrying about hearing their response: 'I got very nervous because I didn't think they'd enjoy it, but they always did.' Despite his reservations, Chappell is convinced that the use of a live audience is beneficial in filming sitcoms: 'A good one will pinpoint where you have done well or timed to perfection, but they will also let you know if the pace of the show is too slow. For the actor, the audience will certainly let them know when they've got it right and it's a magical moment when you trigger that response.'

Vernon Lawrence agrees, though explains the dangers: 'If you've got someone who's inexperienced, they occasionally raise the size of their performance and if you're not careful, you end up with a gross performance. Actors grope for laughs and play large by doing a stage portrayal which ruins the actual size of performance you need for television.' He also points out one other major difference: 'With a sitcom your first exposure to an audience is also your last – you only have one crack at it.'

Certainly, similar as it may seem to the untrained eye, a live filming is not a theatrical performance. The technical concerns are far more complex (and indeed must sometimes overrule other considerations for this is a performance intended to be enjoyed by millions at home, not just the comparative handful invited to attend the recording). As mentioned above, timing is an issue, as is the importance of the actors never breaking character or 'the fourth wall' – the concept that the audience is viewing the performance through an invisible wall, partitioning them off from the events in front of them – and the audience's presence must have been a distraction, albeit one that allowed all those involved the instant gratification so scarcely found in TV and film of knowing their work was well-received.

Actor Don Warrington is not so convinced of the worth of a live audience: 'It gave the show a kind of energy which I suppose worked but at the price of a subtlety that was achieved in rehearsal. In my mind, a subtlety that made the show funnier. It is very, very difficult to get the balance right between the innate theatricality of having an audience and the fact that you're really doing it for the people at home. *They* are the real audience. That kind of disparity is strange and I think it's a balance that's achieved on very few occasions. Len knew what was funny in rehearsal and he timed it, but he was also very good at playing to the live audience while keeping an eye on the camera as well. When you look at it, you can see his energy rise even further, thanks to the studio audience – that was his innate theatricality. Overall, though, I think that an audience makes things just a little bit cruder: I'm not a great believer in them.'

Screened through December 1974 into the January of 1975, the series attracted an average audience of 6.5 million – a healthy, if not startling number. The general consensus was that scheduling was to blame for the somewhat average viewing figures, the show being broadcast on the notoriously awkward Friday night (a time when many potential viewers would leave their front rooms and go out for the evening, determined to wash away the week's work with a few pints or glasses of wine).

Sir Paul Fox commented: 'Despite its Friday evening slot, it did okay. The critics loved the show, of course, and it was very important for us to find a comedy that could play before 9 p.m.

'We received the viewing figures, which were respectable, within 48 hours of airing. London Weekend Television had network control of Friday, Saturday and Sunday, and they elected to play the first series on Fridays. So we took it away from them and gave it to Thames – who gave it a Tuesday evening slot and much greater promotion, which also helped. Things went much better, ratings-wise, from then on.'

Indeed, they would rise to between 8 and 9 million, peaking at a phenomenal 18 million during the show's final series.

It is worth remembering that the TV infrastructure was very different in the 1970s, with ITV split into regions, all of which had a degree of autonomy as to scheduling. This meant that a programme could be seen on different nights entirely depending on where you lived.

And it wasn't just audiences who were to endorse the new show. The British Academy Film and Television Awards (BAFTA) also offered an accolade: the series was selected by the Writers' Guild of Great Britain as one of the comedies short-listed for the Best British Comedy Script in 1975. Eric Chappell was invited to attend the ceremony by his ITV bosses, though they chose not to tell him that the show had been nominated. Arriving at the ceremony at the prestigious Café Royal in London's Regent Street, he was surrounded by many screen luminaries and felt distinctly starry-eyed. He picked up one of the programmes only to learn that *Rising Damp* was up for consideration. The other shows considered were *Last of the Summer Wine, It Ain't Half Hot Mum* and *Porridge.* Though the last won, this would not always prove the case.

Leonard was aware of the strength of what they had all achieved and delighted by the show's success, but he also understood that if the series was to continue then the crew would have to be careful to maintain the high standards already set.

21

Bedsitland

'Situation comedy is supposed to flourish best in a trapped situation. And all those characters in that boarding house are really trapped.'
'They were trapped. In that house, and in their awful lives.'
Dick Clement and Ian La Frenais, screenwriters (interviewed for ITV's 'Comedy Classics': *Rising Damp*)

As previously acknowledged, a great part of the success of *Rising Damp* was due to the environment created onscreen. It was an evocation of the cheap and squalid rooms familiar to many: the kind of bedsit where one only had to reach out from the sofa to stir the can of baked beans that represented that night's hearty meal (in a duvet, naturally, trying to get warm). If the audience hadn't had to endure such a situation themselves, then they likely knew someone who had (or had just deposited their children in one to continue their studies at university, like the character Alan Moore). Naturally, Leonard Rossiter had seen his fair share of bedsits, not just growing up in Liverpool but also on the road during his early days in theatre.

Rising Damp had everything that a successful sitcom needs: a grotesque but immediately recognisable location. Think Derek Trotter's tacky Peckham flat, Basil Fawlty's threadbare hotel on the 'English Riviera' and yes, even Norman Stanley Fletcher's Page Three-decorated prison cell – all places we can immediately identify with, either personally or through a received notion of what such dwellings must be like.

The location of the house was never precisely defined: it was simply a tatty old red-brick, somewhere 'North', giving the place the kind of ubiquitous quality that helped audiences relate to it: Rigsby's home could be in your town, just be glad you don't have to live there.

Colin Piggot was the man hired to bring this world to life in the form of sets. 'It was probably based, if anything, [on] being around Leeds in the sixties and seventies, because it was a pretty grim place then. A lot of houses had arched windows and strange attic rooms; they all looked incredibly damp, horrible and grey.'

Many sitcoms of the day were brightly lit and cheery (however supposedly grim their location): HMP Slade in *Porridge*, for example, never seems so bad a place to while away your sentence. *Rising Damp* kept things dull – dark, heavy colours and more realistic lighting. 'I chose a lot of dark greens,' Piggot explains, 'which was a bit dangerous because green is unlucky as far as some theatrical people are concerned; there was a murmuring about the colour because you couldn't use green in television in those days as some actors would refuse to come on! I remember working on a series with an actress who got her manager to check there was no green anywhere before she came on the set!'

Despite those somewhat absurd considerations – and even a complaint from some corners of the ITV network, who deemed it 'too dark for comedy' – the house, with its dark stairwells and imposing wallpaper, formed a perfect environment for Rigsby and his tenants. Of course, it was a world away from the 'functional, but with a hint of decadence', that its owner laid claim to. In keeping with the level of affection that the series would engender with its audience, Piggot continues: 'I wanted to make it so that no one would want to live there, but in the end people started to like it.'

Leonard, always with an eye to naturalism, can only have been relieved that Piggot was allowed to design the show in the way that he did: for all the practical awkwardness of working in the small sets, you couldn't have asked for a more evocative, truthful foundation to build on.

All the sets were lifted 18 inches off the ground to give an impression of height, allowing shots that would feature the actors ascending (or descending) the stairs to their rooms. The furnishings – in particular, the beds – were deceptive in that many of them were far too small for practical use, allowing the actors room to move – though precious little – and yet appearing perfectly functional onscreen. Things were still incredibly tight: the height of the sets limiting the movement of the cameras, though enabling lower angles than would otherwise have been impossible and a carpenter was always on hand to saw off any extraneous sections that might afford a few more inches for the camera lens to squeeze into.

Watching re-runs of the show, the tight production schedule is also illustrated in the developing clutter of the rooms. The attic space belonging to Alan and Philip starts off rather sparse before slowly filling with rubbish, dirty plates, posters and clothes all joining the perpetual presence of a skeleton hanging by the door that frequently unnerves the building's owner.

If filmed today, *Rising Damp* would no doubt have had the budget and space for a little more leeway but it still stands up as a brave – and predominantly successful – attempt to bring a little more 'real-life' grime to the world of the sitcom.

22

Creating Rigsby

'Although the setting was absurd, it was rooted in a truth – of a lonely man looking for love – which gave it more than just comedy, there was a pathos there, too.'

Neil Pearson, actor, interviewed for ITV's 'Comedy Classics': *Rising Damp*

Despite initial concerns as to whether Leonard Rossiter would be able to carry the show as its leading man, there can be no doubt whatsoever that his performance as Rigsby was a major contributory factor to *Rising Damp*'s enduring success. Interviewed for the arts programme, 'Live from Two' in 1980, Leonard acknowledged that the character resonated with the skills and style he possessed. It was a persona he knew that he could flesh out to the best of his abilities. 'I recognised a lot of things Eric [Chappell] wrote,' he added, 'coming from the North – I come from Liverpool. [That attitude] of being very jealous about the young people of today regarding sex and so on, that's very Rigsby, but I recognised it from when I grew up.'

Certainly, Rigsby was recognisable as a product of his generation, as Don Warrington observes: 'I think he really caught something about the English, a sort of emotional incontinence which one can see in pubs: the man who knows it all but actually knows nothing.'

'He found the character through nuance and observation,' explained renowned scriptwriter Ian La Frenais, who would work with Rossiter on the 1985 movie, *Water*. 'He wasn't a comedian, he didn't look for the gag or the punchline: he had to find the character's voice.' Sir Paul

Fox agrees: 'He was a very distinguished actor and that was the genius of Duncan Wood. He had learned that he didn't want comedians doing a sitcom, he wanted actors.'

Rupert Rigsby wasn't just a vehicle for Chappell's jokes: he was a fully rounded character. As Don Warrington points out: 'Comedy is about what happens between people – it's not about a close-up here or a close-up there, it's about a *relationship*. And that's [how Len and I] worked it. If we found the relationship with the other character, it would be funny.' Eric Chappell concurs: 'He [Rigsby] was a loner, and the thing he had in common with Philip was that he was a loner too. They were both outsiders for different reasons.'

Often there is a degree of vanity with actors. Even when playing the most loathsome character, there is a temptation to ensure they retain a degree of attractiveness. Not so with Rossiter. Like all great character actors, he was only too happy to fully embody the grotesque, from the detail in his costume – the stained cardigan, the plimsolls or slippers he wore to ensure he could creep up on tenants – to the twitch and sneer of his facial expressions. Reviewers of the West End show had been quick to pick on Leonard's habit of standing as if everyone around him possessed 'chronic halitosis': his hands high on his ribs, that backward lean of thirty degrees or so, always rearing away from people.

And yet, like many comic creations before him – Old Man Steptoe or the reprehensible Alf Garnett – Rupert Rigsby earned the affection of an audience, despite his questionable attitudes. 'He [Rigsby] should have been the most unloved character,' notes playwright and author Robert Tanitch, 'instead he was adored by millions. And rightly so, for what came across in Leonard's brilliant, hilarious and memorable performance was not the awfulness of the character, but always the vulnerability.'

Ian La Frenais' co-writer Dick Clement feels that '[Rigsby's] so transparent. You don't feel threatened by him, so you're behind him all the way. We enjoy watching people we don't approve of.'

The audience cannot help but sympathise with Rossiter's Rigsby. For every racist remark or tight-fisted con he offers, we never get away from the fact that this is a very lonely man, desperate to better himself and find the companionship of a woman. Whether we approve of the methods he uses to go about this, we can hardly damn his aspirations.

To Rigbsy, Rossiter also brought the extreme physicality always offered in his performances. 'He was very energetic performer,' recalls Eric Chappell, 'who acted with his whole body. His performance was always a choreographed piece of work. He acted with every fibre of his being – and at such a pace, too.' That pace often proved exhausting for guest performers. 'I remember actors who were appearing in an episode,' Chappell continues, 'saying how much they were looking forward to being on the show, but within a day or two they were growing pale because of the demands thrust upon them. The speed of the production was partly due to the tight schedules but also because of the rate at which Leonard worked.'

That energy was always supported with a precision that ensured every beat counted: every twitch, every pause, was carefully thought out and preserved through rehearsals and eventually onscreen. 'I once saw him play a scene with Richard Beckinsale,' adds Chappell, 'where he was demonstrating how to enter a room in civilised society. He carried the scene off with hardly a word. I saw him do it a dozen times and there was no variation – each scene was an exact replica of the one before and so carefully choreographed I could have been watching Chaplin.' When complimenting Rossiter on the scene, the actor simply replied – not harshly – 'I've spent a long time learning this job.'

Indeed, Leonard's technical precision certainly kept the rest of the cast on their toes. 'He was a wonderful teacher for me,' recalls Don Warrington, 'because it was my first job. He'd take me aside and say, "If you do it like this, it's funny. If you do it the way you're doing it, it's not." And he was right on every occasion. You couldn't help but be dumbfounded by his technical virtuosity.'

'Leonard was one of the great farce actors of all time,' observed Frances de la Tour in a rare interview about her time on the show given just after the announcement of the co-star's untimely death. 'He was nervous, vulnerable, a slave-driver, no more punishable [sic] to others than he was to himself in his drive for perfection.' And certainly all agree that production wasn't always easy, with Rossiter's determination to see the best work produced meaning that he had little time for a lack of work ethic. 'We laughed a lot on set,' de la Tour added, 'but comedy is a serious business and Leonard took it particularly seriously, and rightly so.'

Though commendable in many ways, Rossiter's singular drive also earned him the reputation of being occasionally difficult to work with. 'Comedy can be very tough,' notes Don Clayton, a floor manager on the show, 'especially when you're dealing with some strong personalities. Len Rossiter was brilliant in the role but very intense and not necessarily the funniest man in the world to work with. There was a tension between the director and Len, which I have to say was generated by Len: it wasn't anything malicious on Len's part – it was just that he was such a perfectionist.'

Perfectionism is always hard to deal with creatively, especially in television where there are so many factors to take into account. There is not only the script and the performers to deal with, but also such prosaic complications as shooting schedules. It was impossible to overrun in studio: when the time came to finish the lights would be turned off and everyone would go home; everything ran by a strict clock – and technical problems have a tendency to delay matters just as much as the drive to perfectly perform a scene. However, it must be remembered that Rossiter was always aware of his responsibilities within a production.

As the leading man and to many, the actor who personified the show, Leonard's responsibility within *Rising Damp* was extremely profound. 'Len wouldn't go along with things that he wasn't happy with,' his widow, Gillian Raine, observed in an ITV documentary about the show, 'and had the confidence to say something about it rather than put up with it. Because of his frankness some people thought he was difficult. What people sometimes forgot is that he was playing the lead in many of the productions, which meant he carried a great deal of the responsibility on his shoulders. If something wasn't of the highest possible standard it would reflect badly on him.'

Vernon Lawrence, who took over from Ronnie Baxter as the producer and director on the fourth series, has no such qualms about his working relationship with Leonard: 'I had a great relationship with him and admired him enormously, but if something was wrong he certainly took no trouble in telling you. He could be quite ruthless but had every right to be because he was a genius. I'm not saying he was an unpleasant man – just that he knew what he wanted and what was right for the show. He wasn't a selfish man and didn't insist on having

Leonard in 'Story of a Farm Girl', an episode of Granada TV's 1963 series *Maupassant*, in which a number of Guy de Maupassant's short stories were adapted for the small screen. He played the character of Emile Valin and is seen here with the farm girl of the title, Rose Levesque, played by Angela Morant. ITV / Rex Features

Inspector Bamber chases up leads in a 1963 episode of *Z-Cars*. This was Leonard's first experience of a recurring TV character, something that at his stage of his career he was determined to avoid, preferring the variety of one-off dramas.
Ronald Grant Archive / Mary Evans

Leonard's slimy undertaker Shadrack keeps an eye on his flighty employee Billy Fisher, played by Tom Courtenay, in 1963's *Billy Liar*. It was the first film role to offer Leonard something he could really sink his teeth into. Ronald Grant Archive / Mary Evans

Leonard reads the morning paper in 'Flight from Reality', an ITV *Play of the Week* from 1964. It also featured a young Annette Crosbie, who would later play Victor Meldrew's long-suffering wife, Margaret, in *One Foot in the Grave*.
ITV / Rex Features

Leonard as Eddie, a professional safe cracker, in HTV's 1972 crime thriller *Thick as Thieves*. He would work again with the writers, Bob Baker and Dave Martin, in 1976's *Machinegunner*. ITV / Rex Features

In March 1974, shortly before they would both achieve iconic status in *Rising Damp*, Leonard and Richard Beckinsale appeared in LWT's *If There Weren't Any Blacks You'd Have to Invent Them*, a surreal comic parable written by Johnny Speight. The other actor is Donald Gee. ITV / Rex Features

Leonard seems particularly happy here as *Rising Damp*'s threadbare landlord, Rigsby – no doubt someone's just paid their rent. Running on ITV for four series between 1974 and 1978, *Rising Damp* was the show that saw Leonard transformed from well-respected character actor to TV star. ITV / Rex Features

Oh, Miss Jones... both Frances de la Tour and Leonard would reprise their *Rising Damp* roles for a big screen version in 1979. Unlike many movies based on sitcoms it won a number of awards and, while the cast missed their recently deceased co-star Richard Beckinsale, it was a fitting epitaph to the series and its characters. ITV / Rex Features

In the first series of *The Fall and Rise of Reginald Perrin*, shown on BBC1 in 1976, Reggie disguises himself as a pig farmer, hoping to fool his wife and family after faking his own suicide. **BBC / Ronald Grant Archive / Mary Evans**

Reggie would have hated such crass commercialism but here is Leonard in 1980 at a book signing for *The Better World of Reginald Perrin*, the novelisation of the third series. **Getty Images**

A slightly sinister sketch of Leonard by cartoonist 'Trog', which appeared in *Punch* in December 1981. **Punch / TopFoto**

Leonard as Cyril Dugdale in HTV's *Machinegunner*, shown in 1976. Despite the Bogart-like pose, Dugdale was a rather inept detective, a debt-collector far out of his depth, in Bob Baker and Dave Martin's one-off crime drama. **ITV / Rex Features**

In the seventies there was no clearer sign that you had achieved stardom than being invited to appear in a *Morecambe and Wise Christmas Special*. Here is Leonard in the 1978 show, miming alongside Eric and Ernie as wartime act The Andrews Sisters. **Fremantle Media Ltd / Rex Features**

In 1979 Leonard and his wife, Gillian Raine, starred in *Semi-Detached*, a play that was dear to both their hearts as it was in a 1962 production that they first met. With Leonard co-directing alongside Alan Strachan, the revival sadly met with negative reviews. It would be the only time Leonard tried his hand at directing. Getty Images

A rare shot of Leonard 'at rest', taken at his home in West London in 1982.

© Christopher Cormack / CORBIS

Leonard and Joan Collins became the faces of the Cinzano ad campaign between 1978 and 1983, appearing in ten adverts in all. Here they are shown at the photocall for the final ad in the campaign, with Joan Collins doing all she can to prevent another soaking.

Bill Cross / Daily Mail / Rex Features

Leonard and Gillian seen here with their daughter Camilla in a lovely portrait from 1983.

John Curtis / Rex Features

In his final theatrical role, Leonard played Inspector Truscott, alongside Gemma Craven's Nurse Fay, in the 1984 run of Joe Orton's *Loot*. Leonard had wanted to play the role for many years and while his sad death during a performance can never be overshadowed, it is a small compensation that he finally got his chance, earning some of the finest notices of his career. TopFoto

Leonard Rossiter's last film role was as Sir Malcolm Leveridge in *Water*, a comedy of colonial politics written by Dick Clement and Ian La Frenais, with a cast including Michael Caine and Billy Connolly. The film was released in April 1985, six months after Leonard's death. **Handmade Films / Ronald Grant Archive / Mary Evans**

every other line or taking centre stage all the time. If he felt the script contained something gratuitous and we were running over, he was only too happy to have his own lines cut for the benefit of the show.'

Certainly many of his co-stars seemed comfortable with his methods. 'Leonard was just excellent,' notes Robert Gillespie, who appeared in the second series episode, 'Last of the Big Spenders'. 'He had a particular line of comedy which was unusual in this country – a highly satirical edge. He was an absolute perfectionist, who worked and worked.'

'He was wonderful to watch in rehearsals,' agrees Judy Buxton, who appeared as Alan Moore's girlfriend in the Series Three episodes 'Clunk Click' and 'The Cocktail Hour', 'because he was so precise in everything; he had every little movement off to a tee – I admired him for that. It was a bit nerve-wracking working with him, but I'm glad I had the opportunity.'

Appearing in 'The Good Samaritan' was actor David Swift, who felt that 'To work with Leonard was such a privilege because he was a genius. He knew what he wanted and for someone so exceptionally talented, he was surprisingly restrained.'

Robin Parkinson, who co-starred in the second series episode, 'Moonlight and Roses', went as far as to say: 'I regard him as the best comedy actor this country has produced in the last 30 or 40 years.'

Peter Bowles, who would later go on to star in two more shows written by Eric Chappell, *Only When I Laugh* and *The Bounder*, classed Rossiter as 'a remarkable actor with a unique style. I remember his spring-footedness more than anything. His stylistic approach was very powerful and was something he was unaware of until later in his career, when he began exploiting it.'

Before appearing in *Rising Damp*, Bowles' career had been built on a string of screen villains and straight roles: 'I'd never done situation comedy before and when I made my first entrance, the laughter was so enormous – it surprised me. In fact, it was so enormous they couldn't continue with the recording. The great thing about Leonard was that he always played to the other actors. There's a tendency in situation comedy to play to the audience, but Leonard never did.'

And he certainly had no difficulties in working with Leonard, having appeared with him onstage in the past: 'When filming began I started making suggestions about how scenes could be improved. Everybody seemed to duck for cover but as I expected, he listened and we tried out my ideas. I could never understand why everyone was so nervous of him because if you put forward a good idea that was worth trying, he would never dismiss it.'

Ultimately, it must be noted that when any professional works hard to accomplish the finest job of which he is capable he expects to see those working alongside him do no less. That may cause unrest at times, as working alongside a driven man always does, but almost always it leads to great things. It is clear that the pace he set for the working environment was one that was as draining for him as everyone else involved. 'The effort that he put into those shows was phenomenal,' recalls Don Warrington, 'at the end of it sometimes the man was absolutely exhausted. The passion that was there was frightening.' It is clear that Warrington's admiration for his co-star knows no bounds: 'Every time I saw him, I thought, this man is getting better and better,' he recounts. 'He was amazed at how successful *Rising Damp* was. He'd spent years doing these incredibly difficult parts, and then this part comes along which was as easy as falling off a log for him, and it makes him into a gigantic star.'

As to how much of Rigsby was Rossiter's and how much Chappell's, the writer himself finds it hard to define: 'It's hard thinking back to what I pictured before Len came on the scene. All I know is that he played the character beautifully and in the end I was writing for both Len and Rigsby. At times he would say: "Rigsby would never do that, Eric." Here was the actor telling the writer, who's created the character, what he would or wouldn't do.'

As always in these situations, Leonard would insist he knew best!

23

Black Magic

'From black people, the feeling I got is that they were delighted to see a character such as Philip Smith on television.'

Don Warrington

When Leonard Rossiter introduced the character of Rigsby to the newspaper-reading public he rather controversially associated him with Hitler (and forced a speedy name change for the character in so doing).

There's no doubt that the character was a bigot. Rigsby's initial response to seeing his new tenant was a young black man ('The New Tenant') sets the tone for his attitude to come. Running to Alan Moore shortly afterwards, he quickly airs his old-fashioned attitudes: 'He's probably never had a pair of shoes on before he came here. What's going to happen when he hears the drums? You wait until the next full moon – we'll be locking our doors. You wait until we get the washing of the spears.'

Uncomfortable as much of this may seem to modern-day audiences, it must be remembered that *Rising Damp* was actually one of the first shows on British TV to allow a black character to take the upper hand. For all of Rigsby's jibes, it's Philip who wins out, time and time again. Eric Chappell observes: 'Philip always got the better of the exchanges with his landlord. Don would never have agreed to play the part if he felt it was patronising.'

Director Ronnie Baxter concurs: 'I think most sensible people took it for what it was: a comedy series where the man with all the opinions

153

and views falls flat on his face every time. Most people thought Rigsby was a berk and his arguments always came crashing down around him, anyway. There was always tit for tat between him and Philip, and that's the way to do comedy: Philip always gave as good as he got.'

Indeed, it's true that Philip often put Rigsby in his place. This is outlined particularly early on in the first series episode, 'A Night Out', when the characters take a trip to The Grange, a particularly high-class restaurant, in honour of Miss Jones's birthday. Rigsby is concerned that Philip will embarrass them all with a confusion about cutlery and 'drinking from the finger bowl'. He suggests his new tenant stays close to him, convinced his reputation will be enough to get them through the door despite what he assumes will be disapproval on the part of the restaurant, given Philip's skin colour. In the end it is Rigsby who is unwelcome and only manages to enter because Philip is well known to the maître d', who allows him in as his guest.

Rigsby's attitudes were not exactly unusual for the day, however, as Don Warrington reminds us: 'I never felt any discomfort about it [playing the role] because Rigsby held views that were pretty common. Lots of people had those prejudices so it wasn't anything new to me. What *was* new was that Philip was a response to it and the fact that Rigsby's apparent dislike of Philip is through jealousy. He wanted to be like Philip, because Philip seemed to have all the things Rigsby was desperately struggling for: Miss Jones included, of course. The irony being that it was given to Philip – a man that, according to Rigsby's sensibilities, should be without any of these gifts whatsoever due to the colour of his skin.'

Despite Rigsby's outward bluster, it soon becomes clear that there's a grudging respect between the two of them. 'It's what is underneath most comedy, really,' Warrington agrees, 'a need for the other character. They won't function without the other person being there, so although on the surface there is an animosity, there is something bigger going on beneath. They have a need for each other, a relationship with one another, even if that relationship is hugely dysfunctional.'

Of course, television at the time was hardly without an ample cast of characters who shared Rigsby's attitudes, the medium possessing a long history of racist characters and humour. Alf Garnett, the central character of Johnny Speight's much-lauded (and highly criticised) *Till*

Death Us Do Part had been allowed to air his racist opinions on the BBC since 1965, frequently commenting on the problem of 'coons' in Britain. Speight has talked extensively about the fact that Garnett's opinions were always intended to be risible – and surely he's right – and yet, such was the popularity of the show and indeed, so strong the performance from Warren Mitchell as Garnett, that the character became a much-loved figure, something which rather undercut the fact that we were supposed to find him loathsome. *Till Death Us Do Part* became a long-running success on television, moving from the BBC to ITV and back again through various different series.

Garnett may have been intended as a vehicle to lampoon such attitudes rather than an endorsement of them (his comments about the 'Jews up at Spurs' as in Tottenham Hotspur, a football club known for its sizeable amount of Jewish supporters, being a prime example for Warren Mitchell was both Jewish and himself a fan of the club). But it cannot be denied that the show set a precedent for racist humour in TV comedy. It is notable that Speight was warned against using racist language during the writing of the later series, *In Sickness and In Health*, when produced by the BBC in the mid- to late-eighties. Indeed, a recurring character – Winston (who was both black and openly gay) – was eventually written out. Despite mellowing the opinions of Garnett in his old age, naturally there was a limit to how much he would be able to restrain his language around such a character.

In spite of his insistence that he sought to deride racist opinion rather than concur with it, Speight found even greater controversy with his later series, *Curry and Chips*, featuring Spike Milligan as a blacked-up Irish-Pakistani, Kevin O'Grady. The series, though allegedly seeking to deal with bigger issues, so often fell back on racial slurs that it only ran for six episodes in 1969, amid a great deal of controversy from critics and viewers alike.

To witness Speight's true colours (no pun intended but most certainly accepted), one only has to look at either version of his surrealistic play, *If There Weren't Any Blacks You'd Have to Invent Them*. Originally broadcast in 1968 by London Weekend Television in black-and-white (three years after Speight's Garnett was unleashed), it featured Leslie Sands as a blind man who, after a heated conversation on the subject of equality with a young man (played by John Castle) that he chances to meet in a cemetery, becomes convinced the man is black. Despite his new acquaintance's insistence that isn't the case, the blind man manages to convince others, even those who can see well enough to know better, that it is true. To assist in their delusion, the gathered mob black his face with shoe polish and then force him to become a scapegoat for all their ills.

A disturbing and bizarre play, there is no question that it was way ahead of its time, though the writer's willingness to stick his neck out and be brave is also very much of its time – TV doesn't make a habit of such dramas these days. Six years later, LWT decided to recast and reshoot the play in colour and it is this version that, while shot from an identical script, sticks in most people's minds due to the fact that Leonard Rossiter played the blind bigot and Richard Beckinsale was the young man. Broadcast shortly before *Rising Damp*, it has recently been released on DVD by Network (an ever-reliable source for archive television) alongside the original black-and-white version and is highly recommended.

Johnny Speight was particularly gratified to have Rossiter onboard: 'He had those gifts of talent coupled with consummate craft skills that enable an artist to seize and hold the rapt attention of an audience. He was immensely theatrical without being stagey, and he had a sense of character that gave to everything I ever saw him do a reality that was entirely believable, no matter how bizarre or fantastical the material he was asked to work with.'

And in the case of Speight's script, the material certainly was bizarre: comical, disturbing and with scant care for realism. The writer continues: '[He] brought to it a comic violence that was Chaplinesque in the way that, despite the obvious physical vulnerability of the character, revealed him clearly and comically as the undoubted violent central pivot of the piece.'

In fact, Rupert Rigsby can be counted as the last in a string of roles concerning racism. As well as *If There Weren't Any Blacks You'd Have to Invent Them*, we had already seen Leonard donning turban and face paint as the delusional Mr Marcus in *Drums along the Avon* and trading insults in *Thick as Thives* and *Machinegunner*. This simply shows that racism was a strong theme of the day but it also takes a brave actor to play such parts, one who is happy to give the characters his all, however distasteful to some they may be. Of course, Rossiter was perfect in this regard, never shying away from a truth in his performances and would be obvious casting.

Regardless of how clearly didactic many of these shows were intended to be, others of the era couldn't necessarily say the same. ITV's *The Comedians*, a half-hour showcase of stand-up comedy that ran for 11 series through the seventies and eighties, was no stranger to racist humour – no surprise given that Bernard Manning was a regular! Perhaps the most relevant performer was Charlie Williams, the first mixed-race comedian to achieve a degree of TV success. Despite his ethnicity, Williams' material often revolved around racist stereotypes, with one of his most popular responses to hecklers being, 'If you don't shut up, I'll move in next door to you!'

That latter premise was the backbone to *Love Thy Neighbour*, a sitcom that revolved around a white and black family living next door to one another. As with *Till Death Us Do Part*, a safety net was employed in that it was only the two patriarchs of the families that didn't get on (their wives being perfectly comfortable with one another). Still, it all serves as a reminder that when Rigsby suggests (again, in the first series episode, 'A Night Out') that Philip's favourite meal is probably 'a handful of maize and a bit of burnt Christian', he was hardly the first to cast such out-dated aspersions.

Indeed, such attitudes were common enough in the real world at the time. Though it is amusing to note an anecdote from Don Warrington: 'I remember one incident when Richard [Beckinsale] and I were strolling around the [Leeds] city centre looking for a club to go to and everywhere we went told us we couldn't go in. Richard became furious and asked me if I thought the refusals were because I was black.

'After another refusal he'd had enough and went up to a bouncer and actually asked him that very question. He replied, "No, it's because you're wearing jeans."'

In a way this sums up the seventies, a period when new levels of racial acceptance conflicted with old prejudices to the point where no one was quite sure how to tread. There is no question that Chappell shared any of Rigsby's views – quite the opposite – and *Rising Damp* straddles an era when blatant racism was presented hand-in-hand with an attempt to push it back into the pages of history, where it inarguably belonged. We are never encouraged to share Rigsby's views and dear as the character became to television audiences, he was someone we were encouraged to laugh *at*, rather than *with* from the word go, something Rossiter ensured with his performance.

'Meeting people of a different race was a new experience for many people back in the 1960s and 1970s,' observes Chappell, 'and everyone was having to make adjustments. So I dealt with the subject in a very light-hearted way. But you must remember that the original idea was about a man posing as the son of a chief; with Philip and Rigsby you have two flawed characters and that's what the show was about. Now and again, people ask how I got away with it, and maybe today sensitivities have grown to such an extent that you daren't say anything about race. But people still find the show perfectly acceptable so there can't have been much wrong with it. I feel we must not dodge issues and pretend they are not there because we're writing comedy about life: we're saying laugh at it, don't submit to it.

'It never worried Len, I hasten to add – he went for broke every time. In fact, if I wanted to cut something because I got nervous about it, he wouldn't have it.'

24

Going Out on a High

'The problem with comedy series – as I think most people realise – is that the first one or two [episodes] are normally quite good and then it begins to tail off afterwards,' Leonard Rossiter observed, during a TV interview, 'I reckoned that Eric was capable of writing at least six good scripts so I did the first series without any qualms. The difficulty came afterwards, with the second series, wondering if Eric could keep up the standard he'd set himself. I asked him before we started, was he going to be able to write them? He said: "I didn't think I was going to be able to write the first six!"'

Chappell's concerns soon proved justified, however. He had submitted another sitcom idea at the same time as *Rising Damp*, a show set in an office called *The Squirrels*, which had been bought by another of ITV's regions, ATV. Now faced with the prospect of writing full scripts for both shows, he realised that he had seven weeks to produce five *Rising Damp* scripts and simply couldn't deliver. He suggested to ATV that they brought in other writers to finish off the show, but Leonard was having none of it. He insisted that he had signed on to perform scripts written by Eric Chappell and that was precisely what he intended to do. 'When Len puts his foot down, it stays down,' Chappell later commented. The writer was at his wit's end, but ATV altered the schedule to allow him time off to get over his exhaustion and extra writers were brought in to assist with *The Squirrels*.

In his notes to a book of scripts produced by André Deutsch in 2002, Chappell recalled: 'Len gave me a lecture about saying no to people, but when you're new to the profession you hate turning people down because you're frightened you'll never be asked again.'

Unfortunately this delay meant that filming dates now clashed for Frances de la Tour, who was unable to complete work beyond the first four (of seven) episodes as she had already committed to theatre work. 'It was a blow to lose Frances,' admits Chappell, 'but there was nothing we could do about it. We brought another actress in – Gay Rose, who played Brenda – and it worked well, so Frances leaving didn't actually set us back too much.'

Chappell married Miss Jones off (to Desmond, a rather earnest librarian), much to Rigsby's dismay, and she vanished henceforth from the house. While missed, her absence didn't affect the popularity of the show, now being screened in a more favourable slot. Audience ratings continued to creep up and by the end of the second series run, it was in the Top 20 most popular shows on air at the time. For Chappell, this endorsement was further hit home by the realisation that many of those working at Yorkshire Television at the time would make an effort to secure tickets to watch the live recordings. 'These were people working in the industry who had seen it all,' he says, 'and here they were enjoying my show. I realised that if the professionals liked it, it must be good.'

Rising Damp took a year off from the screens in 1976 due to Leonard's commitment to film *The Fall and Rise of Reginald Perrin*. However, it returned the following year with Frances de la Tour back as Miss Jones. The series showed a slight shift in style in that each episode tended to focus on a new tenant and the regulars' interaction with them. From Mrs Brent and her newborn baby – whom Rigsby mistakes for a child of Miss Jones, working hard to present himself as the perfect father figure – to Peter Bowles as the resting actor Hilary, who insists on referring to Rigsby as 'duckie' and has the rest of the tenants embroiled in acting out scenes from a play he's written.

'Usually the third series of any show goes well,' says Chappell in his notes for the *Rising Damp* script book, 'because it's established itself with the viewers. I found it easier to think up plots for these episodes and I was probably reaching my peak in terms of generating ideas.'

A third series led to a fourth, but this would be the last. Two major changes had occurred behind the scenes, with Ronnie Baxter being replaced by Vernon Lawrence as producer and director, and – more dramatically from the point of the scripts – the unavailability of Richard Beckinsale, who was tied into a West End show, *I Love My Wife*, as well as filming as his *Porridge* character, Lennie Godber, in the short-lived spin-off, *Going Straight*.

The fourth series would feature just six episodes rather than seven, but not because of any other reason other than a mistake in commissioning! Yorkshire Television mistakenly issued a contract for six and when they had noticed their mistake, Chappell politely refused the offer of adding another as the loss of Beckinsale and a sense that their time was up meant he was happy to finish on the series.

Despite these concerns, the fourth series was in no way a letdown in quality, something both Chappell and Rossiter were always determined should not happen: 'I experienced mixed emotions when it came to writing the last episode,' he admits in the script book, 'there was certainly a sense of relief that we'd maintained a high quality throughout, but what worried Len more than anything, and perhaps made him a little tense towards the end, was that we couldn't let the standard drop. I wanted to keep my writing up to a certain level, he wanted to keep his acting up that pitch – neither of us could afford to make a bad show.'

But there was no temptation to continue further: 'I was never going to write a fifth series – Richard had already left the cast and Len wouldn't have done it. He always said that if he wanted to be in a long-running show, he'd have stayed at the insurance office. There was never any question about continuing and I've never regretted the decision, even though writing more would have made me a lot of money. Len and I both felt we had other things to do: we didn't want to hang around until people got fed up with us.'

Vernon Lawrence, perhaps understandably as he was new to the show, had some regrets: 'Personally I was very sorry because I'd only done one series, but in hindsight I think the great job was that we got out on top. We all walked away from a thumping great hit – doing that is very brave. On reflection you ask yourself: "Could we have done another one, another two maybe?" but then the history of British comedy is littered with people who have gone on and made too many shows.'

That year *Rising Damp* beat *Porridge* to win the BAFTA for Best Sitcom, though Ronnie Barker clawed back some of that victory by pipping Leonard to the post to seize the award for Best Light Entertainment Performance.

But Leonard wouldn't have taken this to heart: he considered awards all very nice but not dreadfully important. For him, the only important thing was the finished show and he knew how he felt about that – the opinion of BAFTA wouldn't have mattered, one way or the other. Besides, how could he doubt the popularity of the series when it had completely altered his public life?

25

Oi, Rigsby!

There could have been no way of predicting it but Leonard Rossiter's performance as Rigsby – further exacerbated by the success of Reggie Perrin – took his prized privacy and threw it to the dogs. Some parts come with a guaranteed wave of publicity: if you're taking the lead in the James Bond franchise, for example, you know your life is about to change. Strange as it may seem for a profession that can appear completely extrovert on the surface, it is often one of the most difficult parts of the job for an actor to deal with. Your life changes, everyone knows you, everyone wants to talk to you, they all feel they have a stake in you. For some, this can prove quite intolerable.

Rossiter bore it gracefully enough, careful to keep his home life private and public exposure to a minimum, but things certainly changed around him. 'When I was very young,' recalls his daughter Camilla in an article for *Intelligent Life*, 'I assumed that everyone's father must be on television. Only as I got older did I understand that mine was different and grasp just how well known he was. I realised that to other people he was such a familiar face from their living rooms that they felt they knew him. When we were out and about, total strangers would often just walk up to him and start chatting. He wasn't simply my dad – he was also public property.

'At primary school, I would be asked for his autograph by other children, and occasionally by the teachers. He had a supply of glossy black-and-white photos that he would dutifully sign for me to distribute the following day. The picture was of Dad looking rather jovial and wearing a cravat. If my schoolmates were puzzled that they didn't get one of Rigsby in his moth-eaten cardigan, they never showed it.'

Leonard was pursued for autographs wherever he went. On one memorable occasion while at the seaside, a loaf of bread was shoved at him by a lady who insisted, 'Sign it!' Too surprised to argue, he did.

The recognition also spread to Gillian and Camilla, the latter of whom fondly recalls a time when a pair of ladies stared at them on the bus, clearly recognising Gillian, before one eventually piped up, 'It's that Mrs Damp.'

'As a very private man,' continues Camilla, 'he was never that comfortable with the attention. However, he did relish the fact that he had made a success of his career – and he had no false modesty about it. One evening, he and my mother were due at a friend's first night. They were running late so, as they reached the theatre, rather than stop and oblige the autograph hunters, Dad hurried past, apologising. One woman took great exception and yelled after him, "We put you where you are today, you know!" Dad wheeled round and marched back, retorting: "Oh believe me, you didn't – *I* put me where I am today." '

And no one can argue with the truth of that. As noted earlier by Don Warrington, Leonard had worked for years in the business before the character of Rigsby – one that he found as easy to portray as breathing – suddenly made him a household name. In showbusiness, recognition often comes when you least expect it and in a manner you soon realise that you could do well without.

26

Richard Beckinsale – A Sad Loss

'I always said he was a page waiting to be written on by life. He kept telling me how he wanted to play more mature, sophisticated parts, and I remember saying to him: "You don't need to rush and should enjoy the more innocent roles if that's what you're being offered – after all, there is plenty of time for everything else." Sadly there wasn't.'

Eric Chappell

In 1979, the year after the final series of *Rising Damp* aired (and while the cast and writer were gearing up to the possibility of a feature film) Richard Beckinsale died, at only 31, of a heart attack brought on by a congenital heart defect.

'I was walking along the street that I lived on,' Don Warrington told David Clayton for his 2008 biography, *The Richard Beckinsale Story*, "and somebody shouted to me, "Your mate's dead!", and I just couldn't understand what was being said to me. I went home and put on the television, and it came up on the *Six O'Clock News* that Richard had died. It was a very sad moment, not only for me but also for a lot of people around Richard's age. It was very sad but also very cautionary.'

The news hit everyone who had worked with him deeply, including Leonard. 'Len really loved Richard,' continued Warrington, 'He thought he was wonderful. Whatever mood Len was in, Richard would come in and his mood would change. He was much better than people realised. I would observe him in rehearsals and his skill was to make it look effortless. I've always felt the part of Alan was very difficult to play. I thought he gave it a wonderful charm and innocence, but at the same time, an integrity.'

It is unsurprising that Leonard would respect Beckinsale, for all the clear difference in their working methods. The young man had been an exemplary actor and a perfect foil to Rossiter's performance.

'Richard [Beckinsale] was very laid-back,' says Eric Chappell, 'and he absorbed some of Len's frenetic energy, which was good because we couldn't have had two people like Len in the show.'

Kind and generous, both as a man and performer, there is no doubt that Beckinsale would have gone on to many more great things. There is also the uncomfortable realisation that while Leonard mourned the passing of his friend, robbed too young by a heart condition, only five years were left before a similar fate would befall him too.

27

Rising Damp on the Big Screen

'I wasn't paid a fortune, so didn't feel I had to give it much of my time. The film was basically a regurgitation, with three-quarters of the material coming from the television series.'

Eric Chappell, *Rising Damp: A Celebration* by Richard Webber

The 1970s saw a great deal of successful TV sitcoms turned into movies. At the time British cinema still had a big draw and with fewer repeats and no home video or DVD, considerable sums were to be made in offering audiences the chance to revisit their favourite characters on the big screen.

One of the prime producers of such films was none other than Hammer Studios, today more famous for its horror output. Ever since the 1950s they had transformed such sitcoms as *Life with the Lyons* and *The Army Game* into solid box-office earners. It was with the phenomenal success of their 1971 feature *On the Buses*, based on the LWT sitcom of the same name, that the studio began to dedicate considerable time and money to the genre. They had mixed fortunes, with *That's Your Funeral* (based on a BBC show about comic antics in a funeral home) faring particularly badly – behind the cameras too, when an ageing actor playing a corpse actually died while filming, causing the producer Roy Skeggs to call his family and enquire if they minded him completing his performance for half the fee!

Skeggs, who would later become chairman of Hammer Studios, was involved in many of these pictures, working on all three *On the Buses* movies, *Nearest and Dearest*, *Love Thy Neighbour*, *Man About the House* and *George and Mildred*. By 1980, however, Hammer was on its uppers and now dedicated, rather ironically, to producing TV series sold on the strength of their horror movie brand. Skeggs continued to work in movies, alongside his commitment to the studio, producing a big-screen version of *Rising Damp* to be distributed through British Lion International.

Having secured the agreement from Eric Chappell to write a script, Skeggs had to convince Leonard Rossiter to return. 'He wasn't too keen,' he admits, 'so we took him out to lunch and chatted about it.'

Both Chappell and Rossiter insisted they would only do the film if the script were to reuse storylines from the original series, rather than produce – as Skeggs had hoped – a brand new story. In order to keep both writer and star happy, he was forced to agree.

'I was approached and was delighted to play Rigsby again,' said Rossiter in a later interview. 'It is the funniest character I have ever played. Eric Chappell is a marvellous writer. As we will never make another series, generations will be able to enjoy it – it's not the sort of film to date.'

In fact, the film has arguably dated more than the TV series, though it's far from bad, and certainly the cast seemed to treat it as a perfect way to wrap up their time with the show.

'When the film finishes, I won't be sorry,' admitted Frances de la Tour, when interviewed at the time, 'I have enjoyed the part, but five years is long enough. The film is like the icing on a good cake. And it's nice to go out with a bang and not a whimper.'

'When it was time to begin filming,' says Don Warrington, 'it was really all about whether Len wanted to do it or not, and when he agreed, there was no reason why the rest of us wouldn't want to either.'

But of course there was one omission: Richard Beckinsale. 'It was very difficult to film so soon after Richard's death,' continues Warrington, 'Len found it very difficult because he had a very special relationship with Richard and it was just very hard to do because we missed him so much.'

Eric Chappell created a new character: John Harris, an art student played by Christopher Strauli, who was recommended by Chappell, having worked with him on his new sitcom, *Only When I Laugh*. Initially, Strauli was unconvinced as he had known Beckinsale well, both having trained at RADA at the same time. Eventually, figuring that if someone was going to do it, then it might as well be him, Strauli accepted the part.

But Strauli had some problems working with Rossiter, who wanted him to emulate Beckinsale's performance – something his fellow actor was unwilling to do. 'I told him that, firstly, I was unable to do it and, secondly, I wouldn't want to. Richard had his own unique style and his timing was different from mine. I didn't want to try and do a poor imitation of Richard – I wanted to try and make the character my own.'

Joe McGrath was hired as director, having already worked with Leonard on television. Like Skeggs, he was determined to lift the film from being a straight rehash of previous material and immediately looked to the script: 'Eric would be the first to admit that he didn't put a lot of work into the screenplay,' says McGrath, 'because he thought there wasn't a lot he could do to it. We changed a lot of the stuff, got things moving a bit more than would have been the case on television.'

The script was still written with the technical limitations of the small studio sets in mind, even though there was now no need for such considerations. 'The production manager worked out a rough schedule,' explains McGrath, 'that had Leonard working with the rest of the cast for only one week out of the total five-week shoot. That was because, according to the script, all he did was appear in doorways – something that could have been shot en masse! I said, "Sorry, we're going to have to redo this and bring Leonard into the room so that he can interact with the rest of the actors!"

'I tried to shoot it almost like an old fashioned Laurel and Hardy comedy,' he continues, 'always playing scenes out in wide shots rather than the TV style of intercutting all the time. It all helps to make the film look bigger.' McGrath was determined the film would pull away from its television roots, something Leonard found difficult to begin with. He knew and liked McGrath but because this was Rigsby, he was inclined to stick to the methods he knew in order to play the part.

'The first few days were tricky,' admits McGrath, 'he'd always be asking where the camera was! Leonard admitted that you really are in the hands of a director when you're doing a film. In TV he could ask for monitors so that he could watch to see what was happening as he played a scene out, he was in control (something that didn't make him very popular with TV crews, I hasten to add). He had to lose the feeling that he was still doing a TV show, the sense of a three-sided set with an audience looking on. We got him over that in the end.'

Rossiter had also tried to involve himself in the casting. 'He wanted Denholm Elliott,' explains McGrath, 'and we got him. But Denholm was a seriously experienced film actor and had a completely different way of approaching scenes to Leonard. Leonard knew the character, he knew Rigsby, but Denholm was still finding out things, still defining the character. It was interesting watching the two of them work: Leonard would be prepared to play the scene a certain way the minute we came to it. He would just announce: "I'll start off here by the door, then move to here, say that, then move up here . . ." I used to joke with him, saying, "Okay, what are the rest of us doing?"

'In film, you feel your way a bit more, talk a scene through before shooting, try a few things, see what works, completely different to the TV method where you walk on set and just shoot what you've already blocked. It wound Leonard up to begin with, but then Denholm was quick to take the Mick: he came in one day with all his lines written on pieces of paper and started putting them all over the set, hidden behind jam jars and what have you. He even pinned one on Leonard's chest. Leonard couldn't believe it, asking him what the hell he was doing. Denholm said, "Well, Joe will be over there with the camera behind you so he won't see it, and you know me, I don't like coming in, knowing everything – I don't like knowing all the lines.

'Leonard realised he was having a joke played on him and he did start laughing, "Oh my God!" he said, taking the Mick in return, "Denholm's on another voyage of discovery." But he did settle down and told me in the end that he had really enjoyed it. We became great friends, bizarrely as politically I was like Frances really, a socialist, whereas Leonard was a dyed-in-the-wool Tory. Gillian and Camilla used to say they had no idea how we stayed friends as we were poles apart. We just avoided the subject by drinking lots of wine – he liked wine and so did I, so we got on just fine there.'

The film was a greater success than many such adaptations, doing well at the box office and winning several *Evening Standard* awards:

Best Comedy Film, Best Actor (Denholm Elliott), Best Actress (Frances de la Tour), Best Director and finally, Leonard Rossiter secured the Peter Sellers Award For Comedy.

'With most of my films I get bored after seeing them several times,' admits Roy Skeggs, 'but I never tire of *Rising Damp*.'

Despite everyone's intentions to let *Rising Damp* finish once and for all, it did – like its namesake – threaten to return. Shortly before Leonard's death in 1984, there was a plan to revive the show as a West End theatre production. Famed comedic writer and theatre producer Ray Cooney had begun preparations, with Eric Chappell ready to rework *The Banana Box* with new material. Naturally the loss of the production's intended leading man scotched such plans. Gone were the days when Rigsby could have been played by another actor: the role was so intrinsically linked with Leonard that it would have been a failure to try to give it to someone else. Rigsby was Rossiter, and much as he might have occasionally rankled at the fact, Rossiter was Rigsby.

Part IV

REGGIE PERRIN

28

An Opportunity to Join the Rat Race

JOAN: It's about Mr Perrin, doctor. Do you know what's wrong with him?

DOC MORRISEY: Yes, I do. Middle age, exhaustion, boredom, anxiety, self-disgust, misery, sense of inferiority, dislike of industry, dislike of instant puddings, 25-year itch, fear, insecurity, frustration . . .

JOAN: Well, what can we do about it?

DOC MORRISEY: Haven't the faintest idea . . .

For an actor to feature in a show that will go on to become a revered classic is rare. But to do it twice in quick succession is an amazing feat.

As Rigsby, Leonard Rossiter was firmly entrenched in the public consciousness by the winter of 1975. Two series of *Rising Damp* had aired and the show had built on its solid beginnings to become a ratings success. To many, Rossiter would be inseparable from the seedy landlord, such was the success with which he had embodied the character, but the following year would see him repeat the trick by appearing as Reginald Iolanthe Perrin, a character just as fondly remembered. As Rigsby was the embodiment of the post-war failure, the man who dreams of success and happiness he will never achieve, so Perrin is a man who has achieved all that most men in the 1970s might have wished, but found it lacking. Reggie has a good (though far from great) job, a loving wife, a family and his own corner of suburbia, in which to enjoy them.

'He lived the life that a lot of office commuters would have liked to live,' Leonard noted during a 1980 interview, and he was right. Perrin was, by many people's standards (and certainly Rigsby's) a success – and the suffocating nature of it all was killing him. Driven to a breakdown by a job that lacked fulfilment and a life that ground on and on interminably, he would fake suicide in order to start again and find a life worth living.

It's a tale that resonates to this day – so much so that the series was remade with actor Martin Clunes in the lead role, inspiring runners in the rat race to quit once again. From such common touchstones as the daily commute (with the morning train perpetually eleven minutes late) to the boss who doesn't respect, or even understand him; the meaningless days making products of no creative value (in Perrin's case desserts, but it could so easily be anything, part of the bland, consumer white noise that enriches our life not one jot) to the children whom he loves but can no longer relate to, living as they do a whole chasm of a generation away: Perrin is the ultimate everyman, and like many he struggles for meaning and excitement in the life he has made for himself.

Series writer David Nobbs didn't call on experience to create Perrin's world, though. Interviewed by Richard Webber for his 1996 book, *The Life and Legacy of Reginald Perrin*, he acknowledges that comedy seems an innate part of corporate life: 'There's evidence of this silliness wherever you go. For example, the country is littered with conference hotels, where masses of people gather, wearing little nametags informing others what job they do. To me, there seems a fair amount of farce in the whole thing.' In the same interview he talks of watching commuters head to work while travelling to and from school in Orpington, Kent: 'My train was always teeming with [them] and I spent the whole journey watching everyone with their briefcases, rolled umbrellas and bowler hats heading for the office. Even at that young age, I hoped I would never end up like them.'

It was a future that he would successfully avoid. Having abandoned a brief career in journalism – something he claims to have been atrocious at – Nobbs became a prolific contributor to *That Was The Week That Was*, when David Frost, the show's presenter, recognised his name from time at Cambridge and agreed to read a sketch he had written. More work followed: *The Frost Report, Frost on Sunday* and then *The Two Ronnies*, for whom he penned a number of sketches.

In 1974 the BBC were developing a series of plays that would highlight social issues. Having been asked to pitch an idea, Nobbs submitted a proposal that revolved around a food executive driven mad by the pressure and lack of fulfilment offered by his job. It was subsequently rejected, which he now considers a splendid stroke of luck. Like all good writers, he was determined not to waste a good idea. He was already the author of three novels, *The Itinerant Lodger, Ostrich Country* and *A Piece of the Sky is Missing* (which, as a tale of a man rebelling against his corporate life might be seen as something of a dry run for Perrin), so it seemed logical to see how the idea might work in a different medium.

'I wrote it as a novel with considerable difficulty,' he explains, 'the second half didn't work for ages, but I got it right eventually.'

Indeed, his current publisher – Methuen – rejected the book based on issues with the second half, where the central character ends up in a mental home. After giving the manuscript some further thought, Nobbs – who completely agreed with the criticisms – rewrote the story, introducing the elements that have become so familiar since: Perrin's faked suicide and the eventual remarrying of his wife. His agent, Jonathan Clowes, read the revised text and sent a telegram to Guernsey, where the author was holidaying at the time. 'I didn't get where I am today without knowing a good book when I see one,' it said, signed J.C.

After sending the manuscript to 18 different publishers, the rights were eventually purchased by Victor Gollancz and published as *The Death of Reginald Perrin* (1975). The book did well, garnering excellent reviews:

'The trouble started on page 22, when I got some pretty nasty looks from fellow passengers in a Tube train marooned between Mornington Crescent and Camden Town; later that night my wife complained that my giggles were keeping her awake. It got worse. There's surely no need to say more?'

Jeremy Brooks, *Sunday Times*

'This is delicious entertainment, as comic and sharp as they come, and not a hundred miles away from the world of early Evelyn Waugh.'

Robert Nye, *Guardian*

'Reggie Perrin is a sweaty, charming, paunchy, sad, hilarious man. He inhabits an intriguing, mundane world. A world in which everyone jogs along quite nicely, and then, suddenly out of the blue, nothing happens. But in a most exciting way. A world where the ordinary suddenly occurs when you least expect it. Our world. But, unlike most of us, Reggie sets out to change it. His failure to do so is completely successful. I laughed two hundred and eighty-seven times and cried twice. What a beautiful book.'

Ronnie Barker

That last, from one half of *The Two Ronnies*, was to prove particularly ironic when the novel also attracted an offer from Granada TV. 'Mike Cox from Granada offered to do it as a two-part drama starring Ronnie Barker,' explains Nobbs, 'and I was writing for *The Two Ronnies*, so I was thrilled with the idea until I told my agent, who was remarkably unimpressed and said, "No, no – it's a sitcom at the BBC."' Determined this route would grant his client much greater exposure and having already received an enquiry from the BBC, Jonathan Clowes arranged a meeting with Jimmy Gilbert, head of comedy at the BBC. 'I went along,' continues Nobbs, 'and he said: "Do you have anyone in mind to play the part?" and I said: "Yes, Ronnie Barker," and he said: "Excellent! Leonard Rossiter it is."'

29

Rossiter In Place

'ITV wanted Ronnie Barker because he had three series at the BBC,' David Nobbs explains, 'the BBC didn't want him for the same reasons. They had had enough of him already and Leonard was doing *Rising Damp*, which was demonstrably the best sitcom ITV had done for years, if not ever.'

Certainly after seeing the success of *Rising Damp*, the Corporation were determined to find a vehicle with which to draw Rossiter and Reginald Iolanthe Perrin offered a multi-dimensional comic character that seemed to fit the bill. A far cry from Yorkshire Television's concerns a couple of years previously as to whether Leonard had the skill to hold a sitcom on his shoulders.

'My original thoughts,' Nobbs continues, 'were that he was a very fine actor that didn't at all look like the picture in my head. Though I was in my forties, I was still inexperienced enough to think that mattered so I had slight doubts – which didn't last very long as then I saw *Rising Damp* and decided that, yes, he would be the man.'

Soon afterwards, he met with Rossiter: 'that was in the bar of the BBC, where he said to me: "I really enjoyed your book, it's the second best book by a young English writer that I have read recently." He called me young, which was rather nice. It turned out that the best book he had read was my great friend and colleague Peter Tinniswood [whom Nobbs had met while working as a journalist and since collaborated with]. Len had said this to annoy me, to provoke a reaction. I disappointed him greatly by not being offended – I thought second best was quite good enough. That was typical of Len: he liked to test people.'

Perhaps a man so determined to achieve the very best expected anyone else to feel the same way?

Rossiter invited him to attend a studio run-through of *Rising Damp* that afternoon and the writer was only too happy to attend, though he had slight cause to regret it. '[During the run-through] the director said to Len: "Would you mind moving a little bit to the left?" Len said: "Why am I moving, what's the motivation?" And the director said: "It's because I get a better picture that way," and Len said: "Oh, of course, silly me – I forgot! It's not about comedy, it's not about acting, it's about *pictures*! I'll tell you what, I'll go and sit in the back of the theatre and you can do it without me, it will be a lot better!" So he went and sat at the back with the audience. There was a dreadful silence in the place.

'He eventually came back down, sat next to me and said: "It's going well, isn't it?" There was a sort of manic grin on his face. I thought: do I really want to work with this man? But I have to tell you, we never saw anything like that in *Reggie Perrin*. He was professional, constructive, often very jolly, very social . . . Once or twice the perfectionist appeared if things were not quite right, but nothing like I'd seen that day so I started with the worst!'

Despite those initial reservations, David Nobbs is full of praise for the way Leonard Rossiter brought his creation to life. Speaking to Richard Webber, in his book, *The Life and Legacy of Reginald Perrin*, he states: 'Leonard could express the anxieties Reggie was experiencing in every move, expression and word he uttered. He could also combine pace with subtlety, which is very difficult. Most actors who try being subtle come across as slow, but not Leonard: he could rattle the lines out at a rate of knots while still retaining that delicacy.'

30

Running It Up the Flagpole

The BBC commissioned a pilot episode first, with John Howard Davies assigned as producer. Davies began his association with the entertainment industry as a child actor, playing the title role in David Lean's seminal adaptation of *Oliver Twist* (1948). As a producer and director he worked on such prestigious shows as *Monty Python's Flying Circus* and *Fawlty Towers*, and would eventually take over from Jimmy Gilbert to become head of the BBC's Comedy department between 1977 and 1982. In the BBC's *Comedy Connections: The Fall and Rise of Reginald Perrin*, he recalled his initial impression of the idea: 'Jimmy Gilbert had given me the book to read, and I'd read it and thought it was wonderful [but] I didn't actually see how it was going to be a funny situation comedy.'

Perhaps thinking the same way, David Nobbs' initial draft of the pilot script met with a few problems, as he explained in the same programme: 'I went in to see Jimmy Gilbert. He was less than pleased: he had a long face and he had some assistants with long faces, and they said: "Look, we think you really haven't had enough faith in your own book – you've stuck in all these jokes." I said: "Well, it's a sitcom!" '

Instructing Nobbs to remove the material they considered extraneous, Davies set about casting the rest of his characters. Interviewed later for a documentary about the work of Leonard Rossiter (*Comedy Connections: The Fall and Rise of Reginald Perrin*), Leonard's good friend John Barron recounted how he was offered the part of Perrin's insufferable boss C.J.: 'I was working up in Granada Land [Manchester, where ITV's Granada Studios are based] on *Crown*

Court and staying at a hotel in the country just outside [the city]. A heavy parcel arrived from the BBC and I thought, what on earth could this be? It was a hardback novel of *The Death of Reginald Perrin*. John Howard Davies had attached a note, saying: "Read this. Would you like to play C.J.?" I thought that was very nice of him and started to read it. It got better and better and better, and I closed the last page, picking the phone up almost before I'd put the book down and said "YES!" '

Barron had known Rossiter for many years when he joined the cast of *Reginald Perrin*. 'I first met Len in 1951 at Preston Rep, where he was working as an assistant stage manager,' he told Richard Webber for his *Legacy of Reginald Perrin* book. 'Four years later, I moved to direct plays for the repertory company in Wolverhampton – which was viewed as a promotion – and Leonard came along as a fully fledged actor, and it was obvious then that he was going places. I like to think I helped him through the early days of his career.'

Using the original novel as a draw once again proved successful when Davies offered the role of David Harris-Jones (one of C.J.'s simpering 'yes' men) to actor Bruce Bould. Davies had recently cast Bould as a hippie character in the sitcom, *The Good Life*, and was certain the part of Harris-Jones would suit the actor. Talking in *Comedy Connections: The Fall and Rise of Reginald Perrin*, Bould admits his initial reservations: 'My agent said, "There's three lines – two of them are 'super' and the third is something to do with ice cream." So I said, "I don't think I want to do that. I'll turn it down." Later that day, my agent rang again saying that John Howard Davies had been on the phone saying, "This is a terrible mistake, please go and read the book – it's a very nice part!" ' Bould did just that and realised that Davies was right: should the series go on to be commissioned, the part offered more than had been initially obvious. Though he would certainly have to say 'super' a few more times.

For the part of fellow 'yes' man Tony Webster, Davies approached Trevor Adams, who he had recently cast in an episode of *Fawlty Towers* – as Alan, one half of the 'sexually degenerate' couple that so disgusts Basil in the first series episode, 'The Wedding Party'. Adams also beat a path to the novel on which the series was based, borrowing a copy from his local library to find out what it was like and to 'see what kind of wordage I was likely to end up with'. Webster was the 'great!' to Harris-Jones' 'super!' – a fact that caused an argument between Adams and his fiancée when a woman came up to him in the street, having recognised him from the role, and asked: 'Were you Great! or were you Super!?' A brave man might have answered 'both', but he had enough on his plate explaining to his wife-to-be that the woman was in fact a complete stranger.

For the role of Elizabeth, Perrin's long-suffering wife, Davies approached actress Pauline Yates. 'I always wanted her as number one,' he explained in the *Comedy Connections* documentary, 'because she has an innate stillness, a kind of secretiveness about her. She was able to keep calm under duress.' This time there was no need to use the book to attract her. Having already worked with Rossiter onstage in the 1971 play *Disabled*, Yates relished the opportunity to work with him again, convinced the pilot would be a success with the actor in the central role. Gareth Gwenlan, who would go on to replace John Howard Davies as the show's producer after the former was promoted to head of comedy, picks up the tale: 'Her role was absolutely vital. On first view it appears that she's simply the placid wife at home but in fact Pauline as an actress and the character that David created are much more complex and Pauline's playing of it was absolutely superb.'

Another cast member already familiar with Leonard's work was Tim Preece, who played the role of Perrin's stepson Tom. He had first met Rossiter while attending a one-year course at the Bristol Old Vic Theatre School. 'I played cricket with him,' he recalls, 'I think I bowled him out, but I only *think* – that may be my glorifying it. It was significant meeting Len playing sport as sport was very, very important to Len. He was as fierce and determined a cricketer as he was a squash player.'

Sue Nicholls, now perhaps more well known for her long-standing role as Audrey Roberts in *Coronation Street*, was offered the part of Perrin's secretary (and object of lust): Joan Greengross. At the time she was touring in a production of *Alfie*, with Dennis Waterman playing the role that, years before, had been immortalised by Michael Caine when the production was adapted for the cinema. The only way for her to travel to London and get back in time for the evening performance was to fly and she managed to persuade Davies to meet her at Heathrow as she was too scared to leave in case she missed her returning flight.

Davies cast John Horsley as Doc Morrisey, the medically and psychologically uncertain physician employed at Sunshine Desserts. The interaction between the company doctor and his struggling patient was to provide the series with many of its finest classic moments. 'I think from the point of view of double-acts,' observes Nobbs in *Comedy Connections*, 'of which there were quite a few in the series, the relationship between Reggie and Doc Morrisey was absolutely wonderful, the acting was sublime.'

Certainly the doctor related to his patient just as much as the audience:

DOC MORRISEY: Do you find you can't finish the crossword like you used to? Nasty taste in the mouth in the mornings, can't stop thinking about sex, can't start *doing* anything about sex, wake up with a sweat in the mornings, keep falling asleep during *Play for Today* . . .?

REGGIE: Extraordinary, Doc, that's exactly how I've been feeling.

DOC MORRISEY: So do I – I wonder what it is . . .

John Horsley, a hugely experienced actor of stage and screen, certainly imbued his character with a sense of vagueness that would worry any patient. And according to Gareth Gwenlan that vagueness wasn't always acting: 'I remember while filming the scene of Doc Morrisey examining Martin Wellbourne [Perrin in disguise during the second series], John Horsley kept the stethoscope round his neck the entire time. He forgot to stick the earpieces in his ears and no one noticed, except the audience.'

If there's one screen doctor who could get away with such lackadaisical examination methods, then certainly it was Morrisey. 'I think Doc Morrisey was slightly nervous with Perrin,' Horsley observed for *Comedy Connections*, 'and there was this slight edge with Leonard.' Despite that 'edge', Horsley enjoyed working with Rossiter: 'Jonathan Lynn, who directed him in *Loot*, once said to me: "You always knew if Leonard Rossiter was a friend of yours by the amiable way that he would insult you."'

Geoffrey Palmer was cast as Reggie's stepbrother Jimmy, the ex-military sponger who frequently experienced 'cock-ups on the catering front'. Palmer 'enjoyed playing Jimmy, who, along with everyone else, was larger than life, with a brain that was ready to explode. But there was always a germ of truth and reality in Reggie and the rest of them. Take Jimmy: he's a sad failure in every way but is full of good intentions. He tries to be a public schoolboy and an officer, but fails in both.'

While casting continued, Gareth Gwenlan – already onboard in preparation for Davies' departure – was invited to Rossiter's home to discuss the part of Perrin. Gwenlan was the most junior producer in the department, relatively inexperienced and only in the position due to Davies' specific recommendation. He was therefore somewhat nervous. 'I was shown upstairs to his office,' he explains in Webber's book, *Legacy of Reginald Perrin*, 'next to the wine cellar, which was at the top of the house! Without making it obvious, he began probing me intensely on my knowledge of David Nobbs' book.

'When we started filming series one, each day was like the first day at school. With his usual quiet humour, Leonard was always testing me. I had to make sure I had done just as much homework as he had because if I hadn't, he would soon find out – it was a matter of respect.

'It was a huge learning curve for me but a valuable one: I learnt more about comedy, directing comedy and comedy performance from him in three months than I had in the previous 10 years in TV.'

31

The Fall

The pilot was deemed a success and a full series of seven episodes of *The Fall and Rise of Reginald Perrin* was commissioned, with Gareth Gwenlan now the sole producer.

The titles depicted what was to come with Leonard running onto a deserted beach, the film speeded-up in a manner reminiscent of an old silent movie comedy. He strips off – well, down to a pair of flesh-coloured underpants at least, some modesty was preserved – and heads towards the water. As Rossiter passed over a hump in the shingled coastline he was replaced by stuntman Ken Barker, who had the unpleasant task of dashing out into the waves, his hands the last part of his body to vanish from view. Despite the comedic impression created by the speeded film, it was clear that this was going to be something slightly different.

As a side-note it's worth mentioning that another television project in which Leonard was involved that same year almost saw him vanish into the waves for real. In 1975, while filming *Not the Cheapest but the Best*, a documentary on the life of Isambard Kingdom Brunel, he was nearly washed away, as writer and director Michael Andrews later recalled: 'When we were filming the grounding of the *Great Britain* [a passenger steamship designed by Brunel, "launched" in 1843, only to be trapped in the docks due to its size, merely the first of a history of difficulties that saw the company who owned it go bust three years later], Len was the first one down the cliff path onto the shingle beach and stood gazing out to sea as the surf pounded on the shore. Suddenly, to my horror, I saw an immense wave bearing down on him.

I shouted at the top of my voice and he ran up the beach pursued by a breaking crest, which would have certainly dragged him out to sea had it caught him. Luckily it only caught his legs, but the spray completely drenched him.'

Over the seven episodes of *The Fall and Rise of Reginald Perrin*, audiences followed Reggie's story as it slowly unravelled: driven wild by his fellow commuters and idiotic co-workers, tempted (and then terrified away from) an affair with his secretary before doing the only thing he could think of: faking his own suicide and killing off 'Reginald Iolanthe Perrin' (R.I.P., of course) and commencing a new life. First, as a pig farmer and then, after attending his own memorial service in disguise, as 'Martin Wellbourne', freshly arrived from South America. He falls in love with his wife all over again – and she with him, knowing full well his real identity but happy not to admit as much – and fashioning a whole new start. *Reginald Perrin* was a sitcom like no other, much more a 'novel for television' than was usual in the medium. It challenged its audience almost as much as it had the production crew.

Sue Nicholls (Joan Greengross) recalls her first day on the shoot – and the initial meeting with Rossiter: 'It was only Leonard and myself who were called. Of course I knew who he was, and he must have found out who I was. We were journeyed to this field just out of London. The next thing you know you're running towards each other and in huge clinches, and he was on top of me and I was on top of him – and that was my first meeting with Leonard!'

This footage was one of the many inserted pieces where the audience is shown Perrin's innermost thoughts – one of the most famous, of course, being the image of a hippo that would flash into his mind whenever someone mentioned his mother-in-law. John Howard Davies lays claim to the choice of animal: 'I wanted this thought process of the mother-in-law to come storming through Leonard's vision and into ours, and so I looked at thousands of animals doing all sorts of things but the reason why the hippo got the job is because he wobbled and I wanted a wobbling mother-in-law: mother-in-laws always wobble in my book!'

There would be many iconic moments along the way, not least being a family trip to a safari park where, unhinged by the heat and constant bickering with his son-in-law and grandchildren, Perrin blows his top and leaves the car.

The safari park sequences were the first filming days for Tim Preece, who had been struggling with his characterisation. Having read the book, he pictured Reggie's son-in-law as short and fat, a world away from his tall, thin self. Ultimately he would hit a dry monotone in his performance that was utterly perfect, something he attributes to the unpleasantness of filming on that first day: 'It was so hot and so miserable. I think that's what made Tom the way he is, really.'

Upon stepping out of the car for some fresh air, Reggie finds himself face-to-face with a small pride of lions – a script detail that was far from easy to pull off, as producer Gareth Gwenlan confessed to author Richard Webber: 'I'd ordered three lions for the episode. One was mounted on a plinth, which looked realistic once we put grass around its feet and tied a nylon wire to its tail, which someone swished occasionally. Another was lying down and looked okay, but the third was simply a lion skin. I was wondering how I could use it when a prop boy said: "Don't worry – I'll get inside, wriggle around a bit and and try and look like a lion." He looked too thin so we stuffed straw inside the skin as well and got ready to film. I looked at the other lions: one's tail was swishing, the other was lying down and I was just about to start filming when I noticed a wisp of cigarette smoke coming out of the third lion's mouth: the prop boy was inside, having a fag!

'After apologising, a hand came out of the lion but before he could put the cigarette out, he'd set the tinder dry grass alight – it was a nightmare!'

Such complications were a common theme, according to actor Bruce Bould, talking on *Comedy Connections*: 'The first series was terribly difficult to do – it was full of the sort of technical things that the BBC weren't particularly good at, at the time. All that stuff with the hippopotamus, to try and time that.' Even though the image of the hippo would be edited in after the live recording, Leonard was determined that it should be shown on a screen to the live audience so their response could be captured. 'Len knew what his internal timing would be,' Bould continues, 'but the vision mixer up in his box would have no idea what was going on, so there would be this awful pause and Len would blow up and get terribly cross. We'd rehearse, and rehearse and rehearse . . . the same with the farting armchairs [C.J.'s office offering particularly flatulent furnishings], you sat it in it and nothing . . . it was hell!'

All of which would set Leonard's nerves on edge, determined as ever to create the perfect show. Geoffrey Palmer recalls an example of his insistence on perfection when the sound of a doorbell is supposed to make Reggie jump. 'The doorbell rang and Leonard stopped immediately,' Palmer recalls, 'asking, "Is the bell only going to be that loud?" He repeated the question but still no answer. He then said: "Somebody answer me: is the bell only going to be that loud? If it is, then we're not going to get a laugh." The floor manager told him it was going to be louder, to which he replied: "Let's hear it then, now!" The bell was heard and the scene continued. It was just another example of Len's confidence and desire for getting everything just right. And he was correct, of course: if the bell hadn't been loud enough to startle him or for the audience to hear, then he wouldn't have got the same reaction.'

In a later interview with author Robert Tanitch, Pauline Yates recalled the slight insecurity of working with Rossiter: 'I felt he respected me (otherwise one wouldn't have been there), but I also felt sometimes that he could do the comedy lines better than me, which of course he was right about, but I had to *say* them. So I would say, "Look, Leonard, this is *my* line. I can't do it as well as you, but it happens to be my character's words, so I'll say them in my own way." Then, of course, he would laugh and say, "Okay, Yates, you get on with it then!" In the show, of course, I wouldn't get a laugh! But he never gloated.'

Geoffrey Palmer was also the recipient of advice from Leonard on how to perform the role of Reggie's brother-in-law Jimmy: 'He was a difficult character to get to grips with and I remember during rehearsals Leonard saying, "It's not going to work if you play it like that!" Gradually I realised the character had to be stronger and bigger in his blundering incompetence – he couldn't be bland.'

Sue Nicholls found working with Leonard an enriching experience: 'I liked the way he was very courageous and went with his convictions and, more often than not, they were right: I learned a lot from that. He was lovely to work with: he knew his job – which I always love in people. I learned from him: in fact, all I had to do a lot of the time was speak to him and time my lovely lines correctly. Leonard did the rest!'

It is easy to picture him as a driving force throughout the production, doing his damnedest to ensure that it was as successful as the material warranted. Yes, that attitude was bound to rub certain people up the wrong way from time to time, as indeed had proved the case throughout his career, but it is hard to argue with the quality of the finished product and if that sort of dictatorial approach was what it took to ensure this, then his attention to detail should certainly be applauded. Besides, as everyone involved is happy to admit: Rossiter was frequently right in his demands and the ferocity with which he approached the work drove everyone to greater levels of performance.

'Len was extraordinary,' Palmer continues, 'because you had to get up to his level – I mean he kind of forced you. It was demanding and therefore you gave your best. He was extraordinary: what he set his mind to he did, better than anybody.'

Gareth Gwenlan agrees: 'Anyone working on the production knew they had to try and run as fast as he could, which took some doing. The pace of each episode was so quick and conducive to generating a highly professional atmosphere.'

Rossiter's trademark speedy delivery caused David Nobbs some extra work on the scripts for he had to write what would normally constitute 35 minutes of screen-time in order to compensate for the rate at which the actor delivered his dialogue: 'While we were rehearsing one episode, we realised we only had 28 minutes of script. Len insisted that this would work out at 29 minutes and 30 seconds with all the audience laughter. Of course, when we recorded it he speeded up even more and we finished on 27 minutes!'

Clearly working in these conditions could be extremely draining for Rossiter and everyone else. 'On recording days,' says Bruce Bould, 'he'd start off in the morning relaxed and jokey, but you always knew that by about four in the afternoon someone was going to get it – and usually it was some poor sod in the production team. He had the weight of the series resting on his shoulders and it was the fear that within a few hours we'd be filming in front of a live audience that got to him.'

There is one amusing example of a time when it appears that Rossiter's infallible sense of perfection may have failed him: 'We were in the bar before a show,' David Nobbs explains, 'and I said [to Len]: "I think you're saying this line wrong." He said: "How would you like me to do it then?" So I did it for him. He didn't say anything, but he did it the way I had suggested and it got a big laugh. I said to him in the bar afterwards: "I was right, wasn't I?" "No," he said, "you were wrong – and so were the audience!" '

Leonard could also be extremely generous to the cast and crew, frequently wining and dining them, both at his house and while filming on location. David Nobbs recalled a moment during filming to writer Robert Tanitch:

Len had invited the whole crew for a drink in the bar of the hotel where he planned to stay in Witney, in Oxfordshire.

Len arrived at the hotel, booked in and was handed his room key by the landlord with the memorably welcoming words: 'We don't give front-door keys and we lock the front door at eleven.'

Thank you for your thoughtfulness, said Len courteously. 'It was nice of you to tell me that before I wasted time and energy walking upstairs' – and he picked up his suitcase, walked out and booked a room in the house of a charming old lady on the other side of the green.

We all assembled in the hotel bar. Len arrived late.

What are you all having? he said.

The landlord's eyes glinted.

Oh incidentally, said Len, 'we're having the drinks in a pub across the green. It seems a very nice place.'

Seventy people trooped out, leaving a deserted bar. It was a moment of which Reggie would have been proud.

Despite Rossiter's eternal quest for perfection, the cast is united in their belief that *Reginald Perrin* was a highlight of their careers, not just in terms of the programme's quality but also the pleasure of working together. There is the cliché heard time and again in TV production where the crew is referred to as 'family', an inseparable unit. Often this seems at odds with stories of bust-ups and blazing rows. 'It's a myth that no one gets on in TV,' says David Nobbs, 'they do! John Barron gave a dinner party for Len, his wife Gillian, myself and my first wife and he said: "That's to thank you for the happiest working summer of my life," which sums it up.'

Tim Preece agrees, justifying further – should it be needed – that Rossiter's working methods paid dividends: 'The energy doubled on the recording. For those of us that were outside the doors waiting to come in it was quite difficult because he would be going with much more energy and much faster than in rehearsals and you had to lock into that. It was difficult playing one of the residual characters to keep up. But I think that was right and if anyone complained, they were fools. He was a practical, down-to-earth, serious actor. I hated that he became known as a bit of a monster: the proof of the pudding is in the show.'

Once the series aired, David Nobbs was understandably anxious to know how it had been received. He told the author Richard Webber of an incident in a Leeds hotel that put his mind at rest: 'The reception desk was on the second floor and as I waited for the lift, three businessmen arrived and pressed the lift button again. They waited for a while before one turned to his colleagues and said: "Oh come on, I didn't get where I am today by hanging around waiting for lifts!", to which the other two replied "Great!", "Super!" before heading for the stairs. I couldn't believe my ears: it suddenly struck home that the catchphrases were catching on, which meant the series was making an impact.'

The reviews were quick to roll in, too and, as had been the case with *Rising Damp* before it, *The Fall and Rise of Reginald Perrin* wasn't short of good comments:

'. . . but the joy of watching Leonard Rossiter as Perrin is undimmed. With false nose that isn't, and mouth like the grin of a Hallowe'en pumpkin, his face by itself is a piece of theatre.'

Christopher Hudson, *London Evening Standard*

'As the central character, the bored ice-cream executive, Leonard Rossiter has the splendidly mobile features of a man suffering from a terminal case of social indigestion.'

Peter Dunn, *Sunday Times*

'He spits, pops his eyes, flares his nostrils, and generally comports himself like a crazy ugly. I still haven't worked out why he is funny, but he is.'

Clive James, *Observer*

Given how easy it was for much of the audience to relate to *Perrin*, it should have been no great surprise that the series was a success, as Geoffrey Palmer commented in the BBC's *Comedy Connections*: 'It's an eternal theme, it will appeal to anyone who's doing a job they can't stand. And it goes beyond that into this crazy [sticks his two fingers up] to the world, to the bosses, to the government, to *everybody*, to all institutions. It's wonderfully anarchic in that way.'

Of course there were some who felt the TV series hadn't quite captured the novel – it's a time-honoured cliché that many feel, often quite rightly it must be said, that 'the book is better than the film'. David Nobbs is only too happy to concur: 'A book is a more complex product because it contains subplots, narrative and author's comments, which you can never match to the same degree of detail on the screen. However, adapting a novel for TV injects new qualities such as immediacy and a strength lacking on the pages of a novel. Overall, I was happy how it worked out.

Which is just as well because the success of the first series meant that a second was soon to follow.

32

The Rise

'I didn't really see it as a sitcom, I saw it as the adaptation of the book. It was the story that mattered, and it did sort of move the sitcom on a bit, I think, because of that.'

David Nobbs, creator of Reginald Perrin

Certainly the fact that Perrin's tale unfolded sequentially over the run – like a serial rather than a series of independent episodes – was unusual for the time. It had been common enough practice in sitcoms to allow each episode to remain distinct to another so that they could be broadcast in any order. Not so Perrin: it had to be broadcast in order, in its entirety, or the series wouldn't make sense to an audience. Given the end of the first series showed Perrin (now living under an assumed name) having come to terms with the opportunities offered by a fresh start – albeit with the threat that his old frustrations could take over at any moment – it wasn't immediately obvious how the story could be continued.

'Originally it was only ever seen as one series,' Gareth Gwenlan explains, 'because David's novel reached a natural conclusion. But halfway through filming, things were going so well that I asked David if there was any chance of another.'

Nobbs had to think long and hard: if the story was to continue it must be in a fresh and interesting way, there was little mileage in trying to repeat himself. There was also the realisation that the depth of the first series was in no small part due to its origin as a novel. 'The fact of it starting with the book was very important,' he explains, 'I am not really a sitcom writer – it's not really my métier – and it worked because it wasn't really conceived as a sitcom.'

Leonard Rossiter felt the same way, insisting that if there was to be a second series there should be a second novel as well. 'He demanded a book for each series,' says Nobbs, 'he said: "I will only do them if there is a book."'

'I think it was less to do with the structure,' says Nobbs, 'and more to do with the complexity of the character. The character was created in a medium where you get all his private thoughts, contradictions, disagreements, etc. So I was able to bring them to the script instead of presenting a one-dimensional character, which a lot tend to be.'

The second novel proved particularly difficult to write. Nobbs was determined that it should be about Perrin failing *not* to make a success of himself, however hard he tried. Removed from Sunshine Desserts once more by having his false identity revealed, together with his wife, the unemployed executive makes plans for the future. Deciding that most of the world sells rubbish while pretending it is nothing of the sort, he plumps to sell absolute trash and declaim it as such with total honesty.

This principle sees the opening of 'Grot', his first shop. The shelves are filled with such bizarre items as square hoops, stringless guitars, an LP of silence (titled 'Laryngitis in Thirty Lands, featuring the silence of Max Bygraves, Des O'Connor, the Bay City Rollers, the Sex Pistols and Rolf Harris'), bottomless ashtrays, insoluble suppositories and of course, his son-in-law Tom's parsnip wine. Against all the odds, the shop is a tremendous success: two years later, Grot has become an empire, with 44 shops all over the country and company profits of £750,000 (a small sum by today's standards, inflation being what it is!).

Meanwhile, Sunshine Desserts goes bankrupt and soon Reggie is employing all the old staff – determinedly trying to run the business into the ground, something he singularly fails to do. It doesn't take long before he is once more disillusioned with his lot, infuriated by the public's stupidity in buying his products and the fawning way everyone treats him now that he's a 'success'. He convinces his wife, Elizabeth, to join him on a familiar Dorset beach, where they can shed their clothes and their identities, and start yet another new life together. The final twist in Nobbs' tale comes when, dressed as a pair of tramps, Reggie and Elizabeth come across a fellow Gentleman of the Road, who reassures them that: 'I didn't get where I am today without asking for 10p for a cup of tea.' It is C.J., of course. Glancing down at the coast, they are shocked to see thousands all flinging their clothes aside in order to 'do a Perrin'.

'It was just mind-blowingly clever,' says Gareth Gwenlan of David Nobbs' plot, 'as well as being incredibly funny, the whole thing was also an incredible commentary on consumerism. It wasn't simply a series of gags – David writes with great depth.'

Series Two took the sense of the ridiculous that was present in the first series and expounded on it fully: a bigger, more ludicrous – and yet, as Gwenlan's comment asserts, just as relevant – tale that all involved considered an improvement on the first series.

'The second [series] saw [*Perrin*] hit its peak in terms of invention,' admits Nobbs.

Gareth Gwenan agrees: 'It was unquestionably the best of the three.'

That sense of the absurd played directly into Leonard's skills as an actor, as John Barron commented in a later documentary, *The Unforgettable Leonard Rossiter*, about his work.

'He had an enormous sense of what is ridiculous: he would latch onto it and turn it into reality. He made something that was ridiculous absolutely truthful.'

In itself this is one of the most important touchstones to comedy, as Bruce Bould concurred in the same programme: 'He understood that comedy works out of truth – the more you believe it, the funnier it is.' Which is not to say that comedy must be found in utterly believable situations, but rather impossible situations made convincing. 'As a farce becomes more and more absurd, the belief in it from the actor has got to grow and grow,' continues Bould, 'Len understood that and grew with it, so a manic intensity came out of it which was Len's trademark in a way.'

The book, *The Return of Reginald Perrin*, was published in 1977 alongside the broadcast of the second series.

Rossiter was now in the previously inconceivable situation of having two popular series running at the same time. The characters couldn't be more different, which showcased his abilities wonderfully, with audiences clearly able to see his comic range. Attractive as this was, he was now in the position of having to decide how long he was willing to play Reggie. He had always insisted he wouldn't work on a long-running series and had broken his own rule twice in quick succession. As it was, 1978 would see the final outing for both characters on TV.

33

A Better World

While Reggie would return for a third series in 1977, David Nobbs is far from convinced that he managed to replicate the success he had hit with the second. 'The story didn't translate as well from the book as the first two,' he feels.

This time we follow Reggie's attempts to establish a commune for the 'middle-aged and middle class', where they can learn to live in love and happiness. Again, he finds himself employing his ex-employees from Grot and begins advertising for residents to come and stay at 'Perrins'. 'Want to drop out, but don't like drop-outs?' the advert announces. 'At Perrins the drop-outs are just like you: they're more like drop-ins: so next time you feel like dropping out, why not drop in?'

Activities include such nonsensical activities as 'football with a difference', the difference being there's only one team to encourage people to work together rather than compete (this is not entirely successful, with a disappointing result of 4-1).

The commune becomes a success, attracting everyone from a textiles tycoon to a head of TV comedy, who has lost his sense of humour. In a reversal from the usual Perrin conundrum, however, the commune – which is the first thing Reggie has applied himself to with genuine conviction – is destined for failure. One problem after another besets them until they are forced to close. One by one, all the old employees head off to pastures new – the experience has at least for the most part changed *them* – and Reggie finds himself back where he began: commuting to an office job he loathes, working for Amalgamated Aerosols, owned by C.J.'s brother, F.J.

He has travelled full circle and in the midst of his morning train journey, he stands up and makes a speech: 'Do you, Reginald Iolanthe Perrin, take British Rail's Southern Region for all your dreaded life? For better, for worse, for fuller, for dirtier, in lateness and in cancellation, to retirement or phased redundancy do you part? I do, I *have* to! Place this ring of dirt around your neck, it will be there every day.'

The whole experience seems to have been for nothing and it can only be a matter of time before he once more makes his way to the beach.

'The concept of all the people visiting the community was easier in the book,' Nobbs explained to Richard Webber, 'because I had more time to describe them. On TV, many of the visitors turned into caricatures because time constraints meant we had to skate over them. Also, introducing so many characters meant there were a lot of people taking the comic impetus off the main characters and the whole series at times came across as a compilation of sketches.'

It would seem he had finally found the contrast between mediums too much to overcome, the depth and message of the original novel just not practically condensed into seven half-hour episodes of comedy.

'Reggie Perrin couldn't have gone on forever,' says Geoffrey Palmer (Jimmy), 'it had to be finite, really.'

In fact, the three series have achieved a longevity of their own: the desire to break free of the humdrum and 'do a Perrin' having been felt by most people at some point in their lives. While Rigsby was the perfect example of character comedy, Leonard's Reggie has a soulful quality that makes his character even more potent. His success at portraying a man's gradual breakdown, again finding comedy in something that could have been distinctly tragic, stands as one of his most multifaceted performances.

34

The Legacy of Reginald Perrin

Despite Geoffrey Palmer's comment, Reggie's tale was to enjoy another chapter when, in 1995, David Nobbs wrote both another novel and another TV series, *The Legacy of Reginald Perrin*.

'I thought it would be rather bold and exciting to do a thing about Reggie without Reggie,' he explains, 'I thought the other characters were strong enough and I had a plot idea of a rebellion of old people against the youth culture of the time. I think, in retrospect, it was not such a clever idea – it wasn't perhaps as bold as I had thought.'

The plot dealt with the last will and testament of Reggie – sadly killed by a falling billboard. He has left a great deal of money to his family and former employees but in order to claim it, they must do something utterly absurd. Even from beyond the grave Reggie is determined to shake people out of dullness.

'There was some wonderful stuff in it because David cannot write badly,' says Palmer, 'but to do *Reggie Perrin* without Len Rossiter – what are the other characters without him? Reggie Perrin was Len and the rest of us: it was Reggie and then a whole load of other people. He was on nearly all the time – that's the way David wrote it, one huge central figure who had half the dialogue and the other eight people divided the rest up between them.'

'No one really examined [the idea] too closely,' says Nobbs, 'they were just happy to have something along the same lines, I think – there was never much doubt expressed. I think Jeffery Perkins, who was head of comedy at the time, said: "That's ridiculous without Leonard Rossiter," but when he read the script he thought it could work. But it didn't. The other characters' relationship with Reggie was what made Perrin work and it was a big mistake. I was once asked by Tyne Tees TV to write a sitcom based on Manuel from *Fawlty Towers*: I said no. I would have been on a hiding to nothing and Manuel is a supporting character – it's how furious John Cleese gets with him that makes it funny. I then go and make the same mistake myself within my own work.'

In fact, the series has much to recommend it but perhaps the pre-conceived notion that something was missing would always be a significant hurdle. 'It was tolerable,' is Nobbs' opinion on the matter.

'We missed [Leonard],' says Tim Preece, who returned to the role of Tom for the series, 'it didn't work. It was a nice idea but my own private feeling was that David Nobbs should have put us all through the hoop more. We sat around a bit too much and it should have been more physical and practical – we should have been a bit more daring with it. Len was more physical: just watching him pick up his umbrella and going off to work was a physical experience and I don't think we did enough of that. We all sat around as if he was still there, providing the energy – but he wasn't.'

In 2009, Reggie was resurrected, with David Nobbs co-writing a new version alongside *Men Behaving Badly* creator Simon Nye. Martin Clunes took the central role and despite some initial reservations and mixed reviews – it was always going to be hard to win audiences over – the show was a moderate success and commissioned for a second series. While one cannot help but wish the new Reggie the best of luck, there's no doubt that for most, the original will be the one that is fondly remembered.

'*Reggie Perrin* was one of those extraordinary shows,' explains Gareth Gwenlan, 'that wasn't a major success in audience terms, especially when you compare it with *To the Manor Born* [contemporaneous sitcom starring Peter Bowles and Penelope Keith] that attracted audiences of up to 27 million, and never less than 18 million.' In today's multi-channel landscape, those figures are unheard of and a far cry from the 10.5 million that saw Perrin's audience peak at the climax of Series Two.

'Surprisingly,' Gwenlan continues, '*Reggie Perrin* never won a single award and yet it was – and still is – regarded by many as an important work of comedy.'

In 2004, when the BBC, ITV and Channel 4 organised a nationwide vote to find the UK's favourite sitcom, *The Fall and Rise of Reginald Perrin* ranked 34th (with *Rising Damp* a few places higher at 27). While those numbers may not seem shockingly high, it must be remembered that both shows were over 30 years old and would never have matched the popularity of programmes still being aired at the time of the survey.

Nonetheless, the show is unquestionably one of the most fondly remembered comedies the BBC has ever produced and many of its catchphrases are alive and well today, with the notion of a faked suicide still referred to as 'doing a Perrin'. In David Nobbs' thoughtful and hilarious scripts, Rossiter found another character that would ensure he lived on in our memories.

PART V

I Didn't Get Where I Am Today . . .

35

I Tell You It's Leonard Rossiter

During the latter half of the seventies, Leonard Rossiter was riding higher than ever. He was now that most intangible of things: a celebrity. Not that such an idea was attractive to him: beyond the financial security and the freedom to pick and choose his work, 'stardom' meant nothing.

He continued to enjoy the balance between work and home life: taking regular holidays with Gillian and Camilla, wherever sports facilities could be found. Heaven forbid he was expected to sit in the sun all day! Such inactivity would have driven him wild. He was also terrified of flying, for many years refusing to go anywhere that couldn't be reached by ferry or train. Eventually, for the sake of his family – and no doubt wishing to go somewhere he might pass more unnoticed – he faced his fear and they began to fly abroad, with Leonard gritting his teeth and clutching the armrests in grim terror during take-offs and landings.

The family visited the cinema and the theatre a great deal and Leonard availed himself of a home video recorder – new technology at the time and built like a single bed with a trapdoor in it. The notion of being able to record anything he liked so that it might be kept for posterity was wondrous, something we've all got used to over the years thanks to video rental, DVDs and iPlayers.

Often he would sit down with Camilla and show her some of his favourite films: the Marx Brothers naturally, but also Jacques Tati and Billy Wilder's *Some Like It Hot* with Jack Lemmon, Tony Curtis and Marilyn Monroe. Leonard was also a big fan of British comedies with a black edge to them: *The Lavender Hill Mob*, *Kind Hearts and Coronets*, *The League of Gentlemen* . . . they all matched his sense of humour perfectly, being morally suspect and slightly grotesque!

He was blissfully happy in the role of parent, though occasionally a little over-protective. Camilla recalls one school trip to Hastings where Leonard wouldn't let her take the coach with everyone else: having read of a couple of crashes involving school buses, he drove her instead and waited around all day in the car until it was time to drive her home again. At the time of course, she was deeply embarassed but now recognises that it was simply proof of how much her father cared for her.

As well as his continued games of squash, football and tennis, Leonard decided that it was time to learn the piano. Having announced his intentions, Gillian bought him one for Christmas. After arranging for a tutor to visit, he sat down for his first lesson. However, like windsurfing, the piano was not for Leonard, as Camilla recalls: 'The tutor sat Dad down, hit a note and said: "This is middle C." Dad just looked at him and said: "Why?" There really is no answer to that. Whatever the tutor's explanation, it failed to satisfy Dad. He simply could not accept that a random note was called middle C. Perhaps the perceived lack of logic put him off. The piano sat in our living room for years afterwards and Dad never progressed beyond middle C.'

While TV audiences were still able to enjoy Rossiter either as Rigsby or Perrin, cinema-goers would find him in two Hollywood movies. The first was *The Pink Panther Strikes Again* (1976), the fifth film in the comedy franchise starring Peter Sellers. Sellers' idiotic hero Clouseau is now a chief inspector and his former boss Dreyfus (played by Herbert Lom) wishes him dead. Clouseau visits England on the trail of a missing nuclear physicist and Leonard plays Superintendent Quinlan of Scotland Yard, swiftly shot – accidentally – by Clouseau and on sharpened nerves thereafter. It's not a bad 'Panther' movie, despite the fact that Sellers' relationship with the writer and director Blake Edwards was at an all-time low. 'If you went to an asylum,' Edwards revealed in a later interview, 'and you described the first inmate you saw, that's what Peter had become. He was certifiable.'

The other movie was far less frivolous: *Voyage of the Damned*, also 1976, was based on the real-life voyage of the MS *St Louis*, a cruise-ship of 937 Jews, shipped from Germany in 1939 and allegedly heading for Cuba. It soon becomes clear that the Jews are never expected to disembark, their voyage being a propaganda exercise by the Nazi government. As far as Nazi logic went, when all countries refused to take them as refugees then the world could hardly complain about the eventual fate of all Jews in Germany. Once refused port, their ship would return home whereupon the passengers' lives would be forfeited. The Jews make it clear that they would rather link hands and leap into the ocean than return to Germany and the ship sails on, hoping to find safe port.

Leonard played Commander Udo von Bonin, part of a stellar cast that includes: James Mason, Faye Dunaway, Malcolm McDowell, Max von Sydow, Denholm Elliott and Lee Grant. The movie was nominated for three Academy Awards and six Golden Globes.

As always, the work that continued to bring Leonard the greatest pleasure was not on the screen but rather in the theatre. In the autumn of 1976, he was approached to star in a production entitled *The Frontiers of Farce*, which would feature two one-act plays adapted and directed by Peter Barnes.

Farce, much like the sitcom, is often dismissed snobbishly as a coarse art. Certainly, these days its proliferation at the end of the pier in seaside towns and popularity among amateur dramatic societies marks it as an outdated pleasure. And yes, the humour is often of the broadest kind, relying on such standard conventions as mistaken identity, conversational misunderstanding and a good deal of rushing in and out of doors (narrowly missing one's fellow characters, as a rule). Performances are large, the pace is exhausting and someone usually ends up *in flagrante delicto* with a member of the opposite sex, their spouse mere seconds away from the next swinging door.

On television, *Fawlty Towers* stands as the most obvious example of the art – and certainly one of the most respected – with its regular diet of misunderstandings, beatings and performances that threaten to knock a hole in the set.

Comedy is notoriously difficult to play, farce more so than any other form, requiring pitch-perfect timing and an energy that would reduce many a performer to a breathless wreck. Clearly, it was just the sort of genre that Rossiter excelled at.

'Leonard Rossiter was the best farceur of his generation,' Peter Barnes later declared, 'because [he was] the most serious. On stage, he combined incredible speed with absolute physical and verbal precision. I once asked him to slow down during rehearsals so we could concentrate on certain details but he said that he was only able to think comedically at high speed.'

The two plays offered distinctly different characters for Leonard to get his teeth into. The first, *The Purging*, originally written by the French playwright Georges Feydeau, concerned Follovoine, an inventor who has created what he believes to be an indestructible chamber pot, something he is convinced the French Army will pay handsomely for. Needless to say, the object is not quite as sought-after as he might have hoped. Nor, for that matter, is it remotely indestructible.

The second play was by Frank Wedekind, a major exponent of the 'Theatre of the Absurd', popularised by Samuel Beckett and Harold Pinter. *The Singer* centres on Dhuring, a lunatic composer who has written an opera for a leading tenor of the day. He is determined to corner the man and perform it for him so that he may fall in love with it.

Both roles offered a plethora of the sort of high-octane comic performances that Rossiter was renowned for and his professional skills were immediately appreciated by Barnes: 'His very virtues sometimes made it difficult for other actors who did not share his accelerated metabolism,' he admits. 'He was disturbingly word-perfect in two large parts after just three days of a planned four-week rehearsal. His energy and concentration were prodigious. He always had to change shirts at least once during rehearsals – they became wringing wet after a couple of hours. A hard-edged, high-definition actor, he was at his best exposing the petty meanness of the human spirit.'

His fellow actors were equally impressed. 'Len gave one of the finest comic performances that I have ever seen,' says John Phillips, 'He didn't ask for a laugh. Never conspired with his audience. The laughs came thick and fast because he was totally inside the character and the character, driven by an enormous energy, usually wanted something bigger and better than mere laughs. He was a great comic actor.'

An opinion, John Stride – also in the cast – shared: 'One evening he was so good I couldn't help laughing outright and when he turned to look at me, in the action, the expression of amazement on his face made me laugh even more. He didn't exactly tick me off afterwards but made it clear that that sort of behaviour didn't help.'

Not that Rossiter was above breaking character: during a preview performance the gargantuan false teeth he wore in *The Singer* shot out of his mouth to land in a wastepaper basket on stage. Leonard fished for them while continuing to perform his dialogue – albeit in a manner that suggested he was naught but gums – popped them back in and turned to the audience, whereupon he shrugged and announced: 'What do you expect? This is a preview!'

The reviews were as complimentary as always, with Bernard Levin observing in *The Times*: 'The lunatic frenzy sustained by Mr Rossiter in his scene – some twenty minutes with hardly a breath drawn – is a delight and a wonder to behold, but the nervous energy in it is alarming; I hardly dare to wish the enterprise well, for with seven such performances a week Mr Rossiter will be dead before Christmas.'

Thankfully, Levin's concerns proved unfounded – though it's hard not to think how Leonard would eventually die, with many believing that he had driven himself to it through his extraordinary hard work. The play ran at his old stomping ground, the Bristol Old Vic, before transferring to the Criterion in London for a West-End run, the following February.

Later in 1976 Leonard achieved a personal theatre first, performing a one-man show that had been written especially for him. The Mermaid Theatre was inspired by a radio documentary on the life of the painter and author Benjamin Haydon to commission a play about him. Haydon was one of life's tragic failures, though he himself certainly didn't think so. Trained at the Royal Academy, he was determined to become a renowned painter, producing countless canvases that moved the masses not one jot. He had some small success as a portrait artist, but for the most part his career was one of being an also-ran. One particularly tragic exhibition clashed with the first appearance in London of General Tom Thumb – the stage name of dwarf, Charles Sherwood Stratton. Much to Haydon's dismay, while his exhibition was an utter failure – nobody came –

Stratton's appearance was a sell-out. It was the final straw that pushed him towards suicide.

While he never achieved the success he wished for as a painter, Haydon lectured successfully on art and his biography – what there was of it, for he never completed it – was somewhat well regarded.

John Wells was the writer charged with creating a script. A satirist and actor, he began his career working on *That Was The Week That Was* and had known Leonard from their time together in the follow-up show *BBC 3*. He earned something of a name for himself as an impersonator of Denis Thatcher, the frequently lampooned husband of British Prime Minister, Margaret Thatcher.

Wells had also seen Leonard in *Arturo Ui* and had been so bowled over by his performance that he was in no doubt who he would like to cast as Haydon and wrote the script especially for him. 'What I think Leonard identified with,' he later observed, 'was the energy of the man, and also his gigantic ambition.'

Rossiter worked on the script alongside Wells and Julius Gellner, helping to shape the production with the unerring sense of pace and structure he always brought to his work.

The director was Alan Strachan, who had also witnessed Leonard's performance in *The Resistible Rise of Arturo Ui*: 'It was so mesmerising, a performance of such galvanic power – and so unlike anything else the English stage was offering in the risks it took – that I saw it four times.'

Surrounded by an assortment of easels and paintings designed to emulate both Haydon's studio and by extension, his own chaotic mind, Rossiter performed the two-hour piece through its highs and lows, humour and tragedy – never more so than the climax, which would see Haydon kill himself with a pistol to the head.

'Off stage, we never stopped laughing,' Wells recalled, 'on stage, he was deadly serious, holding his comic talent on a very tight rein: there were moments when he brought the house down with a one-line impersonation or by lolling heavy-lidded on a chaise longue in a mood of sexual reverie. But what stayed in my memory was the perfect control, the sense of a mind working behind tiny details of observed behaviour, all built up very gradually and consciously during rehearsal, a man living through the dramatic moment until the final catastrophe when he turned upstage in a single light, lowering the barrel of the pistol to one temple and spreading the fingers of the other hand with the grace of a dancer. Then there was an explosion, a blackout, and Haydon's signature splashed on a screen in blood.'

'It was,' says Strachan, 'in Len's hands much more than a tour de force and a prodigious feat of memory. He captured not just the absurdity of the man but also something of a tragic grandeur in a spirit whose sense of reality gradually dissolved into terrifyingly isolated madness.'

David Nobbs went to see Leonard in the production when it transferred to the Greenwich Theatre in January the following year. He was utterly blown away by the performance: 'He was truly magnificent – it showed all the qualities in being an actor: versatility, passion, truthfulness, all these things were in his performance that day.'

And the critics agreed. Writing for the *Guardian*, Christopher Dodd said: 'Rossiter's performance is more than a demonstration of the talents of a superb character actor. He gets convincingly inside the sometimes cheerful, sometimes despairing hopelessness.'

In 1979, Strachan would go on to co-direct – with Leonard – the ill-fated revival of *Semi-Detached*.

Meanwhile, on television, another reunion was taking place. Ray Galton and Alan Simpson had written a part for Rossiter in one episode of their new series for Yorkshire Television, *The Galton and Simpson Playhouse*. The show featured seven self-contained, half-hour comedies and Leonard was the star of the sixth: *I Tell You It's Burt Reynolds* (1977).

'It was all true that one,' explains Galton, 'it was based on a mate of mine who did exactly the same thing as Len's character. I come home one night and he's there, pointing at the telly saying, "In a minute I'm going to point someone out and I want you to tell me who it is." We waited a minute, the guy came on and my mate pointed, "There, who is he?" I hadn't a clue and told him as much. "It's Burt Reynolds!" he shouts. It was nothing like him, but my mate wouldn't have it. In the end he called up the *Daily Telegraph* – don't ask me why, but in those days they were like Google, they were supposed to know everything.'

In the TV version, Leonard goes one step further, calling the actor himself and then really losing his rag when even he seems incapable of recognising himself.

It is, as one would expect from Galton and Simpson, a very strong script and perfect material for Rossiter. As an extra twist his co-star is none other than his wife Gillian Raine, who offers a cool and dismissive counterpoint to his building hysteria. It stands up extremely well, never running out of steam despite the single set and simple plot.

Leonard had hit a new phase in his work, selecting each project very carefully, while ignoring the sitcom scripts that piled through his agent's door, offering characters that were carbon copies of Rigsby or Reggie. He had no interest in repeating himself, allowing each new job to offer something fresh.

36

A Suffusion of Herbs and Spices

When asked to recount the roles for which Leonard Rossiter was most famous, there is one more character that people will mention in the same breath as Rigsby or Reggie, though no one will ever be able to tell you his name as he was never given one. But that was okay, he didn't need one for you could always recognise him by his drink: a glass of Cinzano. The fact that Leonard's appearances in what was merely a set of advertisements are so fondly recalled is testament to the performance he brought to them. While many actors might be tempted simply to go through the paces in such work, he could never give anything less than his best and the ten advertisements screened between 1978 and 1983 were no exception.

Leonard was a good friend of the actor William Franklyn, who had starred in a successful series of advertisements for drinks company, Schweppes. 'Leonard said to me once: "What's it like, getting this "Schhh . . . You Know Who? [the catchphrase from the advert] How do you live with it? What's it really like?" And I said: "It's like a mortgage, education for three children, a home for my ex-wife, a home for my parents and a home for me. That's what it's actually like. And if you're not very careful, it might happen to you one day.'

Certainly a lot of actors have managed to achieve considerable sums, not to mention exposure, through appearing in advertising. I once worked with Sir Ian Richardson who, when asked what was under the tarpaulin on his drive, answered: 'A Sky advert' and smiled. (It was, in fact, an extremely desirable Mercedes.)

Few can lay claim to furthering their reputation as an actor through such work, however, and that is what makes the Cinzano commercials such a bizarre aberration.

In the seventies, the leading producer of vermouth was Martini and they had run a series of adverts featuring Bright Young Things quaffing the stuff on golden beaches, determined to convince their audience that Martini was an aspirational drink, something you might sip while fingering the keys to your own yacht. Rival company, Cinzano, decided it might be interesting to spoof these adverts and approached the London agency, Collett, Dickenson, Pearce & Partners, to discuss ideas.

Celebrated director Alan Parker was brought in to direct the first three advertisements. That same year saw the release of his controversial film *Midnight Express* (1978) and there was little doubt that he was a force to be reckoned with. Parker, alongside Ron Collins, the art director for the project, cast Leonard Rossiter for the commercials (Leonard having worked with CDP on an advert for Parker Pens the previous year). They also hired Joan Collins, then at the height of her glamorous fame due to the role of Alexis Carrington Colby in the American TV soap, *Dynasty*.

Scripts had already been written but neither Parker nor Rossiter thought much of them. 'I remember going round to Leonard's house,' says Parker, 'and we agreed the scripts were absolute rubbish. So Leonard said: "What I'd like to do is the old music-hall joke," and we said: "What's that?" So he picked up his cup of tea as we were sitting there in his living room and he looked at his watch, turning the cup over. And we said: "Yeah, that'll be a good joke, especially if it happens to be Joan Collins you're spilling it on!" '

In a later interview, Joan Collins admitted to not having heard of Rossiter prior to meeting the actor. Living and working in America, she had not been aware of his recent successes, though once she began work with him, she immediately recognised his abilities: 'Leonard was such a brilliant comedian that when rehearsing with him, my main problem was to stop shrieking with laughter! His comedy timing was superb, wacky, iconoclastic, and slightly different on every take – the true sign of a marvellous actor. I played a glamorous *femme du monde* to Leonard's buffoon. The first time we rehearsed I was a little bit in awe of him. He was a bit shy of me, and I was a bit shy of him.'

The first commercial was simplicity itself. Collins walks up to Rossiter at the bar. Noticing her, he enthusiastically greets her: 'Melissa, darling! You're early!' He checks his watch, dumping his drink down her cleavage as he does so, then asks her if she would like a Cinzano. 'No thank you,' she replies coldly, 'I've just had one.'

'It worked,' says Alan Parker, 'Boy, did it work! There was a period of time when the commercials were far and away the most interesting thing you could see that evening on television. They were infinitely more entertaining than any of the programmes in those days.'

Designed to launch Cinzano's new 'Bianco' brand, it was an immediate success – something CDP had already foreseen during filming, recognising a good partnership when they saw it. 'I asked who was doing the other two,' Collins recounted, 'and they said possibly Joanna Lumley, possibly Felicity Kendall. When we'd finished there was a huddle in the corner, all the bigwigs whispering. Finally they came over and said: "Would you like to do two more?" And they ran for five years!'

A further two adverts followed, promoting Cinzano's Rosé and Secco brands with Leonard, as always, giving poor Melissa a perfectly delivered soaking.

'People always ask me, "Did Joan object?"' said Rossiter (in regard to Collins' dampness during an interview with ITV's *Sunday, Sunday* in 1984), 'and I'd say: "Why should she object? She's getting paid! No, no, no! We got on very well – well, not *very* well. We got on *quite* well.'

And they certainly did get paid, reportedly £30,000 each. As to whether they got on or not, Collins certainly believed so, despite the fact that Leonard often referred to her as 'the prop'.

'I never found him demanding to anyone,' she claimed, 'other than himself.' Which is certainly a change in his usual working attitude.

In contrast, Terry Lovelock, director of the final two commercials – 'Tiger's Head' (where Leonard trips on a tiger-skin rug and flings his drink at Melissa only to have a group of visiting Japanese businessmen follow suit, believing this to be customary behaviour) and 'Dragoon' (at a fancy-dress ball, where Leonard gives Melissa two sound splashes from his drink when pointing to a woman he considers her double) certainly found his leading man hard work: 'Leonard Rossiter from the theatre – difficult. He felt he was "the main man", the artist of the two. He used to choreograph himself. I know the previous director had some trouble with this, so I had to spend some time with him, just to diffuse what I thought might be some awkward situations. And there was.

'He'd say, "I'm doing this movement, and that movement" and "It'd be nice for the camera to see this and see that". And I said, "Well, I'm going to cut to your foot going in the tiger-skin head on the floor", and he said: "Oh, but they won't be able to see what I'm doing with the rest of me." Joan was thoroughly professional – she got the idea straightaway. She was very intelligent and absolutely unpretentious.'

The adverts became so popular that there was even talk of creating a feature film around the couple though it soon became clear that the idea just wouldn't work. For a plot to develop, the two characters would need to have some sort of relationship and the minute you gave them that depth, the comedy would be lost. They simply wouldn't be together in real life – or in a movie's impression of 'real life' at least – and the changes necessary to make the relationship believable would ruin the pairing. Leonard explained as much to David Lewin of the *Sunday Mirror*: 'If the scripts for the film that we make together were to be ten percent funny and ninety percent romantic, it would deny the expectations of the audience. It is the fact that we are so disparate that makes us interesting and intriguing. In the film, if the girl were a scrubber it wouldn't work. And it wouldn't work if I were upper-crust.'

Movie or not, Rossiter won the award for 'Best Actor in a Commercial' from *TV Times* magazine and the ads – most particularly 'Airliner', where Leonard accidentally trigger's Melissa's seat recline button so that she dumps her drink on herself – are still discussed today.

In 1983, Cinzano reluctantly dismissed the services of CDP after orders from their owners to organise a more 'worldwide' commercial. Leonard, in an act of generosity not untypical of him, took the creators of the last two commercials out for a meal at Tante Claire, near Hyde Park, thought to be one of the finest restaurants in London. One hopes he was careful where he put his drink!

37

Win Some, Lose Some

Now passers-by had three things to shout at Rossiter: they could either tell him that 'They didn't get where they were today . . .', enquire after 'Miss Jones' or ask him if he had Joan Collins' phone number.

Much to his amusement, most barmen would ask if he fancied a Martini, thinking they were being funny, oblivious to the fact that they had the wrong brand entirely. Reportedly, many viewers made the same mistake and Leonard helped Martini sell a fair few bottles of vermouth as well.

As the final series of *Rising Damp* began its broadcast in 1978 (with the last *Reggie Perrin* due to hit TV screens at the end of the year), Leonard took on two distinctly different TV projects: one that would be a success, the other a terrible failure.

The first project concerned Frank Harris, a journalist and biographer, most particularly renowned – or in some cases reviled – for his four-volume autobiography, *My Life and Loves*, which lists his numerous sexual conquests in such graphic detail that it was banned in many countries, including the UK. And nothing sells memoirs (or indeed one's reputation) as being deemed unsuitable for the masses. Harris was described by his friend Oscar Wilde as having been 'received in all the great houses *once*' – notorious then, but easy to relish and a character ripe for portrayal.

Andrew Davies, a screenwriter famous for his literary adaptations – particularly of classic authors such as Dickens, Austen and Brontë – wrote *Fearless Frank (or Tit-bits from the Life of an Adventurer)* for the BBC's 'Play of the Week' series, with Leonard cast as Harris. He recalls the experience: 'We are three or four days into rehearsal. It is my first visit since the read-through. Although there are twenty or thirty people in the room, you notice Rossiter straightaway because he has so much more energy than anyone else. The air around him seems to twitch slightly. He spots me from twenty yards and fixes me with a beady eye.

' "Ah!" he says. "The author! A word with you." I go over. "Think I've found a bit of *bad writing* here."

'His tone is gleefully conspiratorial as he draws me aside, his arm round my shoulder. He is performing the totally confidential discussion with such ferocious panache that the whole room falls silent. I steel myself for whatever is coming: probably a demand for a total rewrite on the last fifty pages or something.

' "I'd like you to consider swapping the order of this word and this word," he says. "And then making this comma into a full stop. Clearer, you see? And funnier, I think."

'He is right, of course. I agree the change.

' "Is that all?" I ask weakly.

' "Yes, that's all. I, er . . . *think* I can make the rest of it work. Just about." The face is dead straight, the timing perfect.

'He did make it work, in an extraordinary way. He blustered, he cajoled, he buttonholed, he fawned, he raged, he leered, he revelled in the life he created as Frank Harris. His work was almost incredibly fast, neat and inventive, and yet he always seemed to have oodles of time to get it all in. Looking for comparisons, one tends to go outside acting, towards boxers, bullfighters, the batting of Viv Richards. And the element of controlled aggression in this comparison is not fortuitous.'

Boxing was to be the theme of the second project, a sitcom called *The Losers*. But this time, the critics didn't pull their punches in their opinion of it, something its writer – Alan Coren – had predicted before the cameras even rolled, Coren had been TV critic for *The Times* for the last seven years and suspected his colleagues, or perhaps rivals might be a better word, would be eager to put the boot in once the series began broadcasting. Certainly, a TV critic unveiling a new sitcom to his peers is rather like a food critic inviting a few colleagues round for dinner. In this case they ate well: 'Here were the country's leading wit and one of the best comic actors,' wrote Stanley Reynolds for Coren's former newspaper, *The Times*, 'and they combined to bore us to death.' Compared to Bernard Davies, writing for *Broadcast* magazine, Reynolds was being kind: 'Leonard Rossiter, who never gives a bad performance, comes very near to doing so in this lamentable series in spite of the fact that he is working like a Trojan. He cannot disguise the poverty of the script nor can he enhance his reputation.'

Harsh words, indeed: and in truth the show could have been better. *The Losers* was about a crooked boxing promoter and the slow-witted young fighter he was always encouraging to throw fights. It was produced by Terence Baker, who went on to achieve some level of notoriety years later when he was involved in the perjury case of Jeffrey Archer, being one of those who gave a false account of Archer's movements to provide him with an alibi. Baker approached Leonard for the lead role of promoter, Sydney Foskett. Happy that the role was a world away from Reggie or Rigsby, he accepted and in turn suggested Joe McGrath as director.

McGrath had an illustrious pedigree in comedy. He had produced and directed Michael Bentine's *It's a Square World* and alongside Dudley Moore, developed *Not Only... But Also...* In cinema, he had worked on the original *Casino Royale* movie – the very strange 'unofficial' version as opposed to the more serious 2006 feature starring Daniel Craig. In fact, it fell to McGrath to handle the awkward casino scenes with Orson Welles and Peter Sellers (where the latter refused to work alongside the former, allegedly due to nerves, insisting on shooting his lines separately). McGrath was to work with Sellers again, both on the unsuccessful attempt to bring *The Goon Show* to television, as well co-writing and directing the incredibly bizarre *The Magic Christian* in 1969. He first worked with Leonard on *Justin Thyme* (1964), which he had co-written along with its star John Bluthal and would later direct him in the *Rising Damp* movie.

Looking for someone to play the role of Nigel, the boxer, both Leonard and McGrath thought of a young actor called Alfred Molina. 'Leonard and I had seen Fred on stage doing a couple of things,' recalls McGrath, 'so when the project came up, we thought he would be an excellent choice.' Of course, Molina has gone on to become incredibly successful Hollywood actor, but at that point he was an unknown face on television.

'I was completely in awe of Leonard Rossiter,' he later admitted. 'For me, he was like one of the comic gods, just a brilliant actor. I was starstruck. He was very nice to me, very considerate. A hard taskmaster, a tough guy to work with, but I loved him because he treated me the same. He didn't make allowances, he didn't give me the benefit of the doubt; he wasn't patronising. I was as green as a cabbage. And I remember being shocked by him. We were in a rehearsal and I was trying something, and he suddenly went, "That's not funny!" He was quite brusque. I didn't say anything, but I wanted to say, "What do you mean, it's not funny? We don't know if it's funny or not – we haven't done it in front of an audience."

'I quickly went on the defensive and then I realised, the second time I tried it – much to his disdain – that he was right. His instinct was spot-on. So, I did myself a favour and decided to trust it rather than fight it. Rather than letting my ego get in the way, I thought, I'll listen to what he says. I watched him like a hawk. And I learned so much: about timing, the way you can change a joke just by the slightest shift of emphasis, the slightest shift in the weight from one syllable to another; the way the coming together of energy and language and voice explodes. All those things come together to make a great comic moment.'

Like Don Warrington before him, Molina had found a nerve-wracking postgraduate course in the shape of Leonard Rossiter. Unlike his fellow actor, however, the show would not launch his career.

Whatever the critics may have thought of *The Losers*, McGrath has fond memories of that time: 'I enjoyed doing it. We managed to convince the TV company to let us shoot 75 per cent of it on film, so we'd only be in the studio with the audience for maybe five to ten minutes of each half-hour show.'

Though the script wasn't as strong as one might have expected considering its source, McGrath is convinced that Rossiter played it for all it was worth, bringing some strong comedy to the show. Certainly, the crew were often laughing.

'One of the episodes featured breakfast in the dining room of a theatrical boarding house,' he recalls, 'and Len passes a table, at which are seated an out-of-work sea lion and its trainer.

'I suggested Len threw a bread roll to the sea lion when he delivered his line of "How's business?" to them, a "bit of business" he was much in favour of. I'd tested the sea lion out earlier so I knew it was up to the job, but Len took so long trying to decide where was best to throw the roll from! Typical perfectionist, he moved from one side to the other, shifting forward and back. By the time he threw it, the sea lion was so nervous that it missed the bread roll entirely and vacated its bowels all over the studio floor. "No wonder you're out of work," said Len, quick as a flash, before turning to me and asking if I'd like to try it again.'

Whatever the critics might have thought, the audience figures were high enough for ATV to request a second series but Coren decided he wasn't interested.

'He said it was too much like hard work!' McGrath laughs, 'not helped by the fact that I'd have to call him during rehearsals every week as Len delivered his lines so quickly I always needed another couple of minutes of material. "Tell him to speak slower!" Coren would say. "No, Alan," I'd reply, "*you* tell him." He wasn't that brave!'

To round off 1978, Leonard was invited to take part in the national institution that was the *Morecambe and Wise Christmas Special*, something he mentioned to Joe McGrath. 'I was working with Eric and Ernie at the time,' McGrath remembers, 'shooting some commercials, so I said to them: "If there's three of you, why not do The Andrews Sisters?" Sure enough, that's exactly what they did.'

The Special featured a black-and-white sequence designed to evoke the wartime era at which the vocal trio were at their height: Eric, Ernie and Leonard miming their way through a performance of "The Boogie-Woogie Bugle-Boy of Company B", one of the trio's most popular songs. They do not make particularly convincing women – however inflated Ernie's bust – and there is a sneer on Leonard's face throughout, a comic sense of a man stranded in the midst of a most disagreeable situation.

'They transcend the mime,' says McGrath. 'It was one of the few times watching *Morecambe and Wise* when my eye wasn't on Ernie – I was watching Leonard!'

38

A Breath of Fresh Air

Having thoroughly endorsed his celebrity status by appearing with Morecambe and Wise, 1979 would see Leonard take on a role distinctly unlike any other that he had played before: that of Joseph Pujol.

Pujol was an entertainer who had risen to huge success in Paris in the latter part of the nineteenth century through a most unusual talent. As a child, he had discovered that he possessed an unconventionally elastic anus and amused his friends with his ability to suck up water and then eject it at high speed. He soon discovered that he could play a similar trick with air, inhaling and then exhaling in a variety of amusing noises, depending on how he constricted himself anally. As a baker, he would amuse his customers by imitating musical instruments while serving behind the counter – something one hesitates to imagine going down well today, if seen at the local supermarket!

Determined to try his luck on the stage, Pujol – under the stage name, *Le Pétomane* (literally translated as 'fartoholic') – appeared in his hometown of Marseilles before travelling on to Paris to join the cast at the much-celebrated Moulin Rouge in 1892. Highlights of his act included the playing of musical instruments such as an ocarina using a length of rubber pipe and lots of concentration. He could also extinguish candles from a great distance.

It's hard to imagine such an act becoming the success it did – though the French have always leaned towards the scatalogical in their humour – but by 1894, Pujol was earning 20,000 francs per show. It was a phenomenal amount and more than double other stars of the theatre, such as the legendary actress Sarah Bernhardt. He was, in fact, the highest paid performer of his generation – and worth every penny it would seem for his shows were phenomenal sell-outs. It was even common practice for nurses to be on standby in case the audience did themselves a mischief by laughing too hard.

Pujol struck out on his own after a disagreement with the manager of the Moulin Rouge over an impromptu performance he gave at the local market to help an ailing friend draw a crowd to his stall. Now performing at his own theatre, the Pompadour, he worked on refining his act, the climax of which was an impression of the San Francisco 1904 earthquake! When the First World War broke out, Pujol – sickened by the violence around him – retired from the business and returned to life in his Marseilles bakery. When he died in 1945, the Sorbonne offered his relatives money for his remains so that they could be studied. Perhaps understandably, the family refused.

Naturally, such an unusual and colourful character interests people even after his death and, as well as a number of books and even a musical about Pujol, Ian McNaughton – who had directed Leonard in the *Rising Damp* pilot – wanted to produce a short film. Working from a script written by Ray Galton and Alan Simpson, the half-hour production floundered briefly in the search for an actor who could bring the Frenchman (and his elastic anus) to life.

'Both Peter Sellers and David Niven wanted to do it,' recalls Galton, 'They thought it was hysterically funny, but were advised against it by their agents! They thought it would be bad for their image. That was the last thing Leonard considered. Was it funny? That's all he cared about. He decided yes, and played it delightfully with great dignity and delicacy. Nobody would have played it better. In the end we were pleased the other two had been warned off.'

Considering its subject matter, the film is handled with a perhaps surprising grace. Leonard approached the role with a sincerity and yes, class that perhaps lesser actors might have avoided altogether, leaping wholeheartedly into a more obvious, crass performance. Despite this,the subject matter was too much for some and certain cinemas fought to get it banned. Now rarely seen, and unavailable on DVD, it represents another in Rossiter's long list of varied and inspired performances and a considerable contrast to his next project: the voice of an animated dog.

Maurice Dodd's *The Perishers* had been running in the *Daily Mirror* since 1958. The three-panel adventures of a group of English children and a shaggy Old English Sheepdog named Boot, originally it was drawn by Dennis Collins and then Dodd himself. A collection of absurdist dreamers – even the dog was convinced he was an eighteenth-century lord trapped in the body of a dog following a gypsy's curse – it was prime material for an animated TV series. In total, 20 x five-minute episodes were made, with Leonard cast as Boot, the dog with a noble pedigree.

That his career continued to be a selection of roles almost specifically chosen for their variety is clear. He was cleansing his palate of five years of sitcom: not that he was ashamed or disliked either performance but there could be no doubting the relish with which he proved there were different performances in his repertoire. From sexual adventurers to farting Frenchmen, an impression of Groucho Marx on Ned Sherrin's *Song by Song* to the voice of a delusional dog for a children's cartoon (that must have pleased the 6-year-old Camilla no end), 1978 proved a varied year.

39

The Male Visitor with the Permanent Head Cold

With so much to celebrate in the last half of the seventies, 1979 brought a chapter in Leonard Rossiter's life that is not so lauded. Indeed, it is only with the publication of *Woman of Today*, broadcaster Sue MacGregor's autobiography in 2002, that we know anything about it.

MacGregor joined the BBC in 1967 as a reporter for Radio 4's lunchtime news show, *World at One*, a role that led her to host the same station's magazine show, *Woman's Hour*, five years later – a post she would retain for 15 years. In 1984, she became one of the hosts of Radio 4's prestigious *Today*, often deemed the most influential news programmes in the country.

Rossiter was invited to appear on *Woman's Hour*, then at the height of his televisual success, thanks to *Rising Damp* and *The Fall and Rise of Reginald Perrin*. The interview went well and MacGregor admits to finding him excellent company, as she writes in her autobiography: 'Although we had seemed to get on rather well, I was completely taken by surprise when the next day he rang me in the office and suggested meeting for a drink. I was also intrigued. Could this be simply a postscript to our meeting of the day before and end in an offer of tickets for his next appearance in the West End? Or was he interested in something more?'

It would seem so as, according to the book, Leonard took MacGregor's phone number and later visited her at her home, where they commenced a sexual relationship. She admits to being flattered and also intrigued by the possibility of getting to know the 'real' man behind his many theatrical personae.

Given that Leonard was so recognisable, their meetings always took place at MacGregor's apartment in Primose Hill, the actor usually covering his face with a white handkerchief as he climbed her steps, leading MacGregor to wonder, 'what my neighbours made of my male visitor with the permanent head cold.' Her feelings for Leonard swiftly developed, finding him: 'quick, clever, funny and an enthusiastic *bon viveur*... I found him immensely attractive.'

But there was never any suggestion that the relationship could develop beyond its rather claustrophobic limitations: 'From the start he made it clear to me that there would never be any question of leaving his wife. I understood this, and assured him that I had always considered myself a determinedly single soul. I would be happy to see him whenever he was free: on the other hand, I would not become the lonely mistress sitting at home waiting for the phone call. I did see other men from time to time, but none of them seemed quite as attractive.'

Of course, with the best will in the world, such arrangements rarely stay so simple and after a year or so of the arrangement, MacGregor found she was dissatisfied with the limitations of the relationship and eager to see more of Leonard than he was either willing or able to provide. This led to a confrontation that saw her leave her apartment in tears after they had argued, with Leonard stressing that he had always been honest about how far their relationship could develop.

After a few days they continued as before, with nothing else said, and they would meet roughly once a week right up until Leonard's death in 1984. In fact, MacGregor only learned of his passing from the BBC News. Shocked and stricken with grief, she relied on the support of her mother, one of the few people who had known of the relationship.

While one cannot help but feel sympathy it is hard to completely separate oneself from the shock and distress these revelations must have caused Rossiter's family just prior to the book's publication. MacGregor wrote to Gillian Raines, Leonard's widow, explaining that she intended to reveal their affair through the pages of her autobiography. One can only imagine what sort of effect such a letter would cause. 'I'm not proud of my relationship with Leonard,' she said, during the publicity around the book launch, 'I don't regret it because I loved him, but it was probably very foolish of me to have got involved. I do think very much about his wife, actually, and his daughter. I feel that they must have been horribly shocked when they heard about it. I don't think they knew anything at all about it.' Of course they didn't: that is until she decided to tell them – along with everyone else.

Naturally, it is a subject that both Gillian and Camilla Rossiter are reticent to discuss, with Camilla commenting to me that, as we only have MacGregor's word to go on, it is a subject she prefers to ignore. It is clear that Camilla believes that MacGregor fabricated the story, wishing only to help sell her book, and there can be no doubt such revelations always help in that regard. Perhaps that is so. Or maybe Leonard did have the affair and left behind a woman who felt a great deal for him to grieve his passing almost alone. Who can say for sure?

On the assumption that the story is true, I can't see that writing about it was altogether necessary – after all, it amounts to little more than a few pages of a book that has plenty more to say. While it is MacGregor's inarguable right to discuss the details of her life, perhaps such an announcement and the untold damage and hurt it will cause those who can do nothing about it – namely Leonard's family – needs more justification than the book itself provides. Were it a central theme, or even the subject of an entire chapter, then perhaps one could understand why it needed to be included. As it is, for all MacGregor's claims of great affection the subject is done and dusted in a handful of literary moments and feels perfunctory. The only people reading about it who could feel any great impact would have been the Rossiters and that leaves a sour taste. Perhaps a relationship carried on in secret for five years should remain a secret. Surely Leonard, were his opinion able to be sought, might have wished it so.

40

Britannia Hospital

The seventies rolled into the eighties, and the UK trembled. The so-called 'Winter of Discontent' of 1978–79 took its toll on the stability of the British government with massive trade union strikes (something Leonard would not have stood for!). Jimmy Callaghan and the left-wing Labour government was dealt a killing blow when a 'motion of no confidence' forced a General Election and Britain came under the control of the Conservatives and its first female Prime Minister, Margaret Thatcher.

While Leonard may have been celebrating, many in his social circle would have felt differently and the period is now looked back on as something of a dark time in British history, with the privatisation of public services and a war over the Falkland Islands. However, there seems little point in denying that Thatcher was the popular choice, reigning for the next 10 years and the political background of the country stimulated the creative industries as it always does, with Leonard taking on roles in a couple of productions that had a distinctly political flavour.

In December of 1981, he appeared as factory foreman Harry Meadows in the David Hopkins' scripted 'Play for Today': *The Factory*. A satire on the relations between management and workers within the UK, it co-starred a young Ray Winstone, fresh from his successes in the controversial Borstal drama, *Scum*, and *Quadrophenia*.

The writer recalls one awkward moment in a later interview:

I was chatting to the director, Gerald Blake, at the 'Acton Hilton' [the nickname for the BBC rehearsal rooms] when the door burst open and in

233

strode Leonard Rossiter, clutching the large brown-paper envelope with its distinctive blue and white sticker, in which the BBC sends scripts around. We had never met before.

He flung the envelope at Gerald's feet and said, 'Who wrote this rubbish? The BBC must be badly off.' Pause. 'And how did you manage to persuade me to do it?'

He then gave me one of those sideways and upward looks, did one of his backward staggers and said, 'Good lord, the author!'

Certainly, this was one way to break the ice during an initial meeting and further proof, if such a thing were needed, of Leonard's willingness to speak his mind. Though knowing his sense of humour, one is inclined to believe he knew exactly what he was doing and was having a joke at Hopkins' expense.

1982 saw Leonard appear on the cinema screens in two distinctly different comedy movies, though they shared one thing in common: a hard time from both critics and audiences alike.

After the death of Peter Sellers in 1980, Blake Edwards, the actor's sometime friend and colleague – as was frequently the case with Sellers, relationships never ran consistently smooth – decided to create a new film in the 'Pink Panther' franchise. In order to surmount the seemingly impossible problem of having a dead leading actor, he constructed the movie from a mixture of new footage, clips and deleted scenes from previous entries in the series, stringing the whole together with a rather messy plot. In fact, the opening titles – featuring the animated Pink Panther, as was often the case – may have put it best: the title 'Story by Blake Edwards' is produced by the cartoon Clouseau urinating the words onto a book cover!

Leonard was seen briefly as Superintendent Quinlan, the role he played in the earlier *The Pink Panther Strikes Again*. The brevity of his screen appearance is a relief when one considers the quality of the film. Despite Edwards' insistence that the project was intended to be a tribute to the late Sellers, the actor's widow Lynn Frederick successfully sued him for over a million dollars, arguing that the work would diminish Sellers' memory.

The second movie saw Rossiter reunited with the director Lindsay Anderson. Anderson's reputation as a filmmaker was built on strong foundations: his first film – and Leonard's second – *This Sporting Life* rose above its commercial failure to be viewed as a last 'hurrah' for the British New Wave movement of 'kitchen sink' dramas. With the 1968 release of *If...*, a surreal satire on the public school system which launched the screen career of actor Malcolm McDowell, Anderson's reputation as an engaging and cine-literate director was assured. The film was to become the first in a loose trilogy featuring Malcolm McDowell as Anderson's 'everyman' Mick Travis. It was to continue with *O Lucky Man!* (1973) before concluding with *Britannia Hospital* in 1982.

Anderson introduced the film at the time by saying: 'The absurdities of human behaviour as we move into the twenty-first century are too extreme – and too dangerous – to permit us the luxury of senti-mentalism or tears. But by looking at humanity objectively and without indulgence, we may hope to save it. Laughter can help.'

A pitch-black comedy taking a swipe at the country's worst excesses via the surreal 'world' of an NHS hospital, *Britannia Hospital* opens with an old man abandoned to die of hypothermia through union action and staff apathy and culminates in the unveiling of a Frankenstein-like creation: a human brain wired to a bank of machinery that proceeds to emotionlessly orate a soliloquy from *Hamlet*.

On opening, the film was harshly received but has gathered a far more favourable opinion in the years since the initial release. Certainly it's not for everyone and while consistently played for laughs unlike Anderson's previous movies, the humour is so gruesome that it's hardly surprising that contemporary audiences were somewhat turned-off by the whole affair.

It features an unwieldy cast, incorporating many familiar faces from Arthur Lowe to Robbie Coltrane, but Leonard was cast as the lynchpin of the whole affair: hospital administrator Vincent Potter. Determined to open a new ward successfully with all the pomp and ceremony he can manage – including a visit from HM The Queen Mother, he is forced to negotiate with striking unions, bloodthirsty surgeons and an undercover film crew. He will do anything, even commit murder, to see things run smoothly, placing the fate and reputation of his hospital above all else. In this, of course, he is a fairly clear metaphor for Anderson – and scriptwriter David Sherwin's – view of the government of the day. It is thanks to Rossiter's ability to play such grotesque excesses with both an eye for the comedy, but more importantly a grounded sense of Potter as a real human being rather than two-dimensional caricature, that the role succeeds. In less controlled hands, it could have easily been a distinctly unpalatable performance but again, this is Leonard's speciality and the material he loves the best, whatever the politic standpoint: comedy so black it makes an audience wince as much as laugh.

'Leonard always acted with his own, absolutely special dynamic,' explains Anderson a few years after the initial release, 'a high-tension artist to whom audiences were drawn as compellingly and fixedly as moths to an incandescent bulb. He never asked for sympathy, he would have scorned that. He guarded his secret: only what he wanted to show, he showed. Only what he wanted to say, he said. When he wanted to make you laugh, he did it with a technique so impeccable that there was no denying him. He was shrewd, very intelligent and had no time for idiots. The world must have driven him mad from time to time with its foolish pretensions. Under the comedy there was a kind of desperation. He was essentially a serious actor, ploughing his own furrow.'

Again we see that key to Rossiter's performance expressed: he was not a comedian, he was an actor with an unerring eye for the comic and the knowledge that the funniest material was always underpinned with a hint of sadness.

41

A Mess in Aisle 3

As the eighties continued, Rossiter maintained his method of picking scripts that confound expectation. He was, as Lindsay Anderson said, still ploughing his own furrow. That would never be clearer than in his choice of television roles he would take on in 1984. Of course, he wasn't to know that those four productions would be his last, though it's unlikely they would have displeased him: a knockabout comedy, Shakespeare, *Alice in Wonderland* and a serious drama that was a throwback to the one-off TV plays that had been such a staple part of his early career.

Liverpudlian writer Brian Cook began his career as a cartoonist but earned his script-writing stripes as a writer on the final series of the popular radio comedy, *Round the Horne*, a vehicle for comedian Kenneth Horne, which also cemented the career of *Carry On* star, Kenneth Williams. Later, working with his writing partner Johnnie Mortimer, Cook had devised such successful sitcoms as *Man About the House*, *George and Mildred* and *Robin's Nest*. In the early eighties he was employed by Thames Television to create a handful of pilot scripts for possible sitcoms, something he enjoyed as it kept his work varied and, should the pilots be successful, he would earn a royalty when they were made into a full-length series. He never got past the writing of the first pilot, however, as *Tripper's Day*, concerning life in a small supermarket, was to entice Leonard back to the world of sitcom.

'Leonard Rossiter was a superb craftsman,' says Cook, 'equal to Ronnie Barker in the sitcom world. He wanted to meet me and I went round to see him at his home in Fulham, a modest terrace house next to a cemetery, a railway line, underneath Heathrow's flight path and in jeering distance of Chelsea's football ground. The match was emptying out as I arrived and thousands of supporters streamed past his front parlour window, occasionally banging on it. The minute he opened his mouth, I realised something I hadn't known before: he came from my home town, Liverpool, so his rhythm and pattern of speech would come very easily to me.

'He sat me down, offered me a glass of wine and indicated a huge pile of scripts on his coffee table. There must have been about fifty. "Why should I do your show rather than these?" he said. I'd handled so many network executives and directors and producers that this question didn't throw me. "Because *I'm* writing it," I replied, not to be outdone in arrogance. He grunted doubtfully at this: "I'd want a rewrite, making the supermarket manager more central to the action."

'This was fair enough – I'd made the show more of an ensemble piece with the manager reacting to events rather than instigating them. "What if I do a rewrite and you decide you don't want to do it?" I said, "That'll reflect on me." "That's a chance you'll have to take," he retorted.'

But he needn't have feared. After rewriting the pilot with Tripper, the manager, now more prominent, Leonard accepted the role. Cook was signed up to write six episodes, the original scheme of creating pilots falling by the wayside, so enthused were Thames to have a comedy star of Rossiter's calibre on one of their shows.

Cook found Leonard a dominating presence. 'He was an opinionated performer,' he says, 'and, considering his successes, why not?'

Not that there wasn't fun to be had at the rehearsals, according to director Michael Mills: 'There were among the cast several cricket-playing enthusiasts including, of course, Leonard himself. In short breaks such as for coffee or rearrangement of the rehearsal room, it was generally the habit to set up an impromptu cricket game with a wastepaper basket as a wicket, a tennis ball and an old cricket bat. When the rest of us went in to bat, we were aware that we were in a rehearsal room and surrounded by non-players. Not so Leonard. When he went in to bat, he played as though he were trying to reach the boundary line at Lords and struck the ball with necessary vigour.

Elderly actresses dropped their knitting and hid behind the furniture; others, more active, bolted for the doors and the ball whistled around their ears. Leonard, of course, was oblivious to all this. A cricket ball (even a tennis ball masquerading as a cricket ball in a rehearsal room) was there to be hit as hard as possible, and Leonard did so.'

And when they weren't playing cricket, they were listening to it, as actor Paul Clarkson recalled: 'Test Match listening was a must and, throughout rehearsals, he insisted on constant updates on England's dismal showing against the West Indies. So disappointed was he by their failure, we embarked on preparation for the inevitable call-up.'

Sadly, it would later seem that the actors enjoyed filming the sitcom more than audiences liked watching it, with the general response to the show being lukewarm at best. Many critics were surprised that an actor of Leonard Rossiter's calibre would have agreed to the role. In an interview with *TV Times* magazine published to coincide with the show, he explained: 'When I was offered *Tripper*, it was pointed out that it wasn't terribly deep stuff, just smash-bang basic comedy in short, sharp scenes. I said I wasn't averse to doing anything if I liked it, and this is fast and funny, and very well written by Brian Cook.'

Perhaps the response was inevitable: there comes a point in most actors' careers when they feel the sharp edge of a critical tongue, accused of not living up to their previous successes. In truth, it would have been hard for *Tripper's Day* to live up to either *Rising Damp* or *The Fall and Rise of Reginald Perrin*, given the quality and reputation of both, and it never tries: it is simply a traditional sitcom, with no higher ambition than to amuse. Unfortunately, and even with Leonard onboard, it often struggles to do so. Perhaps surprisingly given its reception, the show continued for another two series, retitled *Slinger's Day* to reflect the change in manager – and therefore lead character – with Bruce Forsyth now the star.

It was to become a somewhat awkward epitaph as Leonard died between transmission of the second and third episodes. Television audiences were treated to that peculiar form of haunting that occurs with all performers: unscreened appearances are brought forth, the final work of a great actor playing out with an extra air of regret. Now every performance would seek to remind the viewer that, for all the ability and potential, the work was near done. This man's life, like all, was finite and now all that's left are the final few glimpses of what could have been. Thus it was that, by the time Leonard returned to our screens in *The Life and Death of King John* (1984), he was no longer with us.

The BBC's project to adapt all of Shakespeare's plays for television had come about after the producer Cedric Messina decided that Glamis Castle in Angus, Scotland – where he had been working on an unrelated film – would be an excellent location to stage a production of Shakespeare's *As You Like It*. His idea, as good ones have the habit of doing, grew more ambitious: how about producing a series that would feature every single one of Shakespeare's plays? The notion of producing all 37 works was the most ambitious Shakespearian project ever attempted for TV and film. That it was a success, concluding in 1985, after seven series, with the presentation of the bloodthirsty *Titus Andronicus*, is testament to the BBC's tenacity and the skills of the many people involved. The dramas are highly thought of to this day, selling well on DVD and still a frequent touchstone in schools for teachers wishing to bring the text to life for their students.

Though extremely popular in the Victorian era, *The Life and Death of King John* has become one of Shakespeare's lesser-known plays and is rarely performed. The monarch himself is now most commonly pictured as simply the enemy of Robin Hood – the weakling king who signed the Magna Carta and attempted to steal the reign from his brother Richard (the Lionheart) while the latter fought in the Crusades.

Rossiter's performance was posthumously celebrated. Denis Hackett, writing for *The Times*, said: 'His fluttering flights into bravado and retreats into a more natural cowardice – characteristics which, in a comic vein, can be seen in *Rising Damp*, still running on ITV – were entirely appropriate.' While Nancy Banks-Smith, reviewing for the *Guardian*, felt, 'He gave a gloriously eccentric and really very human performance making a funny, pitiful fellow creature out of a cypher.'

The director was David Giles, the principal director behind the BBC's adaptation of *The Forsyte Saga* and *The First Churchills*. Giles had directed four of the historical plays for the BBC Shakespeare series, covering the historically consecutive run between *Richard II* and *Henry V*.

'I found Leonard enormously interesting to work with,' he said in a later interview, 'like a coiled spring, always sniffing about for a way of enlivening every second of the performance. There was always a sense of danger, which gave the comedic elements their edge. He was never easy and could explode. He did twice during rehearsals, but both times with every excuse; and once the explosion was over, it was finished and done with.'

In 1985, 16 years after he had last worked with screenwriters Dick Clement and Ian La Frenais, Rossiter once again appeared on our cinema screens in *Water*. The film centred on the fictional British colony Cascara in the Caribbean, with Michael Caine starring as its 'gone native' governor. When an oil drill hits a supply of fresh mineral water – which, given its quality, is deemed more valuable than the oil – the world begins to take notice of Cascara again. Leonard was cast in the major role of Sir Malcolm Leveridge, a singularly Permaent Secretary from the British Foreign Office.

'I think if I had to choose one adjective to describe Len as an actor,' says Dick Clement, 'it would be "meticulous." He was always prepared when he walked onto the set, having considered every aspect of the role, but he also had a formidable technique, particularly in his ability to absorb great wodges of dialogue. His opening speech in the film is a long tracking shot with Richard Pearson (the Foreign Secretary), where the two of them discuss the fate of the Caribbean island, Cascara. I'd been up half the night fiddling with the dialogue, so I brought in new lines, made excisions and alterations, which would have thrown many actors totally. They took it all in their stride.'

As always, Leonard was happy to bring a few touches of his own to the part. 'There was no false modesty about him,' Clement continues, 'Len knew he was good. But he was also meticulous about the niceties of theatrical etiquette, happy to offer suggestions but aways wanting to be reassured in case it did not fit in with the director's vision. When we shot the scene with Michael Caine at the oil rig, he rehearsed his long walk towards him in front of the watching eyes of the world's press, dressed inappropriately for the tropical heat in his dark Whitehall suit and bowler hat. Halfway there on the first rehearsal, he tripped ever so slightly and then readjusted his bowler minutely as if to restore his dignity. It was a perfect touch, perfectly timed. On the first take he didn't do it.

' "What about the trip?" I asked

' "Oh, you didn't say anything so I assumed you thought it was a bit much."

I reassured him and it was restored.

The film received mixed reviews but as is so often the way, its reputation has mellowed over the years and it is perhaps better received now through the DVD release and screening on television than it was at the time. Certainly Leonard's performance is as flawless as ever and stands as a satisfactory tribute: for most of the world, this would be the last performance he gave.

In the UK, however, where the film was released ahead of international markets, there were two more chances to catch fresh appearances from Rossiter. First, he lent his voice to Harry Aldous' adaptation of Lewis Carroll's *Alice in Wonderland* (1985) for Anglia Television. Rarely seen today, Aldous' version was swamped by similar adaptations released at the same time. In the US, industry veteran Irwin Allen had just produced a TV movie featuring an illustrious list of stars, including Sammy Davis Jnr., Ringo Starr, Anthony Newley and Telly Savalas (as the Cheshire Cat) and the BBC would soon trump Anglia's version with a lavish version of their own produced by *Doctor Who* veterans Barry Letts and Terrance Dicks.

Aldous chose a theatrical puppet adaptation for his inspiration, the renowned Da Silva Puppet Theatre having just staged a version of the tale. The resultant five-part series is therefore a somewhat uncomfortable blend of a live-action Alice – played by 10-year-old Giselle Andrews – talking to clunky puppets in front of CSO backgrounds. CSO, or Colour Separation Overlay, was the frequently used though seldom effective method of superimposing an actor onto a model set. The effect was often the only way a beleaguered TV budget could effect such fantasies but was rarely convincing due to the distinctive blue line around the superimposed actor and the difference in visual quality between the blended images. This criticism aside – and really, it's a churlish one, the production makes the best of what it has – the adaptation is faithful and fun, with many fine actors providing character voices. As well as Leonard's King of Hearts, Bernard Cribbins, Paul Eddington, Michael Bentine and Eric Sykes are present, as is John Barron, sharing a screen credit with Leonard again, this time in his part as 'the Caterpillar'.

Leonard's final TV role couldn't have been more different as he appeared in Peter Ansorge's first television play, *Moon Over Soho*. As both a script editor and producer for the BBC's English Regions Drama Department, Ansorge was involved in such classic productions as Mike Leigh's *Nuts in May* and Alan Bleasdale's *Boys from the Blackstuff*. Later, working with Channel 4, he commissioned *Traffik*, *Tales of the City*, Dennis Potter's *Lipstick on Your Collar* and *G.B.H.*, again by Bleasdale and described by the *Observer* newspaper as 'the UK's best ever drama'.

Moon Over Soho concerned Max (played by Leonard), a German Jew who set up a film magazine to make the woman he loved famous. The actress in question had kept the magazine afloat until her death and now, with bankruptcy looming, Max writes threatening letters to himself hoping they'll convince his mother to bail him out of trouble.

The play was directed by Stuart Burge, already familiar with Rossiter's work, having been artistic director at the Nottingham Playhouse while *The Resistible Rise of Arturo Ui* played there. He was delighted to have the opportunity to work with Leonard again.

'One of Leonard's outstanding talents was an apparent manifestation *of anarchy*,' he explained in a later interview, 'which was, in fact, a meticulously organised and controlled interpretation of the character the author intended. In rehearsal [for *Moon Over Soho*], we were all bowled over by his tireless search for all aspects of a life dominated by [the character's] tragic past, his mother's central European background and an obsession for [German director] Fritz Lang! The result – moving and very funny: he should remain a compelling study for actors of the future.'

While thrilled that Leonard had agreed to play the part, his reputation preceded him, as Ansorge later recalled: 'We did not meet until the day of the read-through, an event I approached in some trepidation. Leonard had a reputation for fastidiousness and even awkwardness at this stage of the production, tact never being uppermost in his mind when questioning young authors on minor or indeed major details in their scripts.

'He strode into the rehearsal room and on being introduced, nodded a greeting by flicking a glance at me rather like a lizard sizing up his prey. After the reading, he sidled across, not unlike the reptilian

Rigsby in *Rising Damp,* and his second sentence to me was: "Peter, there are some details I'm not happy with." For the next hour he probed the script mercilessly. Details were seized on: why had I chosen that particular link in the fourth speech on page 63? What did the stage direction on another page really mean? Instinctively, he uncovered awkward lines and thoughts that had not been remarked on previously by the director, producer or script editor (a very distinguished trio). At the end of the grilling he looked up and announced, "You see, Peter, I'm a great believer in understanding a writer's *intentions.*"

'Over the next few weeks I came to understand the truth of this statement. More questions were asked, even about his fellow actors' roles, but once a satisfactory answer had been given – and only then – a nod of agreement from Leonard would indicate that we were back on course. In this way I believe that Rossiter was able to pin down a character with remarkable precision and vitality. The dedication he brought to his acting is well known, as is the enormous energy with which his creations came to life. Less familiar (at least to me) was the apparent ease by which he could convey stillness, calm and quieter moments, with which he is perhaps not so closely associated.

'That's my earliest memory of the four days in the studio spent recording the play. The most emotional moments were dealt with calmly, directly, with no hint of sentiment, usually in just one take. He lit fireworks elsewhere in the play. It did seem to me that Leonard Rossiter was an actor who respected a writer's intentions.'

42

Curtain!

And, with that, all television shows or movies filmed and stored away in their canisters or chuntering away in the editing suites, Leonard Rossiter returned to the theatre one last time, to play a role that he had always sought: Inspector Truscott in *Loot*. Which brings us back to where we began.

'He was one of those people who came into his own later in life,' says his daughter, Camilla, 'He was never going to be a juvenile lead or romantic lead – he was a character actor. I think it would have been interesting, having the clout that he later achieved, to see what he would choose to do.'

It would have been interesting indeed: one cannot help but ponder on performances that may have been ahead. 'Every time I saw him I thought, this man is getting better and better,' says Don Warrington, 'and getting simpler, too. I know people think of him as a sort of manic performer but I thought he was coming to a second maturity.'

But then perhaps Leonard was always a man to burn bright and then vanish, that energy, that awe-inspiring drive . . . he was not a man to slow down, to creep into inertia as the years went on, much as many who knew and loved him might have wished otherwise.

'Comedy can kill you,' says Don Warrington, 'I think it killed Len.'

Perhaps so, but at least he has left a part of himself behind. 'It's strange,' says Camilla, on watching her father's performances today, 'because it's him and yet it's not, particularly Rigsby as the character is pretty horrible in many ways. But from my point of view it's quite nice to be able to see Dad. Obviously, it's not the same as having him with us, but it's the next best thing: a lot of people whose fathers have died don't have the chance to see them on the television all the time.' True, and certainly Leonard would have been happy to be remembered in this way.

'What he wanted,' continues Don Warrington, 'was for the world to see what he did, not who he was.'

For an actor, they can sometimes be one and the same thing.

The morning after his death, the *Sun* newspaper dedicated space to tributes from many of those who had known him:

> 'I can't believe it is true. I just pray that it is not true, that there is some mistake. Leonard was just such a wonderful man.'
>
> Joan Collins, co-star

> 'Leonard was a gifted comedy character actor who could make bad material good, and good material unforgettable.'
>
> Philip Jones, head of Thames TV

> 'His death is a sad loss – he was a marvellous actor.'
>
> John Barron, co-star and close friend

Jonathan Lynn, the director of his final play – *Loot* – was particularly distraught. 'I don't know why his impact on me was so great,' he said, 'but once Leonard was your friend, he was your friend with the same intensity that he brought to everything else. I grew to love him. When he died, I was more distraught than about any death that I can recall in the whole of my lifetime.

'Gillian asked me to speak the eulogy at his memorial service, which was a very difficult thing to do because I couldn't pretend that he was this easy-going, lovable guy. I couldn't make that kind of speech because the church was going to be full of a thousand people who knew him. So I said that he was a perfectionist and that I hoped God knew what he was in for, and that the Pearly Gates had better open on cue and the Heavenly Choir had better sing in tune, and it made everyone in the church rock with laughter because they all recognised the truth.'

And truth was what Rossiter was all about, as this extract from Lynn's eulogy attests:

The thing about Leonard was that you always knew where you were with him. He could never pretend. He was unable to ingratiate himself with anyone. But he was truthful. And truth is what art is all about. An actor is searching for truth in his way, no less than a philosopher or a clergyman. Leonard constantly searched within himself for the truth of every tiny moment in his performances. And in the process, that imitation of life by a great actor becomes a criticism of life. Truthful acting is truthful criticism, a search for honesty and illumination of how people behave in crisis, or in adversity, at high and low points in their lives.

This is what made Leonard the unique and irreplaceable artist that he was. Those who have nothing to say of their own can have no style because as an actor he genuinely had something to say about the human condition.

And finally, Leonard Rossiter's extraordinary life and career is wrapped up and preserved with Lynn's last comments: 'A true artist puts everything of himself into his work. Leonard, not a man to do anything by half measures, put his whole life and experience into it.'

List of Performances

THEATRE

The Gay Dog
Preston Repertory Company
Royal Hippodrome Preston
9/54
Leonard played Bert Gay
Writer: Joseph H. Colton
Director: Alan Foss

The Little Hut
Preston Repertory Company
Royal Hippodrome Preston
10/54
Leonard played First Stranger
Writer: André Roussin
Director: Anthony Finigan

The Sleeping Prince
Preston Repertory Company
Royal Hippodrome Preston
10/54
Leonard played First Footman
Writer: Terence Rattigan
Director: Geoffrey Wardwell

Come Live With Me
Preston Repertory Company
Royal Hippodrome Preston
10/54
Leonard played Gustave
Writers: Dorothy and Campbell Christie
Director: Geoffrey Wardwell

The Perfect Woman
Preston Repertory Company

Royal Hippodrome Preston
11/54
Leonard played Winkel
Writers: Wallace Geoffrey and Basil Mitchell
Director: Oliver Gordon

Dear Charles
Preston Repertory Company
Royal Hippodrome Preston
11/54
Leonard played Dominique Leclerc
Writer: Alan Melville
Director: Geoffrey Wardwell

The Burning Glass
Preston Repertory Company
Royal Hippodrome Preston
11/54
Leonard played Gerry Hardlip
Writer: Charles Morgan
Director: Geoffrey Wardwell

Loophole
Preston Repertory Company
Royal Hippodrome Preston
12/54
Leonard played Emrys Garron
Writer: Cecil Madden
Director: Geoffrey Wardwell

As Long As They're Happy
Preston Repertory Company
Royal Hippodrome Preston
12/54
Leonard played Hermann Schneider

Writer: Vernon Sylvaine
Director: Geoffrey Wardwell

Thark
Preston Repertory Company
Royal Hippodrome Preston
1/55
Leonard played Jones
Writer: Ben Travers
Director: Geoffrey Wardwell

The Man in Possession
Preston Repertory Company
Royal Hippodrome Preston
1/55
Leonard played Mr McAllister
Writer: H. M. Harwood
Director: Geoffrey Wardwell

The Orchard Walls
Preston Repertory Company
Royal Hippodrome Preston
1/55
Leonard played Godfrey Pritchard
Writer: R. F. Delderfield
Director: Adrian Cairns

When We Are Married
Preston Repertory Company
Royal Hippodrome Preston
2/55
Leonard played Alderman Joseph Helliwell
Writer: J. B. Priestley
Director: Geoffrey Wardwell

The Same Sky
Preston Repertory Company
Royal Hippodrome Preston
2/55
Leonard played Jeff Smith
Writer: Yvonne Mitchell
Director: Geoffrey Wardwell

Angels In Love
Wolverhampton Repertory Company
Grand Theatre, Wolverhampton

4/55
Leonard played Furse
Writer: Hugh Mills
Director: John Barron

A Day by The Sea
Wolverhampton Repertory Company
Grand Theatre, Wolverhampton
4/55
Leonard played David Hanson
Writer: N. C. Hunter
Director: John Barron

The Sleeping Prince
Wolverhampton Repertory Company
Grand Theatre, Wolverhampton
5/55
Leonard played Major-Domo
Writer: Terence Rattigan
Director: John Barron

Peril at End House
Wolverhampton Repertory Company
Grand Theatre, Wolverhampton
5/55
Leonard played Henry
Writer: Agatha Christie
Director: Geoffrey Lumsden

A Question of Fact
Wolverhampton Repertory Company
Grand Theatre, Wolverhampton
5/55
Leonard played Charles Trafford
Writer: Wynyard Browne
Director: John Barron

Both Ends Meet
Wolverhampton Repertory Company
Grand Theatre, Wolverhampton
5/55
Leonard played Sir George Treherne
Writer: Arthur Macrae
Director: John Barron

Rookery Nook
Wolverhampton Repertory Company

Grand Theatre, Wolverhampton
5/55
Leonard played Harold Twine
Writer: Ben Travers
Director: John Barron

The Secret Tent
Wolverhampton Repertory Company
Grand Theatre, Wolverhampton
6/55
Leonard played Inspector Thornton
Writer: Elizabeth Addyman
Director: John Barron

The Living Room
Wolverhampton Repertory Company
Grand Theatre, Wolverhampton
6/55
Leonard played Father James Browne
Writer: Graham Greene
Director: John Barron

Down Came a Blackbird
Wolverhampton Repertory Company
Grand Theatre, Wolverhampton
6/55
Leonard played Ali
Writer: Peter Blackmore
Director: John Barron

Love's a Luxury
Wolverhampton Repertory Company
Grand Theatre, Wolverhampton
7/55
Leonard played Mr Mole
Writers: Guy Paxton and Edward Hoile
Director: Geoffrey Lumsden

A Streetcar Named Desire
Wolverhampton Repertory Company
Grand Theatre, Wolverhampton
7/55
Leonard played Howard Mitchell
Writer: Tennessee Williams
Director: John Barron

Meet a Body
Wolverhampton Repertory Company
Grand Theatre, Wolverhampton
8/55
Leonard played Hawkins
Writers: Frank Launder and Sidney Gilliat
Director: John Barron

Little Lambs Eat Ivy
Wolverhampton Repertory Company
Grand Theatre, Wolverhampton
8/55
Leonard played Corder
Writer: Noel Langley
Director: Hazel Vincent Wallace

Witness for the Prosecution
Wolverhampton Repertory Company
Grand Theatre, Wolverhampton
8/55
Leonard played Leonard Vole
Writer: Agatha Christie
Director: by John Barron

Sabrina Fair
Wolverhampton Repertory Company
Grand Theatre, Wolverhampton
8/55
Leonard played Paul d'Argenson
Writer: Samuel Taylor
Director: John Barron

Beside the Seaside
Wolverhampton Repertory Company
Grand Theatre, Wolverhampton
8/55
Leonard played Wilf Pearson
Writer: Leslie Sands
Director: John Barron

Lady Windermere's Fan
Wolverhampton Repertory Company
Grand Theatre, Wolverhampton
9/55
Leonard played Mr Dumby
Writer: Oscar Wilde
Director: John Barron

It's Never Too Late
Wolverhampton Repertory Company
Grand Theatre, Wolverhampton
9/55
Leonard played Stephen Hodgson
Writer: Felicity Douglas
Director: Roger Winton

I Am A Camera
Wolverhampton Repertory Company
Grand Theatre, Wolverhampton
9/55
Leonard played Clive Mortimer
Writer: John van Druten
Director: John Barron

Seven Year Itch
Wolverhampton Repertory Company
Grand Theatre, Wolverhampton
9/55
Leonard played The Voice of Richard's
Conscience
Writer: George Axelrod
Director: John Barron

Seagulls over Sorrento
Wolverhampton Repertory Company
Grand Theatre, Wolverhampton
10/55
Leonard played Able Seaman Badger
Writer: Hugh Hastings
Director: John Barron

Anna Christie
Wolverhampton Repertory Company
Grand Theatre, Wolverhampton
10/55
Leonard played Chris Christopherson
Writer: Eugene O'Neill
Director: John Barron

Au Revoir
Wolverhampton Repertory Company
Grand Theatre, Wolverhampton
10/55
Leonard played various roles
Writers: Various

Director: John Barron

The Bespoke Overcoat
Salisbury Repertory Company
The Playhouse, Salisbury
11/55
Leonard played Mr Morry
Writer: Wolf Mankowitz
Director: Joan White

The Respectable Prostitute
Salisbury Repertory Company
The Playhouse, Salisbury
11/55
Leonard played The Negro
Writer: Jean-Paul Sartre
Director: Joan White

She Would and She Would Not
Salisbury Repertory Company
The Playhouse, Salisbury
12/55
Leonard played Trappanti
Writer: Colley Cibber
Director: John Barron

Robinson Crusoe
Wolverhampton Repertory Company
Grand Theatre, Wolverhampton
12/55
Leonard played King Neptune and Man
Friday
Writers: Harry Bright and Peter Powell
Director: Peter Powell

Book of the Month
Salisbury Repertory Company
The Playhouse, Salisbury
4/56 Leonard played Dr MacLure
Writer: Basil Thomas
Director: John Barron

Busman's Honeymoon
Salisbury Repertory Company
The Playhouse, Salisbury
4/56
Leonard played Superintendent Kirk

Writer: Dorothy L. Sayers
Director: Basil Foster

I Killed the Count
Wolverhampton Repertory Company
Grand Theatre, Wolverhampton
4/56
Leonard played Samuel Diamond
Writer: Alec Coppel
Director: Peter Aldersley

Simon and Laura
Wolverhampton Repertory Company
Grand Theatre, Wolverhampton
4/56
Leonard played Mr Wolfstein
Writer: Alan Melville
Director: Peter Aldersley

Spring at Marino
Wolverhampton Repertory Company
Grand Theatre, Wolverhampton
5/56
Leonard played Prokovitch
Writer: Constance Cox
Director: Peter Aldersley

My Three Angels
Wolverhampton Repertory Company
Grand Theatre, Wolverhampton
5/56
Leonard played Joseph
Writers: Sam and Bella Spewak
Director: Peter Aldersley

Alibi
Wolverhampton Repertory Company
Grand Theatre, Wolverhampton
5/56
Leonard played Hercule Poirot
Writer: Agatha Christie
Director: Peter Aldersley

All for Mary
Wolverhampton Repertory Company
Grand Theatre, Wolverhampton

5/56
Leonard played Alphonse
Writers: Harold Brooke and Kay Bannerman
Director: Peter Aldersley

Lucky Strike
Wolverhampton Repertory Company
Grand Theatre, Wolverhampton
6/56
Leonard played Charlie Maggs
Writer: Michael Brett
Director: Peter Aldersley

Jupiter Laughs
Wolverhampton Repertory Company
Grand Theatre, Wolverhampton
6/56
Leonard played Dr Drewitt
Writer: A. J. Cronin
Director: Peter Aldersley

The Miser
Wolverhampton Repertory Company
Grand Theatre, Wolverhampton
6/56
Leonard played Harpagon
Writer: Molière
Director: Peter Aldersley

Murder at the Grand
Wolverhampton Repertory Company
Grand Theatre, Wolverhampton
7/56
Leonard played Leonard (the play was specifically written for the company, hence the character shares Leonard's name)
Writer: H. Bromley-Chapman
Director: Peter Aldersley

The Middle Watch
Wolverhampton Repertory Company
Grand Theatre, Wolverhampton
7/56
Leonard played Marine Ogg
Writers: Ian Hay and Stephen King-Hall
Director: Peter Aldersley

Running Wild
Wolverhampton Repertory Company
Grand Theatre, Wolverhampton
7/56
Leonard played Arthur Popplejoy
Writer: Ben Leather
Director: Peter Powell

Appointment with Death
Wolverhampton Repertory Company
Grand Theatre, Wolverhampton
7/56
Leonard played Dr Thodore Gerard
Writer: Agatha Christie
Director: Peter Aldersley

My Wife's Lodger
Wolverhampton Repertory Company
Grand Theatre, Wolverhampton
8/56
Leonard played Willie Higginbotham
Writer: Dominic Roche
Director: Peter Aldersley

The Red-headed Blonde
Wolverhampton Repertory Company
Grand Theatre, Wolverhampton
8/56
Leonard played Jonathan Maxwell
Writer: Val Guest
Director: Kenneth Keeling

Of Mice and Men
Wolverhampton Repertory Company
Grand Theatre, Wolverhampton
8/56
Leonard played Candy
Writer: John Steinbeck
Director: Peter Aldersley

The Food of Love
Wolverhampton Repertory Company
Grand Theatre, Wolverhampton
8/56
Leonard played Owen Thomas
Writer: Christopher Bond
Director: Peter Aldersley

Arsenic and Old Lace
Wolverhampton Repertory Company
Grand Theatre, Wolverhampton
9/56
Leonard played Dr Einstein
Writer: Joseph Kesselring
Director: Peter Aldersley

Springtime
Wolverhampton Repertory Company
Grand Theatre, Wolverhampton
9/56
Leonard played Dick Goddard
Writers: F. Ryerson and C. Clements
(adapted by Basil Thomas)
Director: William Avenell

Ah, Wilderness
Wolverhampton Repertory Company
Grand Theatre, Wolverhampton
9/56
Leonard played Richard Miller
Writer: Eugene O'Neill
Director: Nancy Poultney

Our Wife
Wolverhampton Repertory Company
Grand Theatre, Wolverhampton
9/56
Leonard played Ted Sparrow
Writer: Leslie Sands
Director: Leslie Sands

Shadow of Doubt
Wolverhampton Repertory Company
Grand Theatre, Wolverhampton
10/56
Leonard played Manning
Writer: Norman King
Director: Peter Aldersley

The Happiest Days of Your Life
Wolverhampton Repertory Company
Grand Theatre, Wolverhampton
10/56
Leonard played Rainbow
Writer: John Dighton

Director: Peter Aldersley

One Bright Day
Wolverhampton Repertory Company
Grand Theatre, Wolverhampton
10/56
Leonard played Paul La Barca
Writer: Sigmund Miller
Director: Peter Aldersley

The Tender Trap
Wolverhampton Repertory Company
Grand Theatre, Wolverhampton
10/56
Leonard played Joe McGall
Writers: Max Shulman and Robert Paul Smith
Director: Peter Aldersley

This Year Next Year
Wolverhampton Repertory Company
Grand Theatre, Wolverhampton
10/56
Leonard played Martin Armitage
Writer: Lionel Brown
Director: John Myers

East Lynne
Wolverhampton Repertory Company
Grand Theatre, Wolverhampton
11/56
Leonard played Mr Dill
Writer: Mrs Henry Wood
Director: Peter Aldersley

A Cuckoo in the Nest
Salisbury Repertory Company
The Playhouse, Salisbury
11/56
Leonard played Major George Bone
Writer: Ben Travers
Director: Frederick Peisley

The Food of Love
Salisbury Repertory Company
The Playhouse, Salisbury

11/56
Leonard played Owen Thomas
Writer: Christopher Bond
Director: Frederick Peisley

A Christmas Carol
The Alexandra Theatre, Birmingham
12/56
Leonard played Scrooge
Writer: John Maxwell (based on the novella by Charles Dickens)
Director: John Maxwell

Babes in the Wood
Salisbury Repertory Company
The Playhouse, Salisbury
12/56
Leonard played 'Len (the not-so-bad robber)'
Writer: Henry Marshall
Director: Terence Dudley

Full House
Salisbury Repertory Company
The Playhouse, Salisbury
2/57
Leonard played Mr Rosenblatt
Writer: Ivor Novello
Director: Frederick Peisley

The Cure for Love
Salisbury Repertory Company
The Playhouse, Salisbury
3/57
Leonard played Jack Hardacre
Writer: Walter Greenwood
Director: Terence Dudley

Free as Air
Savoy Theatre, London
6/57
Leonard played two roles: John and Reporter
Writers: Julian Slade and Dorothy Reynolds
Director: Denis Carey

The Iceman Cometh
Touring
11/58
Leonard played Ed Masher
Writer: Eugene O'Neill
Director: Toby Robertson

The Brass Butterfly
Salisbury Repertory Company
The Playhouse, Salisbury
3/59
Leonard played Phanocles
Writer: William Golding
Director: Oliver Gordon

Thark
Salisbury Repertory Company
The Playhouse, Salisbury
3/59
Leonard played Sir Hector Benbow
Writer: Ben Travers
Director: Oliver Gordon

A View from the Bridge
Salisbury Repertory Company
The Playhouse, Salisbury
4/59
Leonard played First Immigration Officer
Writer: Arthur Miller
Director: Oliver Gordon

French without Tears
Salisbury Repertory Company
The Playhouse, Salisbury
4/59
Leonard played Monsieur Maingot
Writer: Terence Rattigan
Director: Oliver Gordon

The Tunnel of Love
Salisbury Repertory Company
The Playhouse, Salisbury
4/59
Leronard played Augie Poole
Writers: Joseph Fields and Peter De Vries
Director: Oliver Gordon

Gigi
Salisbury Repertory Company
The Playhouse, Salisbury
5/59
Leonard played Victor
Writer: Colette, adapted by Anita Loos
Director: Oliver Gordon

Something to Hide
Salisbury Repertory Company
The Playhouse, Salisbury
5/59
Leonard played Inspector Davies
Writer: Leslie Sands
Director: Ian Mullins

Gaslight
Salisbury Repertory Company
The Playhouse, Salisbury
6/59
Leonard played Rough
Writer: Patrick Hamilton
Director: Rolf Dieter

The Love Match
The Richmond Theatre, London
8/59
Leonard played Bill Brown
Writer: Glenn Melvyn
Directed: Jack Williams

The Clandestine Marriage
The Old Vic Company
Theatre Royal, Bristol
9/59
Leonard played Canton
Writers: George Colman and David Garrick
Director: John Hale

Romeo and Juliet
The Old Vic Company
Theatre Royal, Bristol
10/59
Leonard played two roles, Sampson & Friar John
Writer: William Shakespeare
Director: John Hale

The Silent Woman
The Old Vic Company
Theatre Royal, Bristol
11/59
Leonard played Sir John Daw
Writer: Ben Jonson
Director: John Hale

The Long and the Short and the Tall
The Old Vic Company
Theatre Royal, Bristol
12/59
Leonard played Private Bamforth
Writer: Willis Hall
Director: David Scace

Hooray for Daisy!
The Old Vic Company
Theatre Royal, Bristol
12/59
Leonard played Harry Tuck
Writers: Julian Slade and Dorothy Reynolds
Director: Denis Carey

A Taste of Honey
The Old Vic Company
Theatre Royal, Bristol
2/60
Leonard played Peter
Writer: Shelagh Delaney
Director: John Hale

Mary Stuart
The Old Vic Company
Theatre Royal, Bristoeeel
3/60
Leonard played Lord Burleigh
Writer: Stephen Spender (from the original
by Friedrich Schiller)
Director: John Hale

The Woodcarver
The Old Vic Company
Theatre Royal, Bristol
4/60
Leonard played Griff
Writer: Morris Brown

Director: Prunella Scales

She Stoops to Conquer
The Old Vic Company
Theatre Royal, Bristol
5/60
Leonard played Tony Lumpkin
Writer: Oliver Goldsmith
Director: Dudley Jones

The Hostage
The Old Vic Company
Theatre Royal, Bristol
6/60
Leonard played Pat
Writer: Brendan Behan
Director: John Hale

The Comedy of Errors
The Old Vic Company
Theatre Royal, Bristol
6/60
Leonard played Dromio of Syracuse
Writer: William Shakespeare
Director: John Hale

Romeo and Juliet
The Old Vic Company
Theatre Royal, Bristol
7/60
Leonard played Friar Lawrence
Writer: William Shakespeare
Director: John Hale

Rhinoceros
The Old Vic Company
Theatre Royal, Bristol
9/60
Leonard played The Logician
Writer: Eugène Ionesco
Director: John Hale

The Tempest
The Old Vic Company
Theatre Royal, Bristol
9/60
Leonard played Stephano

Writer: William Shakespeare
Director: John Hale

Caesar and Cleopatra
The Old Vic Company
Theatre Royal, Bristol
11/60
Leonard played Rufio
Writer: George Bernard Shaw
Director: Tony Robertson

One-Way Pendulum
The Old Vic Company
Theatre Royal, Bristol
11/60
Leonard played Arthur Groomkiby
Writer: N. F. Simpson
Director: Alan Bridges

Dick Whittington
The Old Vic Company
Theatre Royal, Bristol
12/60
Leonard played Cicely Suett
Writers: V. C. Clinton-Baddely and Gavin
Gordon
Director: Frank Dunlop

Roots
The Old Vic Company
Theatre Royal, Bristol
2/61
Leonard played Mr Bryant
Writer: Arnold Wesker
Director: Duncan Ross

A Passage to India
The Old Vic Company
Theatre Royal, Bristol
4/61
Leonard played Richard Fielding
Writer: Santha Rama Rau (based on the
novel by E.M. Forster)
Director: Alan Bridges

Richard II
The Old Vic Company

Theatre Royal, Bristol
4/61
Leonard played Henry Bolingbroke
Writer: William Shakespeare
Director: John Hale

The Killer
The Old Vic Company
Theatre Royal, Bristol
5/61
Leonard played two roles: The Architect
and Second Policeman
Writer: Eugène Ionesco (translated by
Donald Watson)
Director: John Hale

A Man for All Seasons
The Old Vic Company
Theatre Royal, Bristol
6/61
Leonard played The Common Man
Writer: Robert Bolt
Director: Warren Jenkins

Goat Song
The Old Vic Company
Theatre Royal, Bristol
6/61
Leonard played Celestino
Writer: Martin Shuttleworth
Director: John Hale

North City Traffic Straight Ahead
The Gaiety Theatre, Dublin
9/61
Leonard played Harry Hopkins
Writer: James Douglas
Director: Alan Simpson

The Caretaker
The Leatherhead Theatre Club
11/61
Leonard played Davies
Writer: Harold Pinter
Director: Gareth Davies

The Recruiting Officer
The Playhouse, Nottingham
2/62
Leonard played Sergeant Kite
Writer: George Farquhar
Director: Frank Dunlop

Semi-Detached
Belgrade Theatre, Coventry
6/62
Leonard played Fred Midway
Writer: David Turner
Director: Tony Richardson

Arms and the Man
Belgrade Theatre, Coventry
6/62
Leonard played Sergius Saranoff
Writer: George Bernard Shaw
Director: David Forder

Red Roses for Me
The Mermaid Theatre, London
9/62
Leonard played Brennan o' the Moor
Writer: Sean O'Casey
Director: Julius Gellner

Semi-Detached
Belgrade Theatre, Coventry
9/63
Leonard played Fred Midway
Writer: David Turner
Director: Anthony Richardson

Semi-Detached
Music Box Theatre, New York
10/63
Leonard played Fred Midway
Writer: David Turner
Director: Anthony Richardson

Hamp
The Theatre Royal, Newcastle
8/64
Leonard played Lieutenant Tom Webb
Writer: John Wilson

Director: John Gibson

Ghosts
The Theatre Royal, Stratford East
4/65
Leonard played Pastor Menders
Writer: Henrik Ibsen (translated by Michael Meyer)
Director: Adrian Rendle

Volpone
The Playhouse, Oxford
9/66
Leonard played Corvino
Writer: Ben Jonson
Director: Frank Hauser

The Rules of the Game
The Playhouse, Oxford
10/66
Leonard played Leone Gala
Writer: Luigi Pirandello
Director: James Grout

Volpone
The Garrick Theatre, London
1/67
Leonard played Corvino
Writer: Ben Jonson
Director: Frank Hauser

The Resistible Rise of Arturo Ui
The Citizen's Theatre, Glasgow
9/67
Leonard played Arturo Ui
Writer: Bertolt Brecht (adapted by George Tabori)
Director: Michael Blakemore

The Resistible Rise of Arturo Ui
Lyceum Theatre, Edinburgh
8/68
Leonard played Arturo Ui
Writer: Bertolt Brecht (adapted by George Tabori)
Director: Michael Blakemore

The Strange Case of Martin Richter
The Hampstead Theatre Club,
London 11/68
Leonard played Martin Richter
Writer: Stanley Eveling
Director: Michael Blakemore

The Resistible Rise of Arturo Ui
The Playhouse, Nottingham
4/69
Leonard played Arturo Ui
Writer: Bertolt Brecht (adapted by George Tabori)
Director: Michael Blakemore

The Resistible Rise of Arturo Ui
The Saville Theatre, London
7/69
Leonard played Arturo Ui
Writer: Bertolt Brecht (adapted by George Tabori)
Director: Michael Blakemore

The Heretic
Duke of York's Theatre, London
7/70
Leonard played Giordano Bruno
Writer: Morris West
Directors: Morris West and Joseph O'Connor

Disabled
The Hampstead Theatre Club, London
5/71
Leonard played Barker
Writer: Peter Ransley
Director: Vivian Matalon

Richard III
The Playhouse, Nottingham
9/71
Leonard played Richard III
Writer: William Shakespeare
Director: Peter McEnery

The Caretaker
The Mermaid Theatre, London
3/72
Leonard played the part of Davies
Writer: Harold Pinter
Director: Christopher Morahan

The Banana Box
Adeline Genee Theatre,
East Grinstead
3/73
Leonard played Rooksby
Writer: Eric Chappell
Director: David Scace

The Banana Box
Apollo Theatre, London
6/73
Leonard played Rooksby
Writer: Eric Chappell
Director: David Scace

Abel, Where Is Your Brother?
Act-In Theatre Club, Piccadilly
London
5/74
Leonard played two roles the Narrator & I
Writer: Julius Edliss (translated by Ariadne Nicolaeff)
Director: Amos Mokadi

The Looneys
The Hampstead Theatre Club,
London
10/74
Leonard played Brian
Writer: John Antrobus
Director: Michael Rudman

A Christmas Carol
Touring
12/75
Leonard played Scrooge
Writer: Charles Dickens
Director: Michael Fabian

The Frontiers of Farce
The Old Vic Company
Theatre Royal Bristol

10/76
Two one-act farces, *The Purging* and *The Singer*. Leonard played Flovine in the former and Dhuring in the latter.
Writers: Georges Feydeau and Frank Wedekind (adapted by Peter Barnes)
Director: Peter Barnes

Tartuffe
The Greenwich Theatre, London
12/76
Leonard played Tartuffe
Writer: Molière (translated by David Thompson)
Director: David Thompson

The Immortal Haydon
The Mermaid Theatre, London
12/77
Leonard played Haydon in this one-man show
Writer: John Wells
Director: Alan Strachan

The Immortal Haydon
The Greenwich Theatre, London
1/78
Leonard played Haydon in this one-man show
Writer: John Wells
Director: Alan Strachan

Semi-Detached
The Greenwich Theatre, London (plus tour)
2/79
Leonard played Fred Midway
Writer: David Turner
Directors: Leonard Rossiter and Alan Strachan

Make and Break
The Lyric Theatre, London
3/80
Leonard played Garrard
Writer: Michael Frayn
Director: Michael Blakemore

Make and Break
Haymarket Theatre, London
4/80
Leonard played Garrard
Writer: Michael Frayn
Director: Michael Blakemore

The Rules of the Game
Theatre Royal, Nottingham
8/82
Leonard played Leone Gala
Writer: Luigi Pirandello (translated by Robert Rietty and Noel Gregeen)
Director: Anthony Quayle

The Rules of the Game
Theatre Royal, London
9/82
Leonard played Leone Gala
Writer: Luigi Pirandello (translated by Robert Rietty and Noel Gregeen)
Director: Anthony Quayle

The Rules of the Game
Phoenix Theatre , London
10/82
Leonard played Leone Gala
Writer: Luigi Pirandello (translated by Robert Rietty and Noel Gregeen)
Director: Anthony Quayle

Tartuffe
Churchill Theatre, Bromley
6/83
Leonard played Tartuffe
Writer: Molière (adapted by Miles Malleson)
Director: Peter Coe March 1984, then September 1984

Loot
Ambassadors Theatre, London
3/84
Leonard played Truscott
Writer: Joe Orton
Director: Jonathan Lynn

261

Loot
Lyric Theatre, London
9/84
Leonard played Truscott
Writer: Joe Orton
Director: Jonathan Lynn

TELEVISION

Story Conference
BBC
3/56
Leonard Rossiter (Leo Borowitz)
Other cast unknown
Writer: Donald Wilson (from a story by
Norman Holland)
Director: Victor Menzies
Producer: Victor Menzies

The Nightwatchman's Stories
'The Constable's Move'
BBC
4/2/59
Wally Patch (Bill), Leslie Dwyer (Bob
Grummit), Esma Cannon (Mrs Grummit),
Meredith Edwards (PC Evans) Ann Wilton
(Mrs Evans), Frank Atkinson (Landlord),
Leonard Rossiter (Joe Stocks), Arthur
Brough (Alf Smith)
Writer: Donal Giltinan (from a story by
W.W. Jacobs)
Director: Terence Dudley
Producer: Peter Dews

You Can't Win
'The One That Got Away'
BBC
12/10/61
Frank Finlay (George Lander), John Gill
(Gigs), Humphrey Heathcote (Prison
Officer), Miki Iveria (Woman in Printers),
Virginia Maskell (Elsa Lander), Glyn Owen
(Det. Sgt. Holiday), Leonard Rossiter
(Fenny), Christopher Steele (Craven),
Charles Wade (Waiter), Kenneth J. Warren
(Brewer), Manning Wilson (Falden,

Margery Withers (Mrs Kern)
Writer: Berkely Mather
Director: Alan Bridges
Producer: Alan Bridges

'Studio 4'
The Farquhar Connection
BBC
12/02/62
(also referred to as 'The Intrigue', the title
of the novel upon which the drama was
based)
Anthony Bate (Sege Laurière), Mark
Brackenbury, Leonard Fenton, Frank Finlay
(Fernand Destayac), Louis Haslar, Alfred
Hoffman, Philip Howard, Mary McMillan,
Phyllis Montefiore, Allison Morris (Dark-
haired Girl), Leonard Rossiter (Gérard
Moustier), John Slavid, Marjorie Wilde,
Elaine Williams, Pauline Yates
Writers: Rudolph Cartier, Gerald Hanley,
Roger Smith and Tony Webster from an
original novel by Jacques Natanson,
translated by Mona Andrade
Director: Rudolph Cartier
Producer: Alvin Rakoff

'ITV Television Playhouse'
The Morning After
ATV
16/11/62
Peter Birrell (The Young Man), Annette
Crosbie (Liz), Suzan Farmer (The Young
Actress), Michael Lynch (The Painter),
Juliet Mills, (Carol), April Olrich (Lalage),
Robin Phillips (Alan), Pamela Reece (The
Model), Leonard Rossiter (Harry), Jerry
Stovin (Sam)
Writer: G. C. Brown
Director: John Hale

Z Cars
BBC
9/1/63–27/3/63
'Trumpet Voluntary'
9/1/63
David Andrews (Dennis Gibbs), June Barry

(Olwen Rhys), John Bennett (Ringer), Brian Blessed (PC Smith), Joseph Brady (PC Weir), James Cossins (Sgt. Michaelson), Douglas Cummings (Customer), Peter Duguid (Eddy), Terence Edmond (PC Sweet), Cameron Hall (Rolly), Barry Keegan (Tom Gibbs), Fred Kitchen Jr. (Briggs), Hilary Martin (Joan Longton), Leonard Rossiter (Det. Insp. Bamber), Robin Wentworth (Cooper), Richard Wilding (Customer), Derek Williams (Barman), Frank Windsor (Det. Sgt. Watt)
Writer: Allan Prior
Director: Roger Jenkins
Producer: David E. Rose

'The Hitch-Hiker'
23/1/63
Brian Blessed (PC Smith), Joseph Brady (PC Weir), Terence Edmond (PC Sweet), Robert Keegan (Sgt Blacklitt), Frank Windsor (Det. Sgt Watt), Lynne Furlong (WPC. Stacey), Frank Hawkins (Duty Officer), Hilary Martyn (Joan Longton), Leonard Rossiter (Det. Insp. Bamber), David Warner (Gee), Donald Burton (Det. Con. Little), Ron Falk (Warden), Douglas Harris (1st Garage Attendant), Geoffrey Keen (Fred Parker), Clare Kelly (Winnie Parker), Terry Maidment (PC), Peter Marden (2nd Garage Attendant), George Roderick (Tramp), Brian Tipping (Moped Owner)
Writer: Allan Prior
Director: Michael Leeston-Smith
Producer: David E. Rose

'Act of Vengeance'
6/2/63
Stratford Johns (Det. Insp. Barlow), Brian Blessed (PC Smith), Joseph Brady (PC Weir), Terence Edmond (PC Sweet), Robert Keegan (Sgt Blacklitt), Hilary Martyn (Joan Longton), Leonard Rossiter (Det. Insp. Bamber), Bee Duffell (Mollie Sugden), Edmund Bailey (Roger Hallam),

Gillian Barclay (Evie Scott), Margaret Boyd (Mrs Corbett), Peggy Ann Clifford (Big Annie), Paul Eddington (Stan Ferris), Glenda Jackson (Hospital Nurse), Bert Palmer (Tom Sugden). Ken Perry (Cato Jones), Frank Petitt (Salvation Army Captain), Mairhi Russell (Salvationist), Pauline Williams (Norma Ferris)
Writer: Leslie Sands
Director: Roger Jenkins
Producer: David E. Rose

'The Listeners'
13/2/63
Brian Blessed (PC Smith), Joseph Brady (PC Weir), Terence Edmond (PC Sweet), Robert Keegan (Sgt Blacklitt), Frank Windsor (Det. Sgt Watt), Colin Welland (PC Graham), James Ellis (PC Lynch), Frank Hawkins (Duty Officer), Hilary Martyn (Joan Longton), Leonard Rossiter (Det. Insp. Bamber), Sandra Barry (Fiona), Christopher Coll (Mike), George Coulouris (Watchman), David Hargreaves (Mechanic), Thomas Hethcote (Harry Mather), Bill Horsky (Det. Con. Smethurst), Mary MacKenzie (Martha Mather), Jack Melford (Rigby), Norman Mitchell (PC Adams), Christopher Sandford (Terry)
Writer: Allan Prior
Director: Shaun Sutton
Producer: David E. Rose

'Follow My Leader'
27/2/63
Stratford Johns (Det. Chief Inspector Barlow), Terence Edmond (PC Sweet), Robert Keegan (Sgt Blacklitt), Frank Windsor (Det. Sgt Watt), Colin Welland (PC Graham), James Ellis (PC Lynch), Frank Hawkins (Duty Officer), Michael Forrest (Det. Con. Hicks), Hilary Martyn (Joan Longton), Leonard Rossiter (Det. Insp. Bamber), Peggy Aitchison (Landlady), David Burke (Johnny Oulton), Aletha Charlton (Millie Lovegrove), Leslie Cinrad

(PC), Michelle Hayes (Girl), Ann King (Mrs Auger), George Little (Gurney), Martin Matthews (Owen Sutcliffe), Henry McCarthy (Taggart), Lane Meddick (Garston), Michael Randell (Brian Braddon), Rosemary Rogers (Mrs Dobie), Benn Simons (Gaoler), Maragaret St Barbe West (Mrs carr), Kenneth Waller (Stanley Collins), Tom Watson (Lomax), Brian Wilde (George Webster)
Writer: John Hopkins
Director: Alan Bromly
Producer: David E. Rose

'Members Only'
6/3/63
Brian Blessed (PC Smith), Joseph Brady (PC Weir), Terence Edmond (PC Sweet), Robert Keegan (Sgt Blacklitt), Frank Windsor (Det. Sgt Watt), Colin Welland (PC Graham), James Ellis (PC Lynch), Hilary Martyn (Joan Longton), Leonard Rossiter (Det. Insp. Bamber), Colin Bean (Mr Cowper), Billy Cornelius (Regan), Bill Davies (Councillor Dean), James East (Barman), Joan Frank (Mrs Regan), Jimmy Gardner (Wally Kirkbridge), Richard Jacques (Andy Firsk), Steve Kirby (Bandleader), Reginald Marsh (Reg Peterson), Alex Munro (Robin Dean), Derek Nimmo (Bill Wignall), Lee Richardson (Larry Gilchrist), Janette Richer (Mrs Milburn), Colin Rix (Eddie Milburn), John Walker (George Harvey), Derek Ware (Man in Club)
Writer: John Hopkins
Director: Michael Leeston-Smith
Producer: David E. Rose

'Matter of Conviction'
13/3/63
Stratford Johns (Det. Chief Inspector Barlow), Terence Edmond (PC Sweet), Robert Keegan (Sgt Blacklitt), Frank Windsor (Det. Sgt Watt), Colin Welland (PC Graham), James Ellis (PC Lynch), Lynne Furlong (WPC Stacey), Ken Jones (Det. Con. Smithers), Hilary Martyn (Joan Longton), Leonard Rossiter (Det Insp. Bamber), Leslie Sands (Det. Supt. Miller), Dorothy Gordon (Doris Morris), Mary Hignett (Mrs Jenkins), Dennis Ramsden (Landlord), Marian Spencer (Mrs Morris), John Stratton (Henry Morris)
Writer: Elwyn Jones
Director: Shaun Sutton
Producer: David E. Rose

'Enquiry'
27/3/63
Stratford Johns (Det. Chief Inspector Barlow), Brian Blessed (PC Smith), Joseph Brady (PC Weir), Terence Edmond (PC Sweet), Robert Keegan (Sgt Blacklitt), Frank Windsor (Det. Sgt Watt), Colin Welland (PC Graham), James Ellis (PC Lynch), Leonard Rossiter (Det. Insp. Bamber), Sidonie Bond (Betty Clayton), Stanley Walsh (PC Hodgson), Michael Collins (Gould), Felicity Gordon (Mrs Haywood), Michael Graham (PC Haywood), Robert James (Maison), Diana Oxford (Canteen Girl), Neville Smith (Larry Dodd), Alister Williamson (Garrett), Christopher Wray (PC Anderson)
Writer: John Hopkins
Director: William Slater
Producer: David E. Rose

'ITV Play of the Week'
The Buried Man
Rediffusion
12/2/63
Leonard Rossiter (Robert Bailey), June Brown (Madge Bailey), Gwen Nelson (Mary Bailey), Ray Barrett (Jack Bailey), Michael Williams (Alan Bailey), Charmian Eyre (Joan Morton), Stanley Meadows (Bill Morton), Stan Jay (Workman), Nan Kerr (Vera Shaw)
Writer: David Mercer
Director: Graham Evans
Producer: Peter Graham Scott

Suspense:
'Walk in Fear'

BBC
6/5/63
June Barrie (Rita), Sandra Bryant (Girl), Constance Chapman (Mrs Heath), Peter Claughton (Mr Hodge), Alan Collins (First Youth), Hamilton Dyce (Doctor), Ann Firbank (Helen Treece), Kathleen Michael (Suasan Hartley), Jane Muir (Brenda Robins), Valerie Newman (Office Girl), Leonard Rossiter (Alan Treece), Phyllis Smale (Mrs Robins)
Writer: John Wilkie
Director: Patrick Dromgoole
Producer: Patrick Dromgoole

'Maupassant'
The Story of a Farm Girl
Granada
1/8/63
Geoffrey Bayldon (Clive Marshall), Leonard Rossiter (Valin)
Writer: Doris Lessing (based on a story by Guy de Maupassant
Director: Silvio Narizzano
Producer: Philip Mackie

'ITV Television Playhouse'
The Fruit At The Bottom of The Bowl
ATV
8/8/63
Leonard Rossiter (William Acton)
Writer: Ilona Ference (from a story by Ray Bradbury)
Director:John Hale

'First Night'
It's All Lovely
BBC
22/12/63
Tony Tanner (Charlie), Sally Smith (Janet), Leonard Rossiter (Sammy Love), Dilys Laye (Barbara), Duncan Macrae (Jamie)
Writer: David Proudfoot
Director: Peter Graham Scott
Producer: John Elliott

'The Avengers'
Dressed to Kill
ITV
28/12/63
Patrick Macnee (John Steed), Honor Blackman (Catherine Gale), Alexander Davion (Napoleon), Leon Eagles (Newman), Peter Fontaine (First Officer), John Junkin (Sheriff), Richard Leech (Policeman), Frank Maher (Barman). Leonard Rossiter (Robin Hood), Anneke Wills (Pussy Cat), Anthea Windham (Highwaywoman)
Writer: Brian Clemens
Director: Bill Bain
Producer: John Bryce

Steptoe and Son
'The Lead Man Cometh'
BBC1
21/1/64
Harry H. Corbett (Harold), Wilfrid Brambell (Albert), Leonard Rossiter (Huw the Pew), Bill Maxim (Policeman)
Writers: Ray Galton and Alan Simpson
Director: Duncan Wood
Producer: Duncan Wood

'ITV Play of the Week'
Flight from Reality
ATV
13/4/64
Annette Crosbie (Frances), Richard Leech (Paul), William Lucas (Vincent), Philip Madoc (John), Jean Trend (Rose), Jan Waters (Jill) Leonard Rossiter (Patrick)
Writer: Leo Lehman
Director: John Hale
Producer: Peter Graham Scott

'Festival'
Justin Thyme
BBC
15/4/64
Giselle (Jane Merrow), Daudet (Leonard Rossiter)
Writers: John Bluthal, Robert Fuest and Joe

McGrath
Director: Joe McGrath
Producer: Peter Luke

'Love Story'
Beggars and Choosers
ATV
7/7/64
Nicholas Bennett (Private Horner), James Culliford (Private Mason), Avril Elgar (Louise), Marjie Lawrence (Anne Riley), Patrick Newell (Sgt. Arthur Shrubsole), Leonard Rossiter (Sgt. 'Tubby' Watson
Writer: Douglas Livingstone
Director: Eric Price
Producer: Stella Richman

House of Glass
Unbroadcast
Douglas Livingstone (Private Milton), Bill Owen (Private Wilky), Patrick Westwood (Gunner Tucker) Bryan Marshall (Private Oliver), Neil McCarthy (Guardsman Pollock), Sean Lynch (Fusilier Rice), Derek Benfield (Sapper Maggs), Nicholas Pennell (Private Henry), David Davenport (Sgt. Morrison), Michael Smee (Sgt. Jones), Bob Bryan (Sgt. Williams), Robert Dean (Padre), Leonard Rossiter (Sgt. Golto)
Writer: Mike Watts
Director: Michael Currer-Briggs

'Thursday Theatre': *Celebration*
BBC
4/3/65
Trevor Bannister (Jack Lucas), Angela Crow (Irene Howes), Noel Dyson (Rhoda Lucas), Dudley Foster (Sgt. Maj. Tommy Lodge), Nancie Jackson (Lilian Howes), Leslie Lawton (Stan Dyson), Jane Muir (Christine Lucas), Jenny Oulton (Margo Fuller), Bert Palmer (Edgar Lucas), Linda Polan (May Beckett), Leonard Rossiter (Frank Broadbent), Derek Smee (Lionel Fuller), Brian Smith (Bernard Fuller), Julian Somers (Arthur Broadbent), Jane Tann (Edna Fuller), Joan Young (Alice

Fuller)
Writers: Keith Waterhouse and Willis Hall
Director: Mary Ridge
Producer: Bernard Hepton

***Cluff*: 'The Fire Raiser'**
BBC1
19/6/65
Leslie Sands (Det. Sgt. Caleb Cluff), Michael Bates (Insp. Mole), Olive Milbourn (Annie Croft), John Rolfe (Det. Const. Barker), John McKelvey (PC Arthur Bullock), Jack Howlett (Dr Hamm), Charles Carson (Benjamin Stirk), Kate Coleridge (Polly Stirk), Jane Fergus (Harriet Cobb), Eric Longworth (Fred Robson), Leonard Rossiter (Wilkie), Diana Scougall (April Cobb), Jack Smethurst (Sammy Shaw)
Writer: Gil North
Director: Terence Dudley
Producer: Terence Dudley

'ITV Play of the Week': *Between the Two of Us*
ATV
19/7/65
Angela Crow (Girl), Tommy Godfrey (Publican), Barbara Lott (Woman), Leonard Rossiter (Man), John Woodvine (Detective)
Writer: Rhys Adrian
Director: Graham Evans
Producer: Cecil Clarke

***Redcap*: 'Epitaph for a Sweet'**
ABC
31/11/64
Kenneth Farrington (Sapper Baker), Norman Florence (Asst. Sup. Yacoub), Martin Gordon (Dessouki), Roger Heathcott (Sapper Morse), John Horsley (Major Coulter), Ian McShane (Sapper Russell), Frank Mills (Medical Officer), John Noakes (Sapper Evans), Mike Pratt (Sgt. Bailey), Leonard Rossiter (Sgt. Rolfe), John Thaw (Sgt. John Mann)

Writer: Richard Harris
Director: Peter Graham Scott
Producer: John Bryce

BBC 3
BBC1
Sep/Oct 1965

Performers: John Bird, Eleanor Bron, John Fortune, Bill Oddie, Robert Robinson, David Kernan, Millicent Martin, Cleo Laine, John Wells, Lynda Baron, David Battley, Patrick Campbell, Roy Dotrice, Malcolm Muggeridge, Denis Norden, Harvey Orkin, Leonard Rossiter, Norman St John Stevas
Writers: Christopher Brooker, Caryl Brahms, Peter Dobereiner, David Frost, Willis Hall, Herbert Kretzmer, Peter Lewis, John Mortimer, David Nathan, Peter Shaffer, David Turner, Steven Vinaver, Dick Vosburgh, Keith Waterhouse
Directors: Ned Sherrin and Darrol Blake
Producer: Ned Sherrin

'ITV Play of the Week': *Mr Fowlds*
ATV
15/11/65

Leonard Rossiter (Mr Fowlds), David Cook (Prisoner)
Writer: John Bowen
Director: Vivian Matalon
Producer: Cecil Clarke

'Theatre 625': *Dr Knock*
BBC2
2/1/66

Graham Armitage (Monsieur Bernard), Rosalind Atkinson (Madame Pons), Jimmy Gardner (Jean), Robert Gillespie (Monsieur Mousquet), Patrick Godfrey (Scipio), James Grout (Town Crier), Renee Houston (Madame Remy), Lawrence James (2nd Country Fellow), John Le Mesurier (Dr Parpalaid), Mercia Mansfield (Mariette), Pat Nye (Farmer's Wife), Leonard Rossiter (Dr Knock), Maclolm Taylor (1st Country Fellow), Mavie Villiers (Madame Parpalaid)

Writer: Jules Romains (translated by Harley Granville-Barker)
Director: Herbert Wise
Producer: Cedric Messina

Semi-Detached
BBC
2/1/66

Barrie Ingham (Robert Freeman), William Kendall (Arnold Makepiece), Alison Leggatt (Hilda Midway), Leonard Rossiter (Fred Midway)
Writer: David Turner
Director: Gilchrist Calder
Producer: Cedric Messina

Death is a Good Living
BBC1
22/5/66–12/6/66

Episode One
Geoffrey Toone (Jim Prescott), Don Borisenko (Peter Virtanen), Michael Godfrey (Ramon Aguirre), Dallia Penn (Maria Salvador), Leonard Rossiter (Norman Lynch), Shay Gorman (Security Officer), Jeremy Burnham (Tim Barton), Katharine page (Mrs Lynch), Jack May (Major Gates), Brian Hawksley (Edward Maline), Henry Gilbert (Bartolome Salias), John Slavid (Secretary), Barry Shawzin (Carlo Mestri)
Writers: Brian Degas and Tudor Gates (from a novel by Philip Jones)
Director: Gerald Blake
Producer: Alan Bromly

Episode Two
Geoffrey Toone (Jim Prescott), Don Borisenko (Peter Virtanen), Michael Godfrey (Ramon Aguirre), Dallia Penn (Maria Salvador), Leonard Rossiter (Norman Lynch)
Writers: Brian Degas and Tudor Gates (from a novel by Philip Jones)
Director: Gerald Blake
Producer: Alan Bromly

Episode Three
Geoffrey Toone (Jim Prescott), Don Borisenko (Peter Virtanen), Michael Godfrey (Ramon Aguirre), Dallia Penn (Maria Salvador), Leonard Rossiter (Norman Lynch), Frederick Hall (Airfield Superintendent), David Brooke (Pilot), Jack May (Major Gates)
Writers: Brian Degas and Tudor Gates (from a novel by Philip Jones)
Director: Gerald Blake
Producer: Alan Bromly

Episode Four
Geoffrey Toone (Jim Prescott), Don Borisenko (Peter Virtanen), Michael Godfrey (Ramon Aguirre), Dallia Penn (Maria Salvador), Leonard Rossiter (Norman Lynch), Katharine Page (Mrs Lynch), Brian Hawksley (Edward Maline), Jack May (Major Gates)

'BBC Play of the Month':
The Devil's Eggshell
BBC1
28/6/66
Keith Barron (Dr Quillam), Leonard Rossiter (Prime Minster), David Langton (Sir Leonard Bell), John Philips (Maj. Gen. Atkins), Peter Copley (Home Secretary), Bernard Hepton (Lord Portmanteau), Marian Diamond (Jean Bell), Michael Culver (Holborn), Burt Kwouk (Wu Hsien Ching), Stephanie Bidmead (Maudie), P.J. Kavanagh (Interviewer), Lawrence James (Bland),
Writer: David Weir (from an idea by Alex Comfort)
Director: Gareth Davies
Producer: Cedric Messina

'Thirty Minute Theatre': *Taste*
BBC2
4/1/67
Donald Pleasance (Richard Pratt), Leonard Rossiter (Mike Schofield), Maureen O'Brien (Louise Schofield), Marion Mathie (Margaret Schofield), Robin Hunter (Peter), Clare Nielson (Lydia), Barbara Leake (mary)
Writer: Roald Dahl
Director: John Glenister
Producer: Graeme McDonald

The Revenue Men: 'The Benefactor'
BBC2
9/5/67
Ewen Solon (Caesar Smith), James Grant (Ross McInnes), Clare Nielson (Luke Frazer), Callum Mill (Campbell), Gerry Slevin (John Gillespie), Larry Marshall (Walker), Peter Dawkins (Hugh Evans), Patricia Heneghan (Annie Gillespie), Nancy Gilmour (Gladys), Katie Gardiner (Dot), Harry Hankin (Waterguard Officer), Leonard Rossiter (Ormerod), Paul Kermack (Jason)
Writer: John Pennington
Director: Richard Argent
Producer: Gerard Glaister

'The Wednesday Play': *Drums along the Avon*
BBC1
24/5/67
Leonard Rossiter (Mr Marcus), Valerie Newman (Mrs Marcus), Maureen O'Reilly (Mrs Arnold), Salmaan Peerzada (Jhimma), Anita Mall (Lakshmi), Rafiq Anwar (Lakshmi's father), Surya Kumari (Lakshmi's mother), Norman Tyrrell (Lord Mayor), Peggy Sirr (Jennifer), Phyllis Smale (Gob woman), Helen Downing (West Indian tart), Derek Ware (Motorcyclist), Norman Beaton (Guitarist in club), June Barrie (Woman in club), David Langford (Ambulanceman), Roy Brimble (Ambulanceman), Val Lorraine (Teacher), Georgina Simpson (Schoolgirl), Pat Rossiter (Tart), Liz Towler (Tart), Sally Lewis (Angela), Janet Key (Rosalind), Christine Shelley (Air hostess), Kelly Kelshall (West Indian student), Alan Moore

(Trooper), Colin Fisher (Trooper), Guy Ross (Youth), Clare Sutcliffe (Young girl), P. Ibram (Indian boy), Vincent Mall (Lakshmi's brother), Innocent Mall (Lakshmi's brother), Calvin Lockhart (Bus driver), Peter Andrews (Laughing man), Brian Gear (Policeman), Rumish Amand (Pedlar), Kate Wood (Little girl)
Written by Charles Wood
Directed by James MacTaggart
Produced by Tony Garnett

Goodbye, That's All
BBC
30/9/67
Leonard Rossiter (Man)
Writer: Dennis Woolf
Director: John Robins
Producer: John Robins

Day of the Tortoise
Rediffusion
12/67
Writer: Julian Bond (from the short story by H.E. Bates)
Director: Michael Currer-Briggs
Producer: Antony Kearey

'Thirty-Minute Theatre': *The Unquiet Man*
BBC2
21/2/68
Leonard Rossiter (Andrew), Janet Webb (Wife)
Writer: Michael Keir
Director: Naomi K. Capon
Producer: George Spenton-Foster

'Half-Hour Story': *A View from the Obelisk*
Rediffusion
20/03/68
Gwen Cherrell (Rosemary), Jim Norton (Eoghain), Leonard Rossiter (Owen)
Writer: Hugh Leonard
Directer: Alastair Reid
Producer: Stella Richman

'Theatre 625': *The Fanatics*
BBC2
29/4/68
Alan Badel (David de Beaudrigue), Leonard Rossiter (Voltaire), Rosalie Crutchley (Madame Calas), John Paul (Jean Calas), Alex Scott (Maitre Chalier), Cyril Shaps (Moynier), Tom Criddle (Duke of Choiseul), Richard Caldicot (Saint-Florentin), Hamilton Dyce (Laffiteau), Bernard Hepton (Dr Tronchin), Vivienne Drummond (Madame Denis), Peter Macann (Wagnire), Brian Osborne (Louis Calas), Paul Thompson (Pierre Calas), Matthew Long (Lavaysse), Nan Marriott-Watson (Jeanette), Pamela Cundell (Madame Durand), Gordon Faith (Bergerot), Michael Mundell (Gorse), Edwin Finn (Father Bourges), Robert James (Assesseur), Royston Tickner (Town crier), Milton Reid (Executioner)
Writer: Max Marquis (from 'L'Affaire Calas' by Stellio Lorenzi, André Castelot and Alain Decaux)
Director: Rudolph Cartier
Producer: Michael Bakewell

'Theatre 625': *The Year of the Sex Olympics*
BBC2
29/7/68
Leonard Rossiter (Co-Ordinator Ugo Priest), Suzanne Neve (Deanie Webb), Tony Vogel (Nat Mender), Brian Cox (Lasar Opie), Vickery Turner (Misch), George Murcell (Grels), Martin Potter (Kin Hodder), Lesley Roach (Keten Webb), Hira Talfrey (Betty), Patricia Maynard (Nurse), Trevor Peacock (Custard pie expert), Brian Coburn (Custard pie expert), Derek Fowlds (Custard pie expert), Wolfe Morris (Custard pie expert), Braham Murray (Custard pie expert), Job Stewart (Custard pie expert), Sheila Sands (Artsex girl), Michael Feast (Sportsex contestant)
Writer: Nigel Kneale
Director: Michael Elliott
Producer: Ronald Travers

'ITV Playhouse': *The Double Agent*
Anglia
12/5/69
Leonard Rossiter (Nikolai Krobnevsky),
Brian Blessed (Reg Sugden), Bernard
Archard (Kenneth Ducane), Peter Dyneley
(Col. Golchenko), Edward Judd (Ginger
Ryan), Maureen O'Brien (Nadia Seranova),
Hildegarde Neil (Marion), David Monico
(Georgi Poliakov), Harold Innocent (Tom
Mayhew), Timothy Carlton (Roger List),
Edwin Finn (Mike Parsons) Anthony Roye
(Crowley)
Writer: Anthony Steven (based on the novel
by John Bingham)
Director: John Jacobs

'Saturday Night Theatre': *The Garbler*
Strategy
ATV
2/8/69
Leonard Rossiter ('X'), Willoughby
Goddard (Kell), Anne Cunningham (Helen
Gordon), Michael Lees (Jeff Short), Jeremy
Longhurst (Temple), Jacqueline Maude
(Mrs Davis), Patrick Godfrey (Crawford),
Peter Thornton (Alfred
Writer: Maurice Flanagan
Director: Geoffrey Hughes
Producer: Geoffrey Hughes

'The Wednesday Play': *The*
Italian Table
BBC1
18/2/70
Leonard Rossiter (Mr Jeffs), Isabel Dean
(Mrs Hammond), Moira Redmond (Mrs
Youghal), Ronald Hines (Mr Hammond),
Bridget Brice (Ursula), Libby Granger
(Lucy), John Horsley (Sir Andrew Charles),
Dorothy Frere (Mrs Lynch)
Writer: William Trevor
Director: Herbert Wise
Producer: Irene Shubik

Harry-Kari and Sally
ATV

7/3/71
Leonard Rossiter (Harry)
Writer: Douglas Livingstone
Directer: John Gorrie
Producer: Verity Lambert

Thick as Thieves
HTV
29/2/72
Leonard Rossiter (Eddie), Corin Redgrave
(Trevor), Rosemary McHale (Lynn),
George Woodbridge (Sid), Nina Baden-
Semper, June Barrie, Daphne Heard,
Horace James
Writers: Bob Baker and Dave Martin
Director: Patrick Dromgoole
Producer: Patrick Dromgoole

Steptoe and Son: 'The Desperate Hours'
BBC1
3/4/72
Wilfrid Brambell (Albert Steptoe), Harry H.
Corbett (Harold Steptoe), Leonard Rossiter
(Johnny), J.G. Devlin (Frank), Corbet
Woodall (Newscaster), Tommy Vance (DJ)
Writers: Ray Galton and Alan Simpson
Director: John Howard Davies
Producer: John Howard Davies

'BBC Play of the Month':
The Magistrate
BBC1
20/12/72
Michael Hordern (Mr Posket), Geraldine
McEvan (Agatha Posket), Peter Firth (Cis
Farringdon), Leonard Rossiter (Colonel
Lukyn), Anna Calder-Marshall (Charlotte
Verrinder), Barrie Ingham (Captain Horace
Vale), John Blythe (Wyke), Jan Francis
(Popham), Dudley Jones (Mr Bullamy),
Candace Glendenning (Beatie Tomlinson),
Alan Hockey (Achille Blond), John
Nightingale (Isidore), Peter Whitbread
(Inspector Messiter), Geoffrey Perkins
(Constable Harris), Ken Jones
Writer: Arthur Wing Pinero
Director: Bill Hays

Producer: Cedric Messina

After Loch Lomond
LWT
2/2/73
Leonard Rossiter (Mickey Grant), Kevin
Brennan (Barman), Anne Carroll (Sheila),
Gabrielle Daye (Mrs Buckley), Leslie Dwyer
(Mr Maystead), Joan Hickson (Nancy),
Geoffrey Hinsliff (Geoff), Natalie Kent
(Mrs Maystead), Margery Mason (Brenda),
Richard Moore (Colin), Christine Shaw
(Receptionist), Joy Stewart (Bar lady),
Theresa Watson (Waitress)
Writer: Douglas Livingstone
Director: John Gorrie
Producer: Verity Lambert

'Thirty-Minute Theatre': *The Baby's Name Being Kitchener*
BBC2
26/4/73
Imogen Bain (Young Joanna), Margaret
Courtenay (Sophie), Beth Porter (Joanna),
Leonard Rossiter (Sgt Tax)
Writer: Peter Everett
Director: Michael Hayes
Producer: Tim Aspinall

If There Weren't Any Blacks You'd Have To Invent Them
LWT
3/3/74
Leonard Rossiter (The Blind Man), Michael
Bryant (The Doctor), Richard Beckinsale
(The Young man), Lewis Flander (The
Officer), John Nightingale (The Private),
Donald Gee (The Backwards Man), John
Welsh (The Judge), Geoffrey Bayldon (The
Undertaker), Bob Hoskins (The Sexton),
James Grout (The Priest), Ken Wynne (The
Vicar), Pam Scotcher (The Girl), Mary
Henry (The Jewish Mother), Karen Boyes
(The Senior Nurse), Vicki Michelle
(Nurse), Susan Morrall (Nurse), Pat Peters
(Nurse)
Writer: Johnny Speight

Director: Bill Hays
Producer: Rex Firkin

The Carnforth Practice: The Aristocrat
BBC2
21/4/74
Michael Elwyn (Hon. Grenville Carnforth),
Pamela Salem (Dr Helen Rheinman), Mark
Edwards (Lord Penmore), Gigi Gatti
(Carmelita), Godfrey James (Wally Scott),
Caroline Whitaker (Angela), Tom Chadbon
(PC Henderson), David Daker (Tanker
Driver), Frank Duncan (Magistrate), Jon
Laurimore (Landlord), Irene Peters
(Reporter), Leonard Rossiter (Aaros
Boswell), Cyril Varley (Passer-by), Arthur
White (Sgt. Armstrong)
Writer: Allan Prior
Director: Cyril Coke
Producer: Colin Morris

Masquerade: Mützen ab!
BBC
6/5/74
Leonard Rossiter (Leslie lewis), Mark
Dignam (Fieldman), Thorley Walters
(Bunny), Robert Davey (Brook), Lynne
Frederick (Natalie Fieldman), Neil Hallett
(Trump), Stephen MacKenna (Auctioneer),
David Meyer (Andrew), Frederick Peisley (Sir
Frederick White), Kevin Stoney (Gunther)
Writer: Charles Wood
Director: Graham Evans
Producer: Herbert Wise

'Comedy Playhouse': *Pygmalion Smith*
BBC1
25/6/74
Leonard Rossiter (Smithy), T.P. McKenna
(Brewster), Barbara Courtney (Auriol
Pratt), Maggi Burton (Mrs Kintoul), Laurie
Goode (Auriol's Boyfriend)
Writer: Roy Clarke
Director: Roger Race
Producer: Roger Race

Rising Damp
Yorkshire Television
2/9/74–17/1/75
Pilot: 'The New Tenant'
2/9/74
Leonard Rossiter (Rupert Rigsby), Frances
de la Tour (Ruth Jones), Richard Beckinsale
(Alan Moore), Don Warrington (Philip
Smith)

Series One:
'Black Magic'
13/12/74
Leonard Rossiter (Rupert Rigsby), Frances
de la Tour (Ruth Jones), Richard Beckinsale
(Alan Moore), Don Warrington (Philip
Smith)

'A Night Out'
20/12/74
Leonard Rossiter (Rupert Rigsby), Frances
de la Tour (Ruth Jones), Richard Beckinsale
(Alan Moore), Don Warrington (Philip
Smith) Derek Newark (Spooner), Frank
Gatliff (Manager)

'Charisma'
27/12/74
Leonard Rossiter (Rupert Rigsby), Frances
de la Tour (Ruth Jones), Richard Beckinsale
(Alan Moore), Don Warrington (Philip
Smith) Liz Edmiston (Maureen)

'All Our Yesterdays'
3 /1/75
Leonard Rossiter (Rupert Rigsby), Frances
de la Tour (Ruth Jones), Richard Beckinsale
(Alan Moore), Don Warrington (Philip
Smith), Derek Newark (Spooner)

'The Prowler'
10 /1/75
Leonard Rossiter (Rupert Rigsby), Frances
de la Tour (Ruth Jones), Richard Beckinsale
(Alan Moore), Don Warrington (Philip
Smith) George Sewell (Baker), Michael
Stainton (Policeman)

'Stand Up and Be Counted'
17/1/75
Leonard Rossiter (Rupert Rigsby), Frances
de la Tour (Ruth Jones), Richard Beckinsale
(Alan Moore), Don Warrington (Philip
Smith) Ian Lavender (Platt), Michael Ward
(Labour Candidate), Anthony Sharp
(DeVere-Brown)
Writer: Eric Chappell
Director: Ronnie Baxter
Producer: Ronnie Baxter

Not The Cheapest But The Best
BBC2
4/75
Leonard Rossiter (Narrator/ Brunel)
Writer: Michael Andrews
Director: Michael Andrews
Producer: Tim Aspinall

'Play for Today': *After the Solo*
BBC1
25/11/75
Leonard Rossiter (Dawson), Gerald James
(Peters), John Ringham (Foreman),
Jeannette Hill (Mrs Pritchard), Geraldine
Newman (Mrs Dawson), Nicholas Watson
(Ralph Dawson), Sean Flanagan (Billy),
Barrie Cookson (Fletcher), Iris Russell (Mrs
Fletcher), Margaret John (Mrs Peters),
Stephen Churchett (History teacher),
Simon Gipps-Kent (Gaz Arnold), Nicholas
Cox (Boy), Jean Campbell-Dallas (Woman
in shop), Cy Town (Nephew)
Writer: John Challen
Director: Moira Armstrong
Producer: Ann Scott

Rising Damp
Yorkshire Television
7/11/75 – 26/12/75

Series Two:
'The Permissive Society'
7/11/75
Leonard Rossiter (Rupert Rigsby), Frances
de la Tour (Ruth Jones), Richard Beckinsale

(Alan Moore), Don Warrington (Philip Smith), George A. Cooper (Cooper)

'Food Glorious Food'
14/11/75
Leonard Rossiter (Rupert Rigsby), Frances de la Tour (Ruth Jones), Richard Beckinsale (Alan Moore), Don Warrington (Philip Smith)

'A Body Like Mine'
21/11/75
Leonard Rossiter (Rupert Rigsby), Frances de la Tour (Ruth Jones), Richard Beckinsale (Alan Moore), Don Warrington (Philip Smith)

'Moonlight and Roses'
28/11/75
Leonard Rossiter (Rupert Rigsby), Frances de la Tour (Ruth Jones), Richard Beckinsale (Alan Moore), Don Warrington (Philip Smith) Robin Parkinson (Desmond), Gay Rose (Brenda)

'A Perfect Gentlemen'
5/12/75
Leonard Rossiter (Rupert Rigsby), Frances de la Tour (Ruth Jones), Richard Beckinsale (Alan Moore), Don Warrington (Philip Smith), Henry McGee (Seymour)

'Last of the Big Spenders'
12/12/75
Leonard Rossiter (Rupert Rigsby), Richard Beckinsale (Alan Moore), Don Warrington (Philip Smith), Gay Rose (Brenda), Campbell Singer (Flint), Robert Gillespie (Gasman), Ronnie Brody (Charlie)

'Things That Go Bump in the Night'
19/12/75
Leonard Rossiter (Rupert Rigsby), Richard Beckinsale (Alan Moore), Don Warrington (Philip Smith), Gay Rose (Brenda), Norman Bird (Vicar), David Rowlands (Curate)

'For the Man Who Has Everything'
26/12/75
Leonard Rossiter (Rupert Rigsby), Richard Beckinsale (Alan Moore), Don Warrington (Philip Smith), Gay Rose (Brenda), Larry Martyn (Fred), Elizabeth Adare (Lucy), Helen Fraser (Gwen)
Writer: Eric Chappell
Director: Ronnie Baxter
Producer: Ronnie Baxter

Machinegunner
HTV
24/7/76
Leonard Rossiter (Cyril Dugdale), Nina Baden-Semper (Felicity Rae Ingram), June Barrie (Olive Dugdale), Fazal Bux (Pradesh Son), Ishaq Bux (Mr Pradesh), Adrian Cairns (Mr Wilkins), Shaun Curry (Frank), Hal Galili (Bush), Geoffrey Matthews (Club Barman), Kate O'Mara (Pat Livingstone), Timothy Preece (Des), Gabrielle Rose (Jan), Ewen Solon (Geoff Livingstone), Colin Welland (Jack Bone), Earle Anthony (Club Bouncer), Bob Baker (Scruff No.1), Dave Martin (Scruff No.2)
Writers: Bob Baker and Dave Martin
Director: Patrick Dromgoole
Producer: Patrick Dromgoole

The Fall and Rise of Reginald Perrin
BBC1
8/9/76–20/10/76
Series One:
'Hippopotamus'
8/9/76
Leonard Rossiter (Reginald Iolanthe Perrin), Pauline Yates (Elizabeth Perrin), John Barron (C.J.), Sue Nicholls (Joan Greengross), Sally-Jane Spencer (Linda), Tim Preece (Tom), Geoffrey Palmer (Jimmy), Trevor Adams (Tony Webster), Bruce Bould (David Harris-Jones), John Horsley (Doc Morrisey), Roland MacLeod (Morris Coates), Jacki Piper (Esther Pidgeon), Norman Mitchell (Ron Napier),

Ray Marioni (Waiter)

'Nightmare in the Park'
15/9/76
Leonard Rossiter (Reginald Perrin), Pauline
Yates (Elizabeth Perrin), John Barron
(C.J.), Sue Nicholls (Joan Greengross),
Sally-Jane Spencer (Linda), Tim Preece
(Tom), Geoffrey Palmer (Jimmy), Trevor
Adams (Tony Webster), Bruce Bould
(David Harris-Jones), John Horsley (Doc
Morrisey), Penny Leatherbarrow (Tea
Lady), Abagail Morgan (Jocasta), Robert
Hillier (Adam)

**'The Sunday Extraordinary Business
Meeting'**
22/9/76
Leonard Rossiter (Reginald Perrin), Pauline
Yates (Elizabeth Perrin), John Barron
(C.J.), Sue Nicholls (Joan Greengross),
Sally-Jane Spencer (Linda), Tim Preece
(Tom), Geoffrey Palmer (Jimmy), Trevor
Adams (Tony Webster), Bruce Bould
(David Harris-Jones), John Horsley (Doc
Morrisey), David Warwick (Mark Perrin)

'The Bizarre Dinner Party'
29/9/76
Leonard Rossiter (Reginald Perrin), Pauline
Yates (Elizabeth Perrin), John Barron
(C.J.), Sue Nicholls (Joan Greengross),
Sally-Jane Spencer (Linda), Tim Preece
(Tom), Geoffrey Palmer (Jimmy), Trevor
Adams (Tony Webster), Bruce Bould
(David Harris-Jones), John Horsley (Doc
Morrisey), Tim Barrett (Mr Campbell-
Lewiston), Virginia Balfour (Davina
Letts-Wilkinson), Dorothy Frere (Mrs C.J.),
Tony Sympson (Uncle Percy Spillinger)

**'The Speech to the British Fruit
Association'**
6/10/76
Leonard Rossiter (Reginald Perrin), Pauline
Yates (Elizabeth Perrin), John Barron
(C.J.), Sue Nicholls (Joan Greengross),

Sally-Jane Spencer (Linda), Tim Preece
(Tom), Geoffrey Palmer (Jimmy), Trevor
Adams (Tony Webster), Bruce Bould
(David Harris-Jones), John Horsley (Doc
Morrisey), Dennis Ramsden (Dr Hump),
Tenniel Evans (Elwyn Watkins), John
Rudling (Bill)

**'Trying a Frenchman, Welshman,
Scotsman and an Italian'**
13/10/76
Leonard Rossiter (Reginald Perrin), Pauline
Yates (Elizabeth Perrin), John Barron
(C.J.), Sue Nicholls (Joan Greengross),
Sally-Jane Spencer (Linda), Tim Preece
(Tom), Geoffrey Palmer (Jimmy), Trevor
Adams (Tony Webster), Bruce Bould
(David Harris-Jones), John Horsley (Doc
Morrisey), Anna Cunningham (Jean
Timpkins), Ken Wynne (Mr Deacon),
Hilary Mason (Mrs Deacon), Charmian
May (Miss Pershore), Roger Brierley (Mr
Thorneycroft), Pamela Manson (Barmaid),
John Forbes-Robertson (Henry Possett),
David Millet (Landlord), Vi Kane
(Neighbour), Hamilton McLeod (Waiter),
Bob Sutherland (Major)

'The Memorial Service'
20/10/76
Leonard Rossiter (Reginald 'Reggie'
Iolanthe Perrin), Pauline Yates (Elizabeth
Perrin), John Barron (C.J.), Sue Nicholls
(Joan Greengross), Sally-Jane Spencer
(Linda), Tim Preece (Tom), Geoffrey
Palmer (Jimmy), Trevor Adams (Tony
Webster), Bruce Bould (David Harris-
Jones), John Horsley (Doc Morrisey),
Charmian May (Miss Pershore), Dorothy
Frere (Mrs C.J.), Gerald Sim (Vicar), David
Warwick (Mark), John Forbes-Robertson
(Henry Possett), Peter MacKriel (Waiter)
Writer: David Nobbs
Director: Gareth Gwenlan (Episode One –
John Howard Davies)
Producer: Gareth Gwenlan (Episode One –
John Howard Davies)

'The Galton & Simpson Playhouse':
I Tell You It's Burt Reynolds
Yorkshire Television
31/3/77
Leonard Rossiter (Jim), Patrica Hayes
(Granny), Gillian Raine (Joyce), Ed
Deveraux (Percy), Roy Barraclough (Eric),
Kim Smith (Son), Sally Watkins (Daughter)
Writers: Ray Galton and Alan Simpson
Director: Ronnie Baxter
Producer: Ronnie Baxter

Rising Damp
Yorkshire Television
12/4/77–24/5/77
Series Three:
'That's My Boy'
12/4/77
Leonard Rossiter (Rupert Rigsby), Frances
de la Tour (Ruth Jones), Richard Beckinsale
(Alan Moore), Don Warrington (Philip
Smith), Ann Beach (Mrs Brent), David
Daker (Mr Brent), Daphne Oxenford
(Announcer)

'Stage Struck'
19/4/77
Leonard Rossiter (Rupert Rigsby), Frances
de la Tour (Ruth Jones), Richard Beckinsale
(Alan Moore), Don Warrington (Philip
Smith), Peter Bowles (Hilary)

'Clunk Click'
26/4/77
Leonard Rossiter (Rupert Rigsby), Frances
de la Tour (Ruth Jones), Richard Beckinsale
(Alan Moore), Don Warrington (Philip
Smith), Derek Francis (Mr French), James
Bree (Peppery Man), Judy Buxton
(Caroline)

'The Good Samaritan'
3/5/77
Leonard Rossiter (Rupert Rigsby), Frances
de la Tour (Ruth Jones), Richard Beckinsale
(Alan Moore), Don Warrington (Philip
Smith), David Swift (Gray), John Clive

(Samaritan)

'Fawcett's Python'
10/5/77
Leonard Rossiter (Rupert Rigsby), Frances
de la Tour (Ruth Jones), Richard Beckinsale
(Alan Moore), Don Warrington (Philip
Smith), Andonia Katsaros (Marilyn),
Jonathan Elsom (Douglas)

'The Cocktail Hour'
17/5/77
Leonard Rossiter (Rupert Rigsby), Frances
de la Tour (Ruth Jones), Richard Beckinsale
(Alan Moore), Don Warrington (Philip
Smith), Judy Buxton (Caroline), Diana
King (Mrs Armitage)

'Suddenly at Home'
24/5/77
Leonard Rossiter (Rupert Rigsby), Frances
de la Tour (Ruth Jones), Richard Beckinsale
(Alan Moore), Don Warrington (Philip
Smith), Roger Brierly (Osborne)
Writer: Eric Chappell
Director: Ronnie Baxter
Producer: Ronnie Baxter

The Fall and Rise of Reginald Perrin
BBC1
21/9/77–2/11/77
Series Two:
'Remarried and Back at Sunshine
Desserts'
21/9/77
Leonard Rossiter (Reginald Perrin), Pauline
Yates (Elizabeth Perrin), John Barron
(C.J.), Sue Nicholls (Joan Greengross),
Sally-Jane Spencer (Linda), Tim Preece
(Tom), Geoffrey Palmer (Jimmy), Trevor
Adams (Tony Webster), Bruce Bould
(David Harris-Jones), John Horsley (Doc
Morrisey), Derek Deadman (Man at
Telephone Box), Ken Barker (GPO
Engineer), David Rowley (Owen Lewis)

'Elizabeth's New Admirer'

28/9/77

Leonard Rossiter (Reginald Perrin), Pauline Yates (Elizabeth Perrin), John Barron (C.J.), Sue Nicholls (Joan Greengross), Sally-Jane Spencer (Linda), Tim Preece (Tom), Geoffrey Palmer (Jimmy), Trevor Adams (Tony Webster), Bruce Bould (David Harris-Jones), John Horsley (Doc Morrisey), Ralph Watson (Clerk at Labour Exchange), Christopher Lawrence (House Buyer), Helen Bernat (Girl at Bus Stop)

'Jimmy's Offer'
5/10/77

Leonard Rossiter (Reginald Perrin), Pauline Yates (Elizabeth Perrin), John Barron (C.J.), Sue Nicholls (Joan Greengross), Sally-Jane Spencer (Linda), Tim Preece (Tom), Geoffrey Palmer (Jimmy), Trevor Adams (Tony Webster), Bruce Bould (David Harris-Jones), John Horsley (Doc Morrisey), Glynn Edwards (Mr Pelham)

'The Unusual Shop'
12/10/77

Leonard Rossiter (Reginald Perrin), Pauline Yates (Elizabeth Perrin), John Barron (C.J.), Sue Nicholls (Joan Greengross), Sally-Jane Spencer (Linda), Tim Preece (Tom), Geoffrey Palmer (Jimmy), Trevor Adams (Tony Webster), Bruce Bould (David Harris-Jones), John Horsley (Doc Morrisey), Roland MacLeod (Morris Coates), Jacki Piper (Esther Pigeon), Joan Blackham (Miss Erith), Edward Dentith (Mr Milford), Michael Bilton (Wine Buyer), Cynthia Etherington (Housewife), Del Derrick (Well-Dressed Man), Beatrice Shaw (Elderly Lady), Gilly Flower (Woman with Fur)

'Re-Involvement'
19/10/77

Leonard Rossiter (Reginald Perrin), Pauline Yates (Elizabeth Perrin), John Barron (C.J.), Sue Nicholls (Joan Greengross), Sally-Jane Spencer (Linda), Tim Preece (Tom), Geoffrey Palmer (Jimmy), Trevor Adams (Tony Webster), Bruce Bould (David Harris-Jones), John Horsley (Doc Morrisey), Joan Blackham (Miss Erith)

'Four Untrustworthy Men'
26/10/77

Leonard Rossiter (Reginald Perrin), Pauline Yates (Elizabeth Perrin), John Barron (C.J.), Sue Nicholls (Joan Greengross), Sally-Jane Spencer (Linda), Tim Preece (Tom), Geoffrey Palmer (Jimmy), Trevor Adams (Tony Webster), Bruce Bould (David Harris-Jones), John Horsley (Doc Morrisey), Derry Power (Seamus Finnegan), Sheila Bernette (Gladys), Ken Morley (Arthur), Robert Hillier (Adam), Abigail Morgan (Jocasta)

'Extreme Solution'
2/11/77

Leonard Rossiter (Reginald Perrin), Pauline Yates (Elizabeth Perrin), John Barron (C.J.), Sue Nicholls (Joan Greengross), Sally-Jane Spencer (Linda), Tim Preece (Tom), Geoffrey Palmer (Jimmy), Trevor Adams (Tony Webster), Bruce Bould (David Harris-Jones), John Horsley (Doc Morrisey), Timothy Carlton (Colin Pillock), Blain Fairman (Sheridan Honeydew), Neville Barber (Peregrine Trembleby), Keith Smith (Mr Lisburn), David Rowlands (Mr Herbert)
Writer: David Nobbs
Director: Gareth Gwenlan
Producer: Gareth Gwenlan

Parker Pens commercial
ITV
1977
Leonard played the role of a traffic warden in his first ever television commercial.
Director: Brian Byfield
Producer: Collett, Dickenson, Pearce & Partners, advertising agency

Rising Damp
Yorkshire Television
4/4/78–9/5/78
Series Four:
'Hello Young Lovers'
4/4/78
Leonard Rossiter (Rupert Rigsby), Frances de la Tour (Ruth Jones), Richard Beckinsale (Alan Moore), Don Warrington (Philip Smith), Deborah Watling (Lorna), Alun Lewis (Robin), Robert Dorning (Father)

'Fire and Brimstone'
11/4/78
Leonard Rossiter (Rupert Rigsby), Frances de la Tour (Ruth Jones), Richard Beckinsale (Alan Moore), Don Warrington (Philip Smith), John Clive (Gwyn)

'Great Expectations'
18/4/78
Leonard Rossiter (Rupert Rigsby), Frances de la Tour (Ruth Jones), Richard Beckinsale (Alan Moore), Don Warrington (Philip Smith), Avis Bunnage (Veronica), Andrew Sachs (Snell), Gretchen Franklin (Aunt Maud)

'Pink Carnations'
25/4/78
Leonard Rossiter (Rupert Rigsby), Frances de la Tour (Ruth Jones), Richard Beckinsale (Alan Moore), Don Warrington (Philip Smith), Helen Fraser (Bride), John Quayle (Groom), Joan Sanderson (Mother), Roy Barraclough (Barman)

'Under the Influence'
2/5/78
Leonard Rossiter (Rupert Rigsby), Frances de la Tour (Ruth Jones), Richard Beckinsale (Alan Moore), Don Warrington (Philip Smith), Peter Jeffrey (Ambrose)

'Come On In the Water's Lovely'
9/5/78
Leonard Rossiter (Rupert Rigsby), Frances de la Tour (Ruth Jones), Richard Beckinsale (Alan Moore), Don Warrington (Philip Smith), Brian Peck (Ron), Fanny Rowe (Mother)
Writer: Eric Chappell
Director: Vernon Lawrence
Producer: Vernon Lawrence

BBC2 Play of the Week: Fearless Frank
BBC2
4/10/78
Leonard Rossiter (Frank Harris), Susan Penhaligon (Secretary / Enid / Kate / Jessie / Actress / Schoolgirl), Ben Aris (Whistler), Margaret Courtenay (Mrs Clayton / Mrs Clapton), Andrew Downie (Thomas Carlyle), Donna Evans (Lily Robins / Nursemaid), Katherine Fahey (Laura Clapton), Hal Gilili (Mr Clapton / Cowboy), Keith Jayne (Butcher's boy), Sylvia Kay (Nellie Harris), Denis Lawson (Ernest Dowson / Prof. Byron Smith), Alun Lewis (Kendrick / Young man), Pepsi Maycock (Topsy), Elizabeth Revill (Mrs Mayhew), John Rhys-Davies (Guy de Maupassant), William Russell (Lord Folkestone / Chapman / Headmaster), Philip Sayer (Oscar Wilde), Albert Shepherd (Tibbett / Waiter), Donald Waugh (Shoe-shine boy)
Writer: Andrew Davies
Director: Colin Bucksey
Producer: Louis Marks

Song by Song: 'By Harburg'
Yorkshire Television
8/10/78
Ned Sherrin, Georgia Brown, David Kernan, Clarke Peters, Leonard Rossiter
Writers: Caryl Brahms, Peter Greenwell, Neil Shand and Yip Harburg
Director: Vernon Lawrence
Producer: Deke Arlon

The Losers
ATV
12/11/78– 17/12/78

'A Star is Born'
12/11/78
Leonard Rossiter (Sydney Foskett), Alfred Molina (Nigel), Joe Gladwin (Dennis Breene)

'The Naming of the Parts'
19/11/78
Leonard Rossiter (Sydney Foskett), Alfred Molina (Nigel), Joe Gladwin (Dennis Breene)

'Out of the Strong'
26/11/78
Leonard Rossiter (Sydney Foskett), Alfred Molina (Nigel), Joe Gladwin (Dennis Breene)

'All Down in Black & White
3/12/78
Leonard Rossiter (Sydney Foskett), Alfred Molina (Nigel), Joe Gladwin (Dennis Breene)

'Sitting on a Goldmine'
10/12/78
Leonard Rossiter (Sydney Foskett), Alfred Molina (Nigel), Joe Gladwin (Dennis Breene)

'Togetherness'
17/12/78
Leonard Rossiter (Sydney Foskett), Alfred Molina (Nigel), Joe Gladwin (Dennis Breene)
Writer: Alan Coren
Director: Joe McGrath
Producer: Terence Baker

The Morecambe and Wise Christmas Show
Thames
25/12/78
Eric Morecambe, Ernie Wise, Leonard Rossiter, Harold Wilson (1), Jenny Hanley (Felicity), Anna Dawson (Newsreader/Lola), Jan Hunt, Syd Lawrence, Frank Coda, Jillianne Foot, Denise Gyngell, Yvonne Dearman, Mike Sammes, Frank Finlay, Eamonn Andrews, Nicholas Parsons (Jack Valiant)
Writers: Barry Cryer, John Junkin, Eric Morecambe, Ernie Wise
Director: Keith Beckett
Producer: Keith Beckett

The Fall and Rise of Reginald Perrin
BBC1
29/11/78–24/1/79
Series Three:
'The Great Project'
29/11/78
Leonard Rossiter (Reginald Perrin), Pauline Yates (Elizabeth Perrin), John Barron (C.J.), Sue Nicholls (Joan Greengross), Sally-Jane Spencer (Linda), Leslie Schofield (Tom), Geoffrey Palmer (Jimmy), Trevor Adams (Tony Webster), Bruce Bould (David Harris-Jones), John Horsley (Doc Morrisey), Theresa Watson (Prue Harris-Jones), Brian Coburn (Big Man in Bank), George Tovey (Little Man in Bank), David Hanson (Bank Clerk), Leslie Rhodes (Barman), Ali Baba (Indian in Park), Robert Hillier (Adam), Abagail Morgan (Jocasta)

'Staff Training'
6/12/78
Leonard Rossiter (Reginald Perrin), Pauline Yates (Elizabeth Perrin), John Barron (C.J.), Sue Nicholls (Joan Greengross), Sally-Jane Spencer (Linda), Leslie Schofield (Tom), Geoffrey Palmer (Jimmy), Trevor Adams (Tony Webster), Bruce Bould (David Harris-Jones), John Horsley (Doc Morrisey), Theresa Watson (Prue Harris-Jones), Arnold Peters (Mr Penfold), Joyce Windsor (Mrs Hollies), James Warrior (Mr Babbacombe), Stewart Quentin-Holmes (Passer-by on Canal Towpath)

'The Trickle of Visitors'

20/12/78
Leonard Rossiter (Reginald Perrin), Pauline
Yates (Elizabeth Perrin), John Barron
(C.J.), Sue Nicholls (Joan Greengross),
Sally-Jane Spencer (Linda), Leslie Schofield
(Tom), Geoffrey Palmer (Jimmy), Trevor
Adams (Tony Webster), Bruce Bould
(David Harris-Jones), John Horsley (Doc
Morrisey), Theresa Watson (Prue Harris-
Jones), Glynn Edwards (Mr Pelham), Leslie
Sands (Thruxton Appleby), Frederick
Jaeger (Bernard Trilling), Ronald Pember
(Arthur Noblet), Sally Lahee (Hilary
Meadows)

'Communal Social Evenings'
27/12/78
Leonard Rossiter (Reginald Perrin), Pauline
Yates (Elizabeth Perrin), John Barron
(C.J.), Sue Nicholls (Joan Greengross),
Sally-Jane Spencer (Linda), Leslie Schofield
(Tom), Geoffrey Palmer (Jimmy), Trevor
Adams (Tony Webster), Bruce Bould
(David Harris-Jones), John Horsley (Doc
Morrisey), Theresa Watson (Prue Harris-
Jones), Robert Gillespie (Mr Dent), Peter
Schofield (Mr Winstanley), David Ellison
(Factory Owner), Bunny May (Insurance
Salesman), Janet Davies (Ethel Merman),
Peter Hill (Edwards), Michael Segal (Mr
Jenkins), Andrew Johns (Mr Pennell), Peter
Roberts (Youth), Frank Baker (The Shy
Vet)

'Timebomb'
3/1/79
Leonard Rossiter (Reginald Perrin), Pauline
Yates (Elizabeth Perrin), John Barron
(C.J.), Sue Nicholls (Joan Greengross),
Sally-Jane Spencer (Linda), Leslie Schofield
(Tom), Geoffrey Palmer (Jimmy), Trevor
Adams (Tony Webster), Bruce Bould
(David Harris-Jones), John Horsley (Doc
Morrisey), Theresa Watson (Prue Harris-
Jones), Terence Alexander (Clive 'Lofty'
Anstruther), Hilary Tindall (Deborah
Swaffham), Timothy Carlton (Colin

Pillock), Vincent Bramble (Glenn Higgins),
Gordon Case (Johnson), Frank Baker (Shy
Vet), Kenneth Watson (Superintendent) ,
Leslie Glazer (Merchant Banker)

Untitled
17/1/79
Leonard Rossiter (Reginald Perrin), Pauline
Yates (Elizabeth Perrin), John Barron
(C.J.), Sue Nicholls (Joan Greengross),
Sally-Jane Spencer (Linda), Leslie Schofield
(Tom), Geoffrey Palmer (Jimmy), Trevor
Adams (Tony Webster), Bruce Bould
(David Harris-Jones), John Horsley (Doc
Morrisey), Theresa Watson (Prue Harris-
Jones), Derry Power (Seamus Finnegan),
Joan Peart (Mrs E. Blythe-Erpingham),
Jonathan Fryer (Landlord), Leslie Adams
(Driver)

Untitled
24/1/79
Leonard Rossiter (Reginald Perrin), Pauline
Yates (Elizabeth Perrin), John Barron
(C.J.), Sue Nicholls (Joan Greengross),
Sally-Jane Spencer (Linda), Leslie Schofield
(Tom), Geoffrey Palmer (Jimmy), Trevor
Adams (Tony Webster), Bruce Bould
(David Harris-Jones), John Horsley (Doc
Morrisey), Theresa Watson (Prue Harris-
Jones), John Quayle (Mr Fennel), Linda
Cunningham (Iris Hoddle), Terence
Woodfield (Muscroft), David Sparks
(Rosewall)
Writer: David Nobbs
Directed: Gareth Gwenlan
Producer: Gareth Gwenlan

Cinzano commercials
ITV
1978–1983
Leonard Rossiter (Nebbish), Joan Collins
(Melissa)
Bianco Launch
Art Director: Ron Collins
Copy-writer: John Withers
Director: Alan Parker

Rosé Launch
Art Director: Ron Collins
Copy-writer: John Withers
Director: Alan Parker
Secco Launch
Art Director: Ron Collins
Copy-writer: John Withers
Director: Alan Parker

'Airliner'
Art Director: Neil Godfrey
Copy-writer: Tony Brignall
Director: Hugh Hudson

'Ski Lodge'
Art Director: Neil Godfrey
Copy-writer: Tony Brignall
Director: Hugh Hudson

'Roller Disco'
Art Director: Paul Smith
Copy-writer: Mike Everett
Director: Paul Weiland

'Balcony'
Art Director: Paul Smith
Copy-writer: Mike Everett
Director: Paul Weiland

'Mime'
Art Director: Judy Smith
Copy-writer: Peter Matthews
Director: Peter Levelle

'Tiger's Head'
Art Director: Terry Lovelock
Copy-writer: Terry Lovelock
Director: Terry Lovelock

'Dragoon'
Art Director: Terry Lovelock
Copy-writer: Terry Lovelock
Director: Terry Lovelock

The Perishers
BBC

21/3/79–4/5/79
Voice Actors: Judy Bennett, Sheila Steafel,
Peter Hawkins, Leonard Rossiter
Writer: Maurice Dodd
Director: Dick Horn
Producer: Graeme Spurway

The Prestel Connection
ITV
1979
Commercial
Leonard Rossiter (Harry Lemon)
Director: Len Fulford

'Play For Today': *The Factory*
BBC1
22/12/81
Leonard Rossiter (Harry Meadows),
Gwyneth Strong (Penny Shepherd),
Benjamin Whitrow (James Sellars), Ray
Winstone (Tommy Mason)
Writer: David Hopkins
Director: Gerald Blake
Producer: Innes Lloyd

London Docklands Development
ITV
1982
Leonard Rossiter (Crow 1), John
Barron (Crow 2)
Director: Ken Turner

Escape to the West
HTV
18/7/1982
Joss Ackland, John Abineri, Patricia Brake,
Rosalie Crutchley, Leonard Rossiter,
Norman Bowler
Writer: Dave Martin
Director: Alex Kirby
Producer: Patrick Dromgoole

The Funny Side of Christmas: The Fall
and Rise of Reginald Perrin
BBC
27/12/82
Specially produced segment for this festive

anthology programme.
Leonard Rossiter (Reginald Perrin), Pauline Yates (Elizabeth Perrin), John Barron (C.J.), Sue Nicholls (Joan Greengross), Sally-Jane Spencer (Linda), Leslie Schofield (Tom), Geoffrey Palmer (Jimmy), Trevor Adams (Tony Webster), Bruce Bould (David Harris-Jones)
Writer: David Nobbs

Mick's People
ITV
1983
Commercial for Barclay's Bank
Leonard Rossiter, Mick Ford, Vivienne Ritchie
Director: Jonathan Lynn
Producer: Jeanna Polley for Producers Films

'Play for Today': *Dog Ends*
BBC1
17/7/84
Liz Crowther (Doctor), John Grillo (Vet), Pat Heywood (Beatrice), Charles Lamb (Grandad), Lesley Manville (Vivienne), Bryan Pringle (Henry), Leonard Rossiter (Arthur), David Threlfall (Robert)
Writer: Richard Harris
Director: Carol Wiseman
Producer: Andree Molyneux

Tripper's Day
Thames
24/9/84–29/10/84
'Special Offers'
24/9/84
Leonard Rossiter (Norman Tripper), David John (Laurel), Pat Ashton (Hilda Rimmer), Gordon Gostelow (Alf Battle), Paul Clarkson (Mr Christian), Liz Crowther (Sylvia), Philip Bird (Hardie), Andrew Paul (Higgins), Charon Bourke (Marlene), Vicky Licorish (Dottie)
Writer: Brian Cook
Director: Anthony Parker
Producer: James Gilbert

'Foreign Parts'
1/10/84
Leonard Rossiter (Norman Tripper), David John (Laurel), Pat Ashton (Hilda Rimmer), Gordon Gostelow (Alf Battle), Paul Clarkson (Mr Christian), Liz Crowther (Sylvia), Philip Bird (Hardie), Andrew Paul (Higgins), Charon Bourke (Marlene), Vicky Licorish (Dottie)
Writer: Brian Cook
Director: Michael Mills
Producer: James Gilbert

'Games People Play'
8/10/84
Leonard Rossiter (Norman Tripper), David John (Laurel), Pat Ashton (Hilda Rimmer), Gordon Gostelow (Alf Battle), Paul Clarkson (Mr Christian), Liz Crowther (Sylvia), Philip Bird (Hardie), Andrew Paul (Higgins), Charon Bourke (Marlene), Vicky Licorish (Dottie)
Writer: Brian Cook
Director: Michael Mills
Producer: James Gilbert

'Token of Esteem'
15/10/84
Leonard Rossiter (Norman Tripper), David John (Laurel), Pat Ashton (Hilda Rimmer), Gordon Gostelow (Alf Battle), Paul Clarkson (Mr Christian), Liz Crowther (Sylvia), Philip Bird (Hardie), Andrew Paul (Higgins), Charon Bourke (Marlene), Vicky Licorish (Dottie)
Writer: Brian Cook
Director: Michael Mills
Producer: James Gilbert

'Alarms and Diversions'
22/10/84
Leonard Rossiter (Norman Tripper), David John (Laurel), Pat Ashton (Hilda Rimmer), Gordon Gostelow (Alf Battle), Paul Clarkson (Mr Christian), Liz Crowther (Sylvia), Philip Bird (Hardie), Andrew Paul (Higgins), Charon Bourke (Marlene), Vicky

Licorish (Dottie)
Writer: Brian Cook
Director: Michael Mills
Producer: James Gilbert

'Vatman and Robbin'
29/10/84
Leonard Rossiter (Norman Tripper), David
John (Laurel), Pat Ashton (Hilda Rimmer),
Gordon Gostelow (Alf Battle), Paul
Clarkson (Mr Christian), Liz Crowther
(Sylvia), Philip Bird (Hardie), Andrew Paul
(Higgins), Charon Bourke (Marlene), Vicky
Licorish (Dottie)
Writer: Brian Cook
Director: Michael Mills
Producer: James Gilbert

'BBC Shakespeare': *The Life and*
Death of King John
BBC2
24/11/84
Leonard Rossiter (King John), William
Whymper (Chatillon), Mary Morris
(Queen Elinor), Robert Brown (Earl of
Pembroke), John Castle (Earl of Salisbury),
John Flint (Lord Bigot), John Thaw
(Hubert de Burgh), George Costigan
(Philip – the Bastard), Edward Hibbert
(Robert Faulconbridge), Phyllida Law
(Lady Faulconbridge), Mike Lewin (James
Gurney), Charles Kay (King Philip of
France), Jonathan Coy (Lewis, the
Dauphin), Luc Owen (Arthur – Duke of
Britaine) Gorden Kaye (Lymoges – Duke of
Austria), Claire Bloom (Constance), John
Moreno (Melun), Ian Barritt (French
Herald), Janet Maw (Blanch), Carl Oatley
(English Herald), Clifford Parrish (Citizen
of Angiers), Richard Wordsworth (Cardinal
Pandulph), Ian Brimble (First Executioner),
Ronald Chenery (English Messenger), Alan
Collins (Peter of Pomfret), Tim Brown
(French Messenger), Rusty Livingstone
(Prince Henry), Harry Fielder (Guard)
Writer: William Shakespeare
Director: David Giles

Producer: Shaun Sutton

Moon over Soho
BBC1
18/8/85
Leonard Rossiter, Mary Morris, Lesley
Manville, Ken Campbell, Larrington
Walker, Ivor Roberts, Dave Hill
Writer: Peter Ansorge
Director: Stuart Burge
Producer: Michael Wearing

Alice in Wonderland
Anglia
26/3/85–23/4/85
Giselle Andrews (Alice), Paul Eddington
(White Rabbit), Mary Miller (Baby),
Michael Bentine (March Hare), Jon Glover
(Pat, Mrs Pat, Bill, Knave, Fish Footman,
Frog Footman), Eric Sykes (Mad Hatter),
John Barron (The Caterpillar), John Braban
(Dodo) Eleanor Bron (The Duchess), Leslie
Crowther (The Cheshire Cat), Royce Mills
(Dormouse), Leonard Rossiter (The King of
Hearts), Joan Sanderson (The Queen of
Hearts)
Writer: Harry Aldous (From the books by
Lewis Carroll)
Director: Harry Aldous
Producer: Harry Aldous

FILM

A Kind Of Loving **(1962)**
Alan Bates (Victor Arthur 'Vic' Brown),
June Ritchie (Ingrid Rothwell), Thora Hird
(Mrs Rothwell), Bert Palmer (Mr Geoffrey
Brown), Malcolm Patton (Jim Brown),
Gwen Nelson (Mrs Brown), Pat Keen
(Christine Harris), David Mahlowe (David
Harris), Jack Smethurst (Conroy), James
Bolam (Jeff), Michael Deacon (Les) John
Ronane (Draughtsman) David Cook
(Draughtsman), Norman Heyes
(Laisterdyke) Leonard Rossiter (Whymper),
Fred Ferris (Althorpe), Patsy Rowlands

(Dorothy), Annette Robertson (Phoebe), Ruth Porcher (Mrs Parker), Harry Markham (Railwayman), Peter Madden (Registrar), Kathy Staff (Mrs Oliphant), Jerry Desmonde (TV Compere), Joe Gladwin (Bus Driver), Reginald Green (Contestant), Douglas Livingstone (Window Cleaner), Bryan Mosley (Bus Conductor), Bud Ralston (Pub Comedian), Edna Ridgway (Pub Pianist), Graham Rigby (Pub Politician), Yvonne Buckingham (Barmaid), Helen Fraser (Ingrid's Friend) Kathleen Walker (Woman in dinner queue)
Screenplay: Willis Hall and Keith Waterhouse (based on the novel by Stan Barstow)
Director: John Schlesinger

This Sporting Life (1963)
Richard Harris (Frank Machin) Rachel Roberts (Mrs Margaret Hammond), Alan Badel (Gerald Weaver), William Hartnell ('Dad' Johnson) Colin Blakely (Maurice Braithwaite), Vanda Godsell (Mrs Anne Weaver), Anne Cunningham (Judith), Jack Watson (Len Miller), Arthur Lowe (Charles Slomer), Harry Markham (Wade), George Sewell (Jeff), Leonard Rossiter (Phillips, Sports writer), Katherine Parr (Mrs Farrer), Bernadette Benson (Lynda Hammond), Andrew Nolan (Ian Hammond), Peter Duguid (Doctor), Wallas Eaton (Waiter), Anthony Woodruff (Tom, Headwaiter), Michael Logan (Riley), Murray Evans (Hooker), Tom Clegg (Gower), Ken Traill (Trainer), Frank Windsor (Dentist), John Gill (Cameron), Edward Fox (Restaurant Barman), Glenda Jackson (Singer at Party), David Storey (Rugby Player)
Screenplay: David Storey (based on his own novel)
Director: Lindsay Anderson

Billy Liar (1963)
Tom Courtenay (William Terrence 'Billy' Fisher), Wilfred Pickles (Geoffrey Fisher), Mona Washbourne (Alice Fisher), Ethel Griffies (Florence), Finlay Currie (Duxbury), Gwendolyn Watts (Rita), Helen Fraser (Barbara), Julie Christie (Liz), Leonard Rossiter (Emanuel Shadrack) Rodney Bewes (Arthur Crabtree), George Innes (Stamp), Leslie Randall (Danny Boon) Patrick Barr (Insp. MacDonald), Ernest Clark (Prison Governor), Godfrey Winn (Disc Jockey)
Screenplay: Keith Waterhouse and Willis Hall (based on Waterhouse's novel and their play)
Director: John Schlesinger

A Jolly Bad Fellow (US They All Died Laughing) (1964)
Leo McKern (Prof. Bowles-Ottery), Janet Munro (Delia Brooks), Maxine Audley (Clarinda Bowles-Ottery), Duncan Macrae (Dr Brass), Dennis Price (Prof. Hughes), Miles Malleson (Dr Woolley), Leonard Rossiter (Dr Fisher), Alan Wheatley (Epicene), Patricia Jessel (Mrs Pugh-Smith), Dinsdale Landen (Fred), George Benson (Insp. Butts), Mark Dignam (The Master), Jerome Willis (Armstrong), Ralph Michael (Supt. Rastleigh), Mervyn Johns (Willie Pugh-Smith), Raymond Ray (Waiter), Joyce Carey (Hotel receptionist), Cliff Michelmore (TV commentator), Wally Patch (Landlord)
Screenplay: Robert Hamer and Donald Taylor (based on C.E. Vulliamy's novel *Down Among the Dead Men*)
Directed by Don Chaffey

King Rat (1965)
George Segal (Corporal King), Tom Courtenay (Lt. Robin Grey), James Fox (Peter Marlowe) Patrick O'Neal (Top Sgt. Max), Denholm Elliott (Lt. G.D. Larkin), James Donald (Dr Kennedy), Todd Armstrong (Tex), John Mills (Col. George Smedley-Taylor), Gerald Sim (Lt. Col. Jones), Leonard Rossiter (Maj. McCoy), John Standing (Capt. Daven), Alan Webb (Col. Brant), John Ronane (Capt.

Hawkins), Sammy Reese (Kurt), Michael Lees (Stevens), Wright King (Maj. Brough), Hamilton Dyce (Chaplain Drinkwater), Joe Turkel (Dino), John Merivale (Col. Foster), Geoffrey Bayldon (Squadron Leader Vexley), Reg Lye (Tinker Bell), Arthur Malet (Sgt. Blakeley), Hedley Mattingly (Dr Prudhomme), Dale Ishimoto (Yoshima), John Levingston (Myner), Teru Shimada (The Japanese General), Richard Dawson (Capt. Weaver), Michael Stroka (Miller), William Fawcett (Steinmetz), Roy Duane (Peterson), John Orchard (Pte. Gurble), Larry Conroy (Townsend), John Warburton (The Commandant), David Haviland (Masters), Anthony Faramus (Prisoner), Dick Johnson (Pop), John Barclay (Lt. Spence), Edward Ashley (Prouty), David Frankham (Cox), Louis Neervort (Torusumi)
Screenplay: Bryan Forbes (based on James Clavell's novel)
Director: Bryan Forbes

Hotel Paradiso (1966)

Gina Lollobrigida (Marcelle Cotte), Alec Guinness (Benedict Boniface), Robert Morley (Henri Cotte), Peggy Mount (Angelique Boniface), Douglas Byng (Mr Martin), Robertson Hare (Duke), David Battley (George), Ann Beach (Victoire), Eddra Gale (Hotel Guest), Darío Moreno (The Turk), Derek Fowlds (Maxime), Leonard Rossiter (Inspector), Akim Tamiroff (Anniello), Marie Bell (La Grande Antoinette)
Screenplay: Peter Glenville and Jean-Claude Carrière (based on the play *Hotel du Libre Echange* by Georges Feydeau)
Director: Peter Glenville

The Witches (US The Devil's Own) (1966)

Joan Fontaine (Gwen Mayfield), Kay Walsh (Stephanie Bax), Alec McCowen (Alan Bax), Ann Bell (Sally Benson), Ingrid Boulting (Linda Rigg), John Collin (Dowsett), Michele Dotrice (Valerie Creek), Gwen Ffrangcon Davies (Granny Rigg), Duncan Lamont (Bob Curd), Leonard Rossiter (Dr Wallis), Martin Stephens (Ronnie Dowsett), Carmel McSharry (Mrs Dowsett), Viola Keats (Mrs Curd), Shelagh Fraser (Mrs Creek), Bryan Marshall (Tom)
Screenplay: Nigel Kneale (based on Norah Lofts' novel *The Devil's Own*)
Director: Cyril Frankel

The Wrong Box (1966)

Jeremy Lloyd (Brian Allen Harvey), James Villiers (Sydney Whitcombe Sykes), Graham Stark (Ian Scott Fife), Richard Gregory (Leicester Young Fielding), Nicholas Parsons (Alan Frazer Scrope), Willoughby Goddard (James Whyte Wragg), Valentine Dyall (Oliver Pike Harmsworth), Leonard Rossiter (Vyvyan Alistair Montague), Hamilton Dyce (Derek Lloyd Peter Digby), Hilton Edwards (Lawyer), Timothy Bateson (Clerk), Donald Oliver (Gunner Sgt), Totti Truman Taylor (Lady at Launching), Jeremy Roughton (Bugler), Frank Singuineau (Native Bearer), Michael Lees (Young Digby), Avis Bunnage (Queen Victoria), John Mills (Masterman Finsbury), Michael Caine (Michael Finsbury), Wilfrid Lawson (Peacock – the Butler), Ralph Richardson (Joseph Finsbury), Peter Cook (Morris Finsbury), Dudley Moore (John Finsbury), Nanette Newman (Julia Finsbury), Gwendolyn Watts (Maidservant), Vanda Godsell (Mrs Goodge), Peter Graves (Military Officer), Tutte Lemkow (Strangler), Marianne Stone (Spinster), John Junkin (First Engine Driver), Roy Murray (Fred the Stoker), Donald Tandy (Ticket Collector), Lionel Gamlin (Second Engine Driver), Martin Terry (Stoker), Michael Bird (Countryman), George Selway (Railway Vanman), Josef Behrmann (Railway Vanman), Peter Sellers (Doctor Pratt), John Le Mesurier (Doctor Slattery), Norman Rossington (First Rough), Thomas

Gallagher (Second Rough), Charlie Bird (Benn's Vanman), Thorley Walters (Lawyer Patience), Cicely Courtneidge (Major Martha), Diane Clare (Mercy), Gerald Sim (First Undertaker), Tony Hancock (Inspector), Tony Thawnton (Second Undertaker), Reg Lye (Third Undertaker), George Spence (Workman in Road), Irene Handl (Mrs Hackett), Norman Bird (Clergyman)
Screenplay: Larry Gelbart and Barry Shevelove (inspired by the novel by Robert Louis Stevenson)
Director: Bryan Forbes

The Whisperers (1966)
Edith Evans (Mrs Ross), Nanette Newman (The Girl Upstairs), Harry Baird (The Man Upstairs), Jack Austin (Police Sgt), Gerald Sim (Mr Conrad), Lionel Gamlin (Mr Conrad's Colleague), Glen Farmer (1st Redeemer), Oliver MacGreevy (2nd Redeemer), Ronald Fraser (Charlie Ross), Kenneth Griffith (Mr Weaver), Avis Bunnage (Mrs Noonan), John Orchard (Grogan), Peter Thompson (Publican), Sarah Forbes (Mrs Ross When Young), Penny Spencer (Mavis Noonan), Kaplan Kaye (Jimmie Noonan), Michael Robbins (Mr Noonan), Frank Singuineau (Negro Doctor), Michael Francis (Plain-Clothes Policeman), Shona Lesley (Nurse), Helen Fleming (Nurse), Rosemary Lord (Nurse), Beth Owen (Nurse), Roy Herrick (Young Doctor), Robin Bailey (Psychiatrist), Eric Portman (Archie Ross), George Spence (Caretaker), Leonard Rossiter (Assistance Board Officer), Margaret Tyzack (Hospital Almoner), Terry Eliot (Nurse), George Hillsden (Ticket Collector), Clare Kelly (Prostitute), Charlie Bird (Man in NAB Office), Max Bacon (Mr Fish), Robert Russell (Andy), Max Rawnsley (Man in Street), Allan O'Keefe (1st Attacker), Francis Flynn (2nd Attacker), Michael Lees (1st Young Man), Tom Kempinski (2nd Young Man), Roy

Maxwell (3rd Young Man)
Screenplay: Bryan Forbes (based on the novel by Robert Nicolson)
Director: Bryan Forbes

Deadlier than The Male (1966)
Richard Johnson (Hugh 'Bulldog' Drummond), Elke Sommer (Irma Eckman), Sylva Koscina (Penelope), Nigel Green (Carl Petersen), Suzanna Leigh (Grace), Steve Carlson (Robert Drummond), Virginia North (Brenda), Justine Lord (Miss Peggy Ashenden), Leonard Rossiter (Henry Bridgenorth), Laurence Naismith (Sir John Bledlow), Zia Mohyeddin (King Fedra), Lee Montague (Boxer), Milton Reid (Chang) Yasuko Nagazumi (Mitsouko), Didi Sydow (Anna), George Pastell (Carloggio), Dervis Ward (Henry Keller), John Stone (David Wyngarde), William Mervyn (Chairman of the Phoenician Board)
Screenplay: Jimmy Sangster, David Osborn, Liz Charles-Williams (based on characters created by H.C. McNeile)
Director: Ralph Thomas

Deadfall (1967)
Michael Caine (Henry Stuart Clarke), Giovanna Ralli (Fé Moreau), Eric Portman (Richard Moreau), David Buck (Salinas), Leonard Rossiter (Fillmore), Geraldine Sherman (Delgado's Receptionist), Carlos Pierre (Antonio), Vladek Sheybal (Dr Delgado), Renata Tarrago (Guitar Soloist), Nanette Newman (Girl), Emilio Rodríguez (Police Captain), Carmen Dene (Masseuse), Reg Howell (Spanish Chauffeur), John Barry (Symphony Orchestra Conductor), Santiago Rivero (Armed Guard)
Screenplay: Bryan Forbes (based on the novel by Desmond Cory)
Director: Bryan Forbes

2001: A Space Odyssey (1968)
Keir Dullea (Dr Dave Bowman), Gary

Lockwood (Dr Frank Poole), William Sylvester (Dr Heywood R. Floyd), Daniel Richter (Moon-Watcher), Leonard Rossiter (Dr Andrei Smyslov), Margaret Tyzack (Elena), Robert Beatty (Dr Ralph Halvorsen), Sean Sullivan (Dr Bill Michaels), Douglas Rain (HAL 9000), Frank Miller (Mission Controller), Bill Weston (Astronaut), Ed Bishop (Aries-1B Lunar shuttle captain), Glenn Beck (Astronaut), Alan Gifford (Poole's father), Ann Gillis (Poole's mother), Edwina Carroll (Aries-1B stewardess), Penny Brahms (Stewardess), Heather Downham (Stewardess), Mike Lovell (Astronaut)
Screenplay: Stanley Kubrick and Sir Arthur C. Clarke (based on his short story 'The Sentinel')
Director: Stanley Kubrick

Oliver! (1968)
Ron Moody (Fagin), Shani Wallis (Nancy), Oliver Reed (Bill Sikes), Harry Secombe (Mr Bumble), Mark Lester (Oliver Twist), Jack Wild (The Artful Dodger), Hugh Griffith (The Magistrate), Joseph O'Conor (Mr Brownlow), Peggy Mount (Mrs Bumble), Leonard Rossiter (Sowerberry), Hylda Baker (Mrs Sowerberry), Kenneth Cranham (Noah Claypole), Megs Jenkins (Mrs Bedwin), Sheila White (Bet), Wensley Pithey (Dr Grimwig), James Hayter (Mr Jessop), Elizabeth Knight (Charlotte), Fred Emney (Chairman – Workhouse), Edwin Finn (Pauper – Workhouse), Roy Evans (Pauper – Workhouse), Norman Mitchell (Arresting Policeman), Robert Bartlett (Fagin's Boy), Graham Buttrose (Fagin's Boy), Jeffrey Chandler (Fagin's Boy), Kirk Clugston (Fagin's Boy), Dempsey Cook (Fagin's Boy), Christopher Duff (Fagin's Boy), Nigel Grice (Fagin's Boy), Ronnie Johnson (Fagin's Boy), Nigel Kingsley (Fagin's Boy), Robert Langley (Fagin's Boy), Brian Lloyd (Fagin's Boy), Peter Lock (Fagin's Boy), Clive Moss (Fagin's Boy), Ian Ramsey (Fagin's Boy), Peter Renn (Fagin's Boy), Billy Smith (Fagin's Boy), Kim Smith (Fagin's Boy), Freddie Stead (Fagin's Boy), Raymond Ward (Fagin's Boy), John Watters (Fagin's Boy)
Screenplay: Vernon Harris (based on Lionel Bart's musical adaptation of Charles Dickens' novel *Oliver Twist*)
Director: Carol Reed

Diamonds for Breakfast (1968)
Marcello Mastroianni (Grand Duke Nicholas Wladimirovitch Goduno), Rita Tushingham (Bridget Rafferty), Elaine Taylor (Victoria), Margaret Blye (Honey), Francesca Tu (Jeanne Silkingers), The Karlins (Triplets), Warren Mitchell (Popov), Nora Nicholson (Anastasia Petrovna), Bryan Pringle (Police Sgt), Leonard Rossiter (Inspector Dudley), Bill Fraser (Bookseller), David Horne (Duke of Windemere), Charles Lloyd Pack (Butler), Anne Blake (Nashka)
Screenplay: Simpson, Rouve and Harwood
Director: Christopher Morahan

Otley (1968)
Tom Courtenay (Gerald Arthur Otley), Romy Schneider (Imogen), Alan Badel (Sir Alex Hadrian), James Villiers (Hendrickson), Leonard Rossiter (Johnston), Freddie Jones (Philip Proudfoot), Fiona Lewis (Lin), James Bolam (Albert), James Cossins (Geffcock), James Maxwell (Rollo), Edward Hardwicke (Lambert), Ronald Lacey (Curtis), Phyllida Law (Jean), Geoffrey Bayldon (Insp. Hewett), Frank Middlemass (Bruce), Damian Harris (Miles), Robert Brownjohn (Paul), Maureen Toal (Landlady), Barry Fantoni (Larry), Bernard Sharpe (Tony), Paul Angelis (Constable), David Kernan (Ground steward), Sheila Steafel (Ground stewardess), Katherine Parr (Newsagent), Kathleen Helm (Dietician), Norman Shelley (Businessman), John Savident (Businessman), Ken Parry (Businessman), Jonathan Cecil (Young man at party),

Georgina Simpson (Young girl at party), Ron Owen (Hotel waiter), Stella Tanner (Traffic warden), Robin Askwith (Kid No.1), Kevin Bennett (Kid No.2), Kenneth Cranham (Kid No.3), Robert Gillespie (Policeman), Don McKillop (Police driver), Pete Murray (Himself – Radio Presenter (voice)), Jimmy Young (Himself – Radio Presenter (voice))
Screenplay: Dick Clement and Ian La Frenais (based on the novel by Martin Waddell)
Directed: Dick Clement

Luther (1973)

Stacy Keach (Martin Luther), Patrick Magee (Hans), Hugh Griffith (John Tetzel), Robert Stephens (Johan von Eck), Alan Badel (Thomas de Vio), Julian Glover (The Knight), Judi Dench (Katherine), Leonard Rossiter (Brother Weinand), Maurice Denham (Johann von Staupitz), Peter Cellier (Prior), Thomas Heathcote (Lucas), Malcolm Stoddard (King Charles), Bruce Carstairs (Duke of Saxony), Matthew Guinness (monk), Tom Baker (Pope Leo X)
Screenplay: Edward Anhalt (based on the play by John Osborne)
Directed: Guy Green

Barry Lyndon (1975)

Ryan O'Neal (Barry Lyndon/Redmond Barry) Marisa Berenson (Lady Lyndon), Patrick Magee (The Chevalier), Hardy Krüger (Captain Potzdorf), Steven Berkoff (Lord Ludd), Gay Hamilton (Nora Brady), Marie Kean (Barry's Mother), Diana Körner (German Girl), Murray Melvin (Reverend Runt), Frank Middlemass (Sir Charles Lyndon), André Morell (Lord Wendover), Arthur O'Sullivan (Captain Feeny,), Godfrey Quigley (Captain Grogan), Leonard Rossiter (Captain Quin), Philip Stone (Graham), Leon Vitali (Lord Bullingdon), John Bindon (Recruiting soldier), Roger Booth (King George III), Billy Boyle (Seamus Feeny), Jonathan Cecil (Lt. Jonathan Fakenham), Peter Cellier (Sir Richard), Geoffrey Chater (Dr Broughton), Anthony Dawes (British Soldier), Barry Jackson (British Soldier), Wolf Kahler (Prince of Tübingen), Ferdy Mayne (Colonel Bulow), David Morley (Bryan Patrick Lyndon), Pat Roach (Toole), Dominic Savage (Young Bullingdon), George Sewell (Barry's Second), Anthony Sharp (Lord Hallam), John Sharp (Doolan)
Screenplay: Stanley Kubrick (based on the novel by William Makepeace Thackeray)
Director: Stanley Kubrick

The Pink Panther Strikes Again (1976)

Peter Sellers (Chief Inspector Clouseau), Herbert Lom (Dreyfus), Lesley-Anne Down (Olga), Burt Kwouk (Cato Fong), Colin Blakely (Drummond), Leonard Rossiter (Quinlan), André Maranne (François), Byron Kane (Secretary of State), Dick Crockett (The President), Richard Vernon (Fassbender), Briony McRoberts (Margo Fassbender), Dudley Sutton (McClaren), Hal Galili (Danny Salvo), Robert Beatty (Admiral), Bob Sherman (CIA Agent), Phil Brown (Virginia Senator), Jerry Stovin (Aide), Paul Maxwell (CIA Director), Michael Robbins (Jarvis), Vanda Godsell (Mrs Leverlilly), Norman Mitchell (Mr Bullock), Patsy Smart (Mrs Japonica), Tony Sympson (Mr Shork), George Leech (Mr Stutterstutt), Deep Roy (Italian Assassin), Geoffrey Bayldon (Dr Duval), Graham Stark (Munich Hotel Clerk), Anthony Chinn (Chinese Assassin), Ivan Hunte (Piano Player), Josh Little (Drummer), Joe Sampson (Bass Player), Gordon Hunte (Guitar Player), Kevin Scott (MC), John Clive (Chuck), Chris Langham (Police Driver), James Warrior (Police Constable), Gordon Rollings (Inmate), Joan Rhodes (Daphne), Damaris Hayman (Fiona), Patrick Jordan (Detective), Richard Bartlett (Young Man), John Sullivan (Tournier), Dinny Powell (Marty the Mugger), Terry

Richards (Bruce the Knife), Bill Cummings (Hindo Harry), Terry Yorke (Cairo Fred), Terence Plummer (1st Kidnapper), Peter Brace (2nd Kidnapper), Cyd Child (Bouncer), Eddie Stacey (West German Assassin), Herb Tanney (Norwegian Assassin), Joe Powell (Taxi Passenger), Fred Haggerty (Munich Hotel Doorman), Terence Maidment (West German Assassin), Julie Andrews (Ainsley Jarvis (singing voice)), Omar Sharif (Egyptian Assassin)
Screenplay: Frank Waldman and Blake Edwards
Director: Blake Edwards

Voyage of the Damned (1976)

Faye Dunaway (Denise Kreisler), Oskar Werner (Professor Egon Kreisler), Lee Grant (Lili Rosen), Sam Wanamaker (Carl Rosen), Lynne Frederick (Anna Rosen), David de Keyser (Joseph Joseph), Della McDermott (Julia Strauss), Genevieve West (Sarah Strauss), Luther Adler (Professor Weiler), Wendy Hiller (Rebecca Weiler), Julie Harris (Alice Fienchild), Nehemiah Persoff (Mr Hauser), Maria Schell (Mrs Hauser), Paul Koslo (Aaron Pozner), Jonathan Pryce (Joseph Manasse), Brian Gilbert (Laurenz Schulman), Georgina Hale (Lotte Schulman), Adele Strong (Mrs Schulman), Milo Sperber (Rabbi), Max von Sydow (Captain Schroeder), Malcolm McDowell (Max Gunter), Helmut Griem (Otto Schiendick), Keith Barron (Purser Mueller), Anthony Higgins (Seaman Berg), Ian Cullen (Steinman, Radio Officer), Donald Houston (Dr Glauner), David Daker (First Officer), Constantine Gregory (Navigation Officer), Don Henderson (Engineering Officer), Ina Skriver (Singer), Orson Welles (José Estedes), James Mason (Dr Juan Remos), Katharine Ross (Mira Hauser), Victor Spinetti (Dr Erich Strauss), Michael Constantine (Luis Clasing), José Ferrer (Manuel Benitez), Ben Gazzara (Morris Troper), Fernando Rey (President

Bru), Bernard Hepton (Milton Goldsmith), Günter Meisner (Robert Hoffman), Marika Rivera (Madame in Bordello), Janet Suzman (Leni Strauss), Frederick Jaeger (Werner Mannheim), Denholm Elliott (Admiral Canaris), Leonard Rossiter (Commander von Bonin), Philip Stone (Secretary)
Screenplay: Steve Shagan and David Butler (based on the book by Steve Shagan and David Butler)
Director: Stuart Rosenberg

The Waterloo Bridge Handicap (1978)

Leonard Rossiter (Charles Barker), Gorden Kaye (Chubby Chap), Lynda Bellingham (Likely Lady), Patricia Hodge (Gossiping girl), John Quentin (Austin Reed), Brough Scott (Commentator), Ian Marter (Lincoln's Inn), Zoot Money (Red Hair), Azad Ali (Station Master), Brian Croucher, Tricia George (Gossiping girl), Bill Kerry, Lucita Lijertwood (Ticket Collector), Count Prince Miller (Ticket Collector), Seretta Wilson (Tourist)
Screenplay: Ross Cramer
Director: Ross Cramer

Le Pétomane (1979)

Leonard Rossiter (Monsieur Joseph Pujol), Madelaine Bellamy, John D. Collins, Michael Cronin, Alexandra Dane, Kalman Glass, John Harvey, Alun Lewis, Victor Lucas, Roland MacLeod, Nancy Nevinson, Michael Ripper, Gordon Rollings, Graham Stark, Bob Todd
Screenplay: Ray Galton and Alan Simpson
Director: Ian MacNaughton

Rising Damp (1980)

Leonard Rossiter (Rigsby), Frances de la Tour (Miss Jones), Denholm Elliott (Seymour), Don Warrington (Philip), Christopher Strauli (John), Carrie Jones (Sandra), Glynn Edwards (Cooper), John Cater (Bert), Derek Griffiths (Alec), Ronnie Brody (Waiter), Alan Clare (Accordionist),

Jonathan Cecil (Assistant), Bill Dean (Workman), Pat Roach (Rugby player)
Screenplay: Eric Chappell
Director: Joe McGrath

***Britannia Hospital* (1982)**
Leonard Rossiter (Vincent Potter), Brian Pettifer (Biles), John Moffatt (Greville Figg), Fulton Mackay (Chief Superintendant Johns), Vivian Pickles (Matron), Barbara Hicks (Miss Tinker), Graham Crowden (Professor Millar), Jill Bennett (Dr MacMillan), Peter Jeffrey (Sir Geoffrey), Marsha A. Hunt (Nurse Amanda Persil), Catherine Willmer (Dr Houston), Mary MacLeod (Casualty Sister), Joan Plowright (Phyllis Grimshaw), Robin Askwith (Ben Keating), Dave Atkins (Sharkey), Malcolm McDowell (Mick Travis), Mark Hamill (Red), Frank Grimes (Sammy / Voice of Genesis), Peter Machin (Peter Mancini), Marcus Powell (Sir Anthony Mount), John Bett (Lady Felicity), Gladys Crosbie (Queen Mother), Rufus Collins (Odingu), Ram John Holder (Aide), Jim Findley (Aide) Pauline Melville (Clarissa), Kevin Lloyd (Picket), Robert Pugh (Picket), Robbie Coltrane (Picket), Dandy Nichols (Florrie), Glenn Williams (Whoolie), Brian Glover (Painter), Mike Grady (Painter), Tony Haygarth (Fraser), Jagdish Kumar (Sen), Patrick Durkin (Blodgett), Paddy Joyce (Feeney), Richard Griffiths (Cheerful Bernie), Dave Hill (Jeff), Charmian May (Miss Diamond), Valentine Dyall (Mr Rochester), Roland Culver (General Wetherby), Betty Marsden (Hermione), Adele Strong (Old Lady), Ted Burnett (Taxi Driver), Gabrielle Lloyd (Private Nurse), Barbara Flynn (Private Nurse), Val Pringle (President Ngami), Robert Lee (Mr Banzai), Errol Shaker (Captain Mbwami), Alan Penn (Padre), Liz Smith (Maisie), Robin Davies (Adrian), John Gordon Sinclair (Gregory), Bob Hornery (BBC Cameraman), Paul McCleary (Assistant), Paul Kember (Sound Recordist), Jane Stonehouse (PA), Patricia Healey (Intensive Care Sister), Rosemary Martin (Casualty Nurse), Robert Owen (Ambulanceman), Ellis Dale (Man in Wheelchair), Maggie Ollerenshaw (Miss Rowntree), Elizabeth Bennett (Nurse / Demonstrator), Patsy Byrne (Nurse), Brenda Cavendish (Nurse), David Daker (Guest Workman), Edward Peel (Guest Workman), Alan Bates (Macready), Arthur Lowe (Guest Patient), T.P. McKenna (Theatre Surgeon), Michael Medwin (Theatre Surgeon), Edward Hibbert (Theatre Surgeon), Peter Holmes (Theatre Surgeon), Salmaan Peerzada (Theatre Surgeon), Janette Foggo (Theatre Nurse), Cora Kinnaird (Theatre Nurse)
Screenplay: David Sherwin
Director: Lindsay Anderson

***Trail of the Pink Panther* (1982)**
Footage of Leonard from 1976's *The Pink Panther Strikes Again* was used in this 'tribute' to Peter Sellers' Inspector Clouseau
Screenplay: Blake Edwards
Director: Blake Edwards

***Water* (1985)**
Michael Caine (Governor Baxter Thwaites), Valerie Perrine (Pamela Weintraub), Brenda Vaccaro (Dolores Thwaites), Leonard Rossiter (Sir Malcolm Leveridge), Billy Connolly (Delgado Fitzhugh), Dennis Dugan (Rob Waring), Fulton Mackay (Reverend Eric), Jimmie Walker (Jay Jay), Dick Shawn (Deke Halliday), Fred Gwynne (Franklin Spender), Trevor Laird (Pepito), Chris Tummings (Garfield Cooper), Stefan Kalipha (Cuban), Alan Igbon (Cuban), Kelvin Omard (Nado), Oscar James (Miguel), Charles Thomas Murphy (Ken), Felicity Dean (Sarah), William Hootkins (Ben Branch), Alan Shearman (Charlesworth), Bill Bailey (Hollister), Richard Pearson (Foreign Secretary), Maureen Lipman (Prime Minister), Paul Heiney (Kessler), Glory Annen (Hostess), Bruce Boa (US Advisor), Danny Brainin (Film Director), Jacqueline De Peza (Lucille), Harry Ditson (Spenco

off

off

289

Executive), Benjamin Feitelson (French
Reporter), Darcy Flynn (TV Production
Assistant), Christopher Gilbert (US Marine),
Rashid Karapiet (US Secretary General), Sabu
Kimura (Japanese Reporter), Julie Legrand
(French Business Executive), Lucita
Lijertwood (Delgado's Mother), Alfred
Molina (Pierre), Bill Persky (TV Director),
Manning Redwood (US General), Bill
Reimbold (Texan), Bob Sessions (US
Admiral), Ruby Wax (Spenco Executive)
The Singing Rebels Band: Eric Clapton, Ray
Cooper, Jon Lord, Mike Moran, Chris
Stainton, Ringo Starr, Jenny Bogle,
Anastasia Rodriguez
Screenplay: Dick Clement, Ian La Frenais
and Bill Persky
Director: Dick Clement

RADIO

Semi-Detached
9/63
A recording of the stage production
produced for radio.
Writer: David Turner
Director: Anthony Richardson

Paths Of Glory
1/65
Adaptation of the Humphrey Cobb novel
(adapted eight years earlier for the screen
by Stanley Kubrick).

Steptoe and Son: The Lead Man Cometh
2/66
It was common for the BBC to adapt
successful sitcoms for the radio and *Steptoe
and Son* was no exception. This was a
slightly revised version of the original script
performed again by Wilfrid Brambell,
Harry H. Corbett and Leonard Rossiter.

No Exit

4/73

Close Encounters of the Worst Kind
7/83

ALBUMS/SPOKEN WORD

Free as Air
6/57
Original Cast Recording of the musical *Free
as Air* performed at the Savoy Theatre.
Released on Oriole Records.

Hooray for Daisy!
12/59
Selected songs from the Bristol Old Vic
show released on the His Master's Voice
label.

Jeeves: A Gentleman's Personal Gentleman
1980
Featuring: Gerald Harper, Frank Duncan,
Keith Alexander, Andrew Sachs, Kenny
Lynch, Norris McWhirter, Wilfrid
Brambell, Leonard Rossiter and Annie
Haslam.
Writer: C. Northcote Parkinson

A Christmas Carol
1981
An abridged version of the Dickens novella,
narrated by Leonard Rossiter.

Rising Damp
1/80
End title song for the movie as performed
by 'Leonard Rossiter and the Rigsbyettes'.
Credited as 'Leonard Rossiter & The
Rigsbyettes'
Music: Brian Wade
Lyrics: Eric Chappell
Released on the Chips label.

Sources

The following books and TV programmes have been invaluable in the writing of this biography and I would recommend them to anyone who wants to find out more about Leonard Rossiter and his work.

BOOKS

Leonard Rossiter
By Robert Tanitch, published by Robert Royce, 1985
A 'pictorial tribute' to Leonard published shortly after his death. Numerous quotes from people who worked with him throughout his career (including many who are now sadly passed on) appear alongside the most comprehensive and evocative selection of photographs one can imagine. The book is unfortunately out of print but is well worth hunting down secondhand.

Rising Damp: A Celebration
By Richard Webber, published by Boxtree, 2001
The name fairly gives it away. Webber has written extensively on the sitcom and his work always hits that tricky balance of being incredibly informative but still a humorous, pleasurable read. An absolute necessity for any fan of *Rising Damp*, covering the show in far more depth than I was able to here. It is sadly out of print but can be found online through the usual second-hand sources.

Rising Damp: The Complete Scripts
By Eric Chappell, edited by Richard Webber, published by Granada Media, 2002
Some scripts fall flat when read, needing the spark of live performance

to bring them off the page. Not so here and with Eric Chappell's extensive notes this book is a positive treasure. And something of a whopper. Still in print.

The Life and Legacy of Reginald Perrin: A Celebration
By Richard Webber, published by Virgin Books, 1996
This book does for Perrin what the previous volume did for Rigsby . . . albeit in a slightly more lavish manner and five years earlier. Another excellent book now sadly out of print.

The Richard Beckinsale Story
By David Clayton, published by The History Press, 2008
Clayton finally does Beckinsale the service of a biography. Comprehensive and well written, it's unreservedly recommended as a valuable look at an actor whose gentle, casual performances lulled people into thinking that what he was doing was easy. Still in print.

Woman of Today: An Autobiography
By Sue MacGregor published by Headline Books, 2003
I could have hardly written that chapter in Leonard's life without this.

TV PROGRAMMES

The Unforgettable Leonard Rossiter
ITV, 25 September 2000
A short tribute documentary first broadcast on ITV but now available on DVD (in a box set alongside other fine actors Ronnie Barker, Kenneth Williams and Sid James). Directed by Ashtar Alkhirsan.

Comedy Connections: The Fall and Rise of Reginald Perrin
BBC1, 19 July 2004
An episode of the series produced by BBC Scotland and directed by Kevin McMunigal which looks at the making of popular BBC sitcoms. This is included on the BBC DVD set of all of the Perrin series, adding to its already not inconsiderable value!

Comedy Classics: Rising Damp

ITV, 23 September 2008
Similar format to the above but produced for ITV, sadly not available on the DVD of the series released by ITV but as everything else is (including the award-winning movie), one can hardly complain!

All of these are in addition to the many TV shows and movies featuring Leonard Rossiter that are currently available on DVD.

Index

Wallace, Hazel Vincent 111, 112
Wardle, Irving 101, 102
Warren, Barry 76
Warrington, Don 19–20, 126, 133,
    135–6, 141, 147, 148, 149, 152,
    153, 154, 157, 165–6, 168, 245,
    246
Waterhouse, Keith 55, 73
Watson, Theresa 50
Watson, Tom 63
Watts, Mike 60
Wells, John 67, 85, 212
West, Timothy 30, 35
Whitehouse, Mary 97
Williams, Charlie 157

Williams, Kenneth 6, 237
Williams, Michael 16–17
Wilson, John 62
Windsor, Frank 45
Winstone, Ray 233
Wolverhampton Repertory
    Company 27, 28, 30, 31, 182
Wood, Charles 94
Wood, Duncan 132, 133, 137, 148
Woodthorpe, Peter 112, 123

Yates, Pauline 102, 183, 190

Zulu 93